The Aesthetic Turn

Eliot Deutsch

The Aesthetic Turn

Reading Eliot Deutsch on Comparative Philosophy

Edited by Roger T. Ames

OPEN COURT

Chicago and Lasalle, Illinois

To order books from Open Court, call 1-800-815-2280.

Open Court Publishing Company is a division of Carus Publishing Company.

©2000 by Carus Publishing Company

First printing 2000

Printed and bound in the United States of America.

Library of Congress Cataloging-in-Publication Data

The aesthetic turn : reading Eliot Deutsch on comparative philosophy / edited by Roger T. Ames.
    p.   cm.
    Includes bibliographical references and index.
    ISBN 0–8126–9405–8 (cloth : alk. paper)
    1. Deutsch, Eliot.   I. Ames, Roger T., 1947–
B945.D3974A37   1999
191—dc21

                                          99–42789
                                            CIP

CONTENTS

ACKNOWLEDGMENTS

This volume began, as do most celebratory volumes, with a remarkable career, and it is to acknowledge this event—this Eliot Deutsch—that the book has been written by a few of his many friends.

Daniel Cole has once again set aside his many responsibilities as the Coordinator of the University of Hawai'i's Center for Chinese Studies for as much time as it has taken to transform a manuscript into a handsome volume that does fair credit to its title, *The Aesthetic Turn*. He has stepped up to the ramparts to press the war against those fickle technologies that have threatened to overwhelm this editor as we have pursued the process of camera-ready production.

The photograph of Eliot that serves as frontispiece was selected by Marcia Roberts-Deutsch, his wife and intellectual companion of these many years. She also lent her counsel to the selection of an appropriate cover. Yet once again, Eliot and all of us are much enhanced by Marcia and her sense of what is right.

As always, I am indebted to Open Court's Editorial Director David Ramsay Steele for his encouragement, and especially to my Editor, Kerri Mommer, professional and friend, who has steered this project through from its inception. And once again, Steve Coutinho has done a fine job on the index.

Introduction

Eliot Deutsch has been at the center of the comparative philosophy movement in this generation. In many ways, his biography is intimately embedded within the broader story of the Philosophy Department at the University of Hawai'i, and it is with this story that we must commence.

The first chapter begins with his precursors, Charles A. Moore and Wing-tsit Chan, who, with the support of their then president, Greg Sinclair, shared a vision and a place in the 1930s. The University of Hawai'i, like the community it served, was coming of age, and was marked by an extraordinary diversity of languages and cultures. With a student body of more than 70 percent Asian-Americans and Pacific Islanders, there was some considerable pressure on the faculty to provide an inclusive education that was relevant to the lives of all of its clientele.

The Philosophy Department, from the outset, was committed to teaching philosophy within a Western philosophical context, but with the distinct mission of providing access to the non-Western philosophical traditions of South Asia, China, Korea, and Japan, as well as Buddhism and Islam as more pan-geographical phenomena. This definition of philosophy certainly served local needs, and was ambitious enough. But the mission of Charlie and Wing had just begun.

In 1939 the Philosophy Department hosted the first of the East-West Philosophers Conferences, bringing to the islands the wise grey heads of East and West to reflect on and discuss issues of then contemporary relevance. The first several of these summer conferences in 1939, 1949, and 1959 were small and long, collecting some twenty to thirty scholars for six weeks of intensive discussion. Among the distinguished representatives of world culture were William Ernest Hocking, F.S. C. Northrop, D. T. Suzuki, Hu Shih, S. Radhakrishnan, Thomé H. Fang, John Findlay, Hajime Nakamura, Richard McKeon, John Smith, Tang Chun-i, and

T.R.V. Murti, with a host of younger philosophers attending as well, several of whom have made contributions to this very volume.

Moore and Chan had laid the foundation for an intellectual movement—a very difficult job. And their initial vision was indeed a noble one: to construct a synthetic world philosophy negotiated out of the best of each tradition by distinguished scholars from around the world to serve as a philosophical charter for world peace and prosperity.

Each of these world congresses produced a volume of papers that chronicled the exchanges among the philosophers present, extending the impact of these meetings for decades beyond the conferences themselves. And in 1950, with the same goal of widening the influence of global philosophy, Charlie Moore published the first issue of *Philosophy East and West*, a quarterly journal of comparative philosophy that was over time to become the central voice for the community of scholars who joined the discipline.

There is a wonderful story of how Eliot first met Charlie Moore. He was in India in 1963–64 as a young assistant professor doing research on classical Vedānta philosophy. In order to meet many of the leading Indian philosophers of the day, Eliot made his way to Chandigarh in northern India to attend the All-India Philosophy Conference. Charlie Moore had been invited to this conference as a special guest, and at its conclusion, Eliot and Charlie prepared to fly back to New Delhi from Chandigarh. Having hitched a ride with the delegation of senior scholars escorting Moore to the airport, Eliot waited with Charlie the usual Indian time for the plane to arrive. Finally, the arrival of the plane was announced, and yet it proceeded to fly on overhead without making the slightest gesture of landing at the small Chandigarh airport. On inquiry, it was discovered that Charlie and Eliot were the only two passengers to have reservations, making it hardly worthwhile for the plane to land—a point quite beyond dispute.

Charlie and Eliot were provided a car and driver, and an otherwise distressing six hours of negotiating an automobile through a sea of color and kind that only travelers through India will ever know was softened by the happy opportunity of two philosophers to engage in their art. The animated conversation continued through the evening and over breakfast the next day—and three years later Deutsch was invited from his position at Rensselaer Polytechnic Institute in New

York to join the University of Hawai'i Philosophy Department, and to succeed Charlie as Editor of *Philosophy East and West*.

Inheriting the mantel from Moore in 1967, Eliot has carried the project of promoting Western literacy on non-Western philosophical traditions into the second half of the twentieth century. And on his watch, the earlier rather romantic vision of a world philosophy gradually gave way to a rather different project. The search for a unifying sameness has been transformed into the celebration of philosophical and cultural differences as a safeguard against the homogenizing forces of technologies and economic structures that have come to define modern living. In philosophy generally, there has been increasing disillusionment with the quest for certainty, driven as it has been by ambitious methodologies and assumptions about acultural, ahistorical, and a-ethnographic standards of evidence. In this sea change, the alternative cultural experiences that give traditions their character have become a resource from which to draw for contemporary philosophical reflection and adjudication.

Charlie Moore had worked hard to build up the subscription base of *Philosophy East and West*, but starting up a new journal for a discipline on the margins of philosophy was not easy; in 1967 it was still a cottage industry with only minimal professional and institutional support. It lacked a community.

It was the professional eyes of the young Deutsch that established and nurtured *Philosophy East and West* as the voice of comparative philosophy within the Western academy, challenging the entrenched provincialism of Anglo-American philosophy with peer reviewed essays and special topical features expressing the rich differences that distinguish the cultural traditions of our world. And it was around *Philosophy East and West* that a community of sixty-eight founding members gathered to establish the Society for Asian and Comparative Philosophy in 1967. With the assistance of Karl Potter, Richard Robinson, and Hans van Buitenen, Eliot undertook the organizing of SACP. In its more than thirty years of existence, the Society has organized over a hundred panels at meetings held in conjunction with the Association for Asian Studies, the American Philosophical Association, and the American Academy of Religion. It has sponsored three major research conferences, and a monograph series edited by Henry Rosemont and published by the University of Hawai'i that now boasts over twenty titles.

By the time that Eliot in 1987 decided to step down from his twenty years of editing *Philosophy East and West*, the journal had expanded from under 200 mostly individual readers to 1200 primarily library subscribers, and the participating membership in the Society had grown to over 400 scholars.

In addition to the journal, from 1969 Eliot took on the responsibility of continuing the conference series with smaller meetings of an East-West nature on specialized topics such as law, logic, and representative individual philosophers: Wang Yangming on the 500-year anniversary of his birth, and Martin Heiddeger on his eightieth birthday. In fact, the field of comparative philosophy had by now matured to the point where greater in-depth critical engagement could be carried forward. The first of these conferences, for example, was on "Aesthetics East and West," and included such luminaries as Albert Hofstadter, Stephen Pepper, and Donald Keene.

Throughout this period, Hung Wo Ching, an enlightened local businessman, had made raising financial support for these meetings his business, and he did it well. In 1987 with the assistance of Wing-tsit Chan, now close to his ninetieth year, and with the steady support of businessman Hung Wo Ching, plans were laid for the next large Sixth East-West Philosophers Conference on the theme, "Culture and Modernity." For Eliot, a whole new generation of scholars had arisen from the days of the earliest meetings, and the time was ripe for new introductions. In 1989, a conference of 130 scholars coming from over thirty-three countries, including for the first time Africa and Latin America, was convened under Eliot's directorship, and like so many other of his ventures, it was a ringing success. By now, with the cumulative affect of the conference program, the conference volumes, and the journal, the commonplace among Western philosophers that Asian traditions might have something to say about religion but not philosophy, had been fully discredited. Not only were many of the leading Western philosophers in attendance, but six of the last eight presidents of the American Philosophical Association had joined the discussion.

And so these conferences continue, where scholars of good-will proceed, with civility and critical intelligence, to contribute what insight and knowledge they can bring to bear on the pressing issues of our changing times. And *Philosophy East and West* continues, with the year 2000 marking its fiftieth year.

Deutsch's own philosophical career has been a motive force in the comparative philosophy movement. The narrative divides into two rather distinct phases. In his first incarnation, he was a student of Indian culture, publishing translations and interpretative studies on the high philosophies of South Asia. His translation of the *Bhagavad Gītā* (1968), his *Advaita Vedānta: A Philosophical Reconstruction* (1969), and his *Source Book on Advaita Vedānta* (1971), belong to this earlier period. Each of these works reflects both a philological command of the original texts, and an uncanny ability to understand them and to say what they mean.

Although never really abandoned, this more historical beginning gave way to a sustained creative reflection through which Deutsch has entered the realm of philosophy proper as a philosopher in his own right. Funding the development of his own philosophical positions with a broad range of human experience, Deutsch has borrowed widely from Chinese, Japanese, Indian, Buddhist, and of course, Western philosophical literatures. In this mode, he has published book-length comparative studies on metaphysics, aesthetics, truth, freedom, the construction of person, and philosophy of religion.

As a defining signature of his work, Deutsch has moved away from the familiar centrality of metaphysics and epistemology to consistently take aesthetics as the starting point of his philosophical enterprise. Creativity and personal freedom are key values in Deutsch's vision of the project of becoming human. There is a real sense in which the philosophy of Deutsch, in a way analogous to several of the East Asian traditions from which he draws so expertly, can be fairly described as an aestheticism.

In celebration of Deutsch's very distinguished career, leading figures in comparative philosophy have directed their combined critical gaze at Deutsch's creative philosophizing, and have produced the collection of essays gathered herein. The table of contents not only rehearses several of Deutsch's major themes and theses, but further reads as a *Who's Who* of comparative philosophy. In fact, many of these mature and established scholars are the young faces in the old black and white photographs that remember the East-West Philosophers Conferences of the days gone by. They were there then, and are here now in this volume, because the community that gathered around this changing vision and its visionaries, among

The Aethetic Turn: Reading Eliot Deutsch

them Deutsch himself, has always included the luminaries and the boomers, the older generation and the young and scrappy, as its formula for the most effective way to carry on the project of comparative philosophy.

The virtue of this particular "Critics and Their Critics" series is that the authors under review get to engage their critics, and Deutsch makes fair use of the opportunity in his responses. One might say that the logic of this volume is the academic narrative of Deutsch's career, the engagement of his ideas by his peers and his students, and his warm yet critical responses. Yet Eliot is first and foremost an aesthetician, and it is the beauty of this man and his career rather than its logic, that this volume chooses to celebrate.

Roger T. Ames

Honolulu

PART
1

Mysticism and Aesthetics in Eliot Deutsch's Thought

Arthur C. Danto

Eliot Deutsch and I got to know one another through the circumstance that, to a philosophy department whose members had only the most distant interest in Asian thought, he submitted a dissertation which, in part, dealt with the modern Indian philosopher, Sri Aurobindo. It was required, then as now, that the approval of three members of the department be secured in order that the dissertation go on to defense, and I found myself enlisted as a very junior third member of Eliot's committee because I had an avowed if spotty interest in what was innocently designated Oriental thought. My interests and Eliot's were poles apart. I had found considerable meaning in certain Daoist ideas, as well as in those of Zen, which it seemed at the time one could apply to one's life without having to change one's life. Since Orientalism has fallen under attack as a concept in recent times, we have come to appreciate that there is no single set of ideas common and peculiar to the philosophical traditions of the Near, the Middle, and the Far East, and that even a burning interest in Zhuangzi [Chuang Tzu] and the Ox-Herding pictures will not entail a corollary keenness for the kind of thought that Sri Aurobindo practiced. But such are the ways of *Geworfenheit* that Eliot and I became friends despite the vast distance between the objects of our disjunctive enthusiasms.

I have, to this very day, no clear idea what drove Eliot to devote to Sri Aurobindo the kind of time writing a dissertation exacts. But my overall sense is that he had a certain belief in mystical experience, that he perhaps had such an experience, and that his preoccupations were, centrally, religious in nature. I think that Aurobindo combined a respect for religious cognitions together with a sense of secular duties—he established an ashram in Pondicherry, but he also founded an important university in Calcutta, and participated in the political and educational debates of his era. This may in part have been what drew Eliot to him—the idea that one might have a genuine mystical calling without foregoing the secular imperatives of life. Come to think about it, our general views on religion and ordinary life were not so disparate. I had not the slightest inclination to turn my back on the world to follow a specifically Zen discipline. Or I thought living in the world could be practiced as a Zen discipline. I never pressed Eliot on the matter of religious experiences, but whatever his attitude, it did not keep him from the defining dharmas of career and family and the pleasures of living in the world.

In addition to a responsiveness to certain dimensions of what an earlier generation would have considered the Wisdom of the East, Eliot and I shared an interest in art without either of us aspiring to be aestheticians. I was inspired by analytical philosophy, in which, with the exception of Ernest Nagel, the Columbia department had as faint an idea as it had of the *Vedānta Sūtras*. But I found nothing in the analytical literature which seemed enlightening in regard to the art which also inspired me, and it was only later, in the mid-1960s, that I was able to perceive an evolution in art which made it possible to apply to it an analytical methodology. I think, by contrast, that Eliot never felt a gap between philosophy and art, and found, from the beginning, a certain internal relationship between artistic and religious experience. So his overall thought at the time was very little different from what it became when he published his most mature writing on art, *Essays on the Nature of Art* in 1996. As often happens, we had less in common than we would have supposed we had, when, with our wives, we attended various cultural events together, talked about them over Irish coffee at the Algonquin Hotel, and invited one another to dinner parties. I respect, without entirely being able to accept, the general views on art Eliot advances in that book, as well as in his 1975 *Studies in Comparative Aesthetics*. Taking those books together with my 1981 *The Transfiguration of the Commonplace* (an exceedingly Zen title!) would itself be an exercise in comparative aesthetics. The distance between these two systems of aesthetic thought was probably already present when we first became friends, even if there was no way in which one could see it at the time other than as a difference in personality, attitude, and taste.

In my case, at least, the gap between our aesthetic sensibilities would have become pronounced only when I think about the very different structures of Contemporary Art that have evolved out of Modernism. I feel that Modernism was, and remains, a deeply gratifying body of attitudes to Eliot Deutsch. But Modernism is very little help to me in thinking through the problems of contemporary art, in which it proved possible for works of art and quite ordinary objects to look so alike that there need be no relevant perceived difference between them. My tirelessly invoked examples came from Andy Warhol, but in truth they could have come from almost anywhere in the transformative course of the art world in the sixties. My questions regarding art were more or less ontological. Wittgenstein once asked, in regard to human action, "What remains when, from the fact that I raise my arm, the fact that my arm goes up?" The art of the sixties made it possible to ask the same kind of question about it. "What remains when I subtract from a work of art everything it has in common with an ordinary object which happens entirely to resemble it?" This implies that just as an action is a bodily movement plus X—or a bodily movement an action minus X—a work of art is an object plus Y and an object a work of art minus Y. The parallel philosophical tasks are to solve for X (Wittgenstein appears to have thought that X=0) and for Y. The difference between Eliot's view of art and mine is that, for him, such problems do not arise. He has a very clear idea of what a work of art is, as something that could hardly be confused with an ordinary object, in connection with which the kind of aesthetic analysis he develops has no special application. Whereas my idea would be that there need be no aesthetic differences between works of art and commonplace objects—in just the way in which there need be no observable difference between someone practicing a Zen discipline by brushing his teeth and—someone just brushing his teeth. Zen is another term for the transfiguration of the commonplace. Whereas art in Eliot's scheme is something apart from the ordinary in much the way in which the object of a religious experience would be. These differences were present at the inception of our friendship, but they would hardly have been accessible to consciousness because art had not as yet produced the kinds of works that made the differences vivid.

I recently read an interview with the contemporary avant garde artist, John Armleder. The interview concerns music rather than the visual arts, but since the kind of problem which concerns me arises as spontaneously with music as with visual art, it is worth quoting a fragment of the discussion between Armleder and a writer named Spark Vett. They have been listening to *Gagaku*, the traditional Japanese court music for which certain dances had evolved.

S.V. Turn down the music. I can't hear the tape with that noise.

J.A. You mean turn down the music and leave the noise?

S.V. That's not music.

J.A. I wrote an essay once titled "The Music Inevitable." Of course there was a paragraph on John Cage—any sound is music, and so on. I remember Cage quoting Alan Watts so often. One day I asked Alan Watts what he thought about music, Cage, and so on. He just mumbled something about modern western music as electronically generated stupidness, and that music was harmony, not noise. (*Parkett* 50/51, 1997, p. 42)

What Vett considers noise, Armleder knows is *Gagaku*. He points out that "we used to play it a lot during our happenings in the late sixties." But he states this because there is, in his view, an analogy between the noise-music problem and certain problems which relate to "the configuration of my installations today." With qualifications—Eliot does not mumble!—Armleder's exchange with Watts resembles an imagined exchange between Eliot Deutsch and me.

I would suppose Armleder's use of music would present counterparts to his use of visual form, just as Cage's most distinctive work was inspired by the celebrated white canvas painted by Robert Rauschenberg at Black Mountain College in 1956. Cage described that canvas as a "landing field," in that most of the transient modifications—light and shadows which play across its surface, which we commonly subtract from our experience of the work—are in fact part of the work, which changes from instant to instant. The white canvas was a way of redeeming visual aspects of the world for art which, in other contexts would have been *merely* lights and shadows or (in the case of accidents) coffee stains or lipstick smears. Or a fly lighting for an instant. Or an inadvertent finger-smutch. That is precisely what Cage allowed to happen with *4´33˝*, in which whatever you hear is the music rather than the noise it would be were any one to hear it under other auspices.

George Leonard, in *Into the Light of Things: The Art of the Commonplace from Wordsworth to Cage*, quotes a witness to the second performance of *4´33˝*, by David Tudor, at Carnegie Recital Hall:

He opened up the piano lid and put his hands on the keys as if he was going to play some music. What we expected. We were waiting. And nothing happened. Pretty soon you began to hear chairs creaking, people coughing, rustling of clothes, then giggles. And then a police car came by with its siren running, down below. Then I began to hear the elevator in the building. Then the air conditioning going through the ducts. Until one by one by one all of us, everyone one of that audience there . . . began to say "Oh. We get it. Ain't no such thing as silence. If you just listen, you'll hear a lot. . . ." It made available to a number of us not just the sounds but all phenomena. Then the question is, now that everything's available, what do you do?

Cage, in an interview with Leonard, acknowledged the influence of Zen, which he got, as so many in the art world of that time did, from D. T. Suzuki, improbably teaching his famous seminar, the same from year to year, in 716 Philosophy Hall. He said "I've thought of music as . . . an activity of sounds in which the artist found a way to let the sounds be themselves." There is a lot of difference between the sounds which became 4′33″ in Carnegie Recital Hall, and those made by pelting rain on the roof of the shed in which the "premier" of Cage's piece took place (in Woodstock, New York!). However dissimilar the sets of noises, the piece is (always) the same. What gives it its identity has nothing to do with the sounds which fill four minutes and thirty-three seconds. If the silence happened to be filled with the sound of a chamber group in the next building, playing a piece by Bach, that music would be, as much and for the same reason as the crash of garbage cans outside, among the adventitious sounds of life. My sense is that the message is not quite that there is no such thing as silence. It is rather that some silences are music and some are not, just as with sounds which are noises when not music without sounding different in any way from when they occur as music.

There is something deeply Zen about Cage's work. I recall a story about a Zen monk spitting on a statue to the Buddha. Reprimanded in the obvious way, he responds by saying that he had been taught that Buddha is everywhere—so how can one spit without spitting on the Buddha? There are no, so to speak, non-Buddha zones. The idea that a statue is a thing apart—as a work of art is a thing apart—blinds us to the problem I have already outlined. A musical sound is an ordinary sound plus Z; an ordinary sound is a musical sound minus Z. What then is Z? I am uncertain that Cage addressed the question he daringly raised. And I wonder if it is humanly possible to regard all sounds as modifications of some undifferentiated auditory substance—a cry for help, a scream, the breeze in the palmettos, the hiss of tires on wet pavement. As if art exists not in anything whatever but in certain special things selected out for that status. Buddhism is not as easy a philosophy to live by as it sounds. I knew some Chinese who felt they could not become Buddhists, compelled as they were by the teaching, because to be human means to be attached to certain humans, whose welfare impinges our own. This, too, is not a question Cage entirely addressed. Nor is it one that I have properly considered. Jack Miles writes, "What John Cage eventually heard in the silence he had created was the sound of the world dying, and he could not bear to hear it." The Buddhist response might simply be "So?" The test of authenticity was whether it matters not in the least whether the monk treads his way among the ash-pits and cinders of a world destroyed, or along the precipitous path in one of Wang Meng's dizzying mountainscapes.

I am very proud to have figured in the narrative John Leonard tells, in which Cage and Suzuki and I are situated in a tradition stretching at least as far back through Ruskin and Carlyle to Wordsworth. The world in which Ruskin and Wordsworth lived was not dying, by contrast to the world in which Cage and I have lived. To feel the world that way leaves one, Jack Miles feels, no alternative to environmental activism, by contrast with the radical passivity of the Buddhist attitude. But the philosophical problem remains, whatever one's response, of solving for Y or Z when the work of art and the mere real thing look so alike that it is difficult to bring to bear on the problem the aesthetic structures Eliot makes to serve in his essentialist definition of art.

I was pleased, going through *Essays on the Nature of Art*, to read Deutsch's robust affirmation of essentialism. He announces, indeed, at the preface to his book that it is "at once an essentialist account of the nature of an artwork and a contextualized characterization of aesthetic experience and the role of art in society" (p. ix). It is a very bold thing to identify oneself as an essentialist in the present intellectual climate, in which it is the received attitude that art works mean such different things to different cultures, genders, races, and religions, that there is no overarchingly invariant thing art can possibly be. And it is striking that Deutsch wishes to maintain that however deep the impulses of art may be inflected by these differences, there is a residual and crucial sense in which art is everywhere and always the same. As Deutsch puts it, "A work of art, even though culturally embedded, thus has it own intentionality" (p. 33)—by which he means that the work of art, as such, satisfies the conditions his essentialist account of art lays out as the definition of art. The latter, finally, is to be developed "against the background of an ontology, stated or not . . . for any discussion of what art is can be addressed only through various presuppositions concerning what there is" (p. 5).

I am in entire agreement with many of these controlling assumptions. I too am an essentialist; I too am convinced that an adequate philosophy of art must be ontological. I am essentialist in the respect that a definition of art must be compatible with art of every sort, irrespective of cultural differences. Wittgensteinians, who sought to make an aesthetics out of Wittgenstein's ideas, believed that there could be no general rule or principle which all the artworks exemplified, any more than, to use his paralyzing example, there are properties peculiar to all and only games. He said famously that if we look, we will see that games fit together rather as a family, and, by implication, that the class of artworks is a family-resemblance class with no uniting properties. And hence no definition is possible. But happily, they feel, no definition is needed, for we all know, in virtue of knowing our language, which are the artworks. We can pick them out effortlessly, give or take certain marginal, essentially contested cases. My book, *The Transfiguration of the Commonplace* was intended to put paid to the Neo-Wittgensteinian philosophy of art as part of preparing the ground for exactly what it rejected in principle: a definition of art. And it would have been through working out such a definition that I supposed I might meet the argument from multiculturalism and against essentialism. A definition of art must be compatible with all the works of art, however they might differ culturally or in terms of gender or whatever. A definition of art could not single out a group of artworks, insisting that these have a greater claim to the status of art than those to be found elsewhere in the highly disjunctive extension of the expression "work of art." Everything that is art is so in the same degree and in the same way. The Wittgensteinians were dazzled by the disjunctiveness of that extension. They simply could not see how that disjunctiveness would entail conditions on the concept of art making it compatible with whatever is art. So I am entirely responsive to Eliot Deutsch's philosophy of the philosophy of art. We differ, however, in our respective philosophies of art, and, in my view, we differ in our ontologies.

The ontology I accept is grounded in the discoveries of contemporary art since Cage and Rauschenberg, Warhol and Beuys, Duchamp and Armleder. My ontology holds that there is no object which cannot be a work of art: a siren sound, a fortuitous shadow, a Brillo box, a block of fat, a urinal, a truck tire which rings some plants, such as we find in red-neck neighborhoods. This sets ontological limits, not to the extension of "work of art"—there are, we now see, largely through the work of the artists here enumerated, no such limits. The limits, rather, are set to the intension of the expression. Whatever we understand the concept of art to be, it must be compatible with any object being a work of art. Hence, no characterization of one set as against another can form part of the concept, or play a role in the intension. And my problem with Eliot's definition of art is that he seems to believe that there are constraints on which objects can be works of art.

Let me take this to a further point. It does not follow from the fact that anything can be a work of art that everything is one. For in addition to the object one needs to solve for X. There is always the question of what it is in addition to the object a work of art has to have in order to be a work of art. This is precisely the ontology of art. The ontology of Jesus is that he is a man plus God. The ontology of an action is that it is a bodily movement plus—and here philosophers will differ. The ontology of a work of art is that it is an object plus—and here Eliot and I will say different things. And my question is whether what he says is really compatible with the discovery that anything can be a work of art. I think it cannot. And for that reason I find his philosophy of art unsatisfactory. I hope this is not because, or merely because—it is not my philosophy of art.

I believe Eliot is vulnerable through his essentialism, not because essentialism is wrong, but because I find it difficult to see how the definition, when it is put in place, can be extended to cover the art from which I have taken my philosophical inspiration. For particular example, consider beauty as a component in the essence of art. "If beauty were absent," he writes, "the object would simply fail as an artwork" (p. 29). There is a difference between a failed artwork, and an object which fails to be an artwork. The first is a critical failure, the second an ontological failure. On my ontology, according to which an artwork is an object plus X, an object fails to be an artwork (philosophically) when it lacks X. But once an artwork, it can fail critically. In some cases it can fail because it lacks beauty. But it can lack beauty and still be an artwork, for beauty does not pertain to the essence of art, as can be seen from the kinds of examples I cited. A tire with plants in it would be an emblem not of beauty but of squalor. A lump of lard, as Beuys used it, would not be beautiful—unless every lump of lard was beautiful. Duchamp's circle, under the leadership of Walter Arensberg, tried to claim that the urinal out of which *Fountain* was constituted was beautiful, and that Duchamp meant to draw attention to its gleaming whiteness and elegant curvatures. Duchamp, by contrast, meant, through the readymades, to put aesthetics entirely out of play. His philosophical contribution was to show that aesthetic qualities cannot belong to the definition of art because the readymades failed if they were beautiful—though they did not fail as art for that reason. Deutsch writes that "The meaning of a work is its aesthetic content." One could argue that the absence of beauty is the aesthetic content of the readymades—but that, apart from putting an unusual spin on "beauty," entails that the absence as well as the presence of beauty is compatible with the status of art, and hence that beauty is no part of art's essence. Of course, Deutsch uses the term *beauty* in his own way: "A work of art is beautiful to the degree to which it presents as its own presence a formal achievement, a radiance and splendor of form, that is appropriate to it." This concept of beauty may, he might urge, be as true of *Fountain* as of Giorgione's *La Tempesta* or Piero's *Resurrection*. But that would not be the beauty aestheticians have had in mind in thinking of art as beautiful. It rather mounts alongside standard usage an exclusionary usage of Deutsch's own.

This is perhaps as far as I wish or need to carry the analysis. As I see it, there are too many works of art which fail to fit Deutsch's essentialist definition, or which satisfy it only incidentally. On the other hand, there are undoubtedly many works which do satisfy it, and these may in truth be the works Deutsch thinks of when he thinks of art, or upon the basis of which he regards art as spiritually important. His definition may then be said to present the essence of these works—magnificent, glorious, radiant (to use his term), splendid (to use his concept). But this is not the essence of art as art. I, of course, have my own definition, but I was inspired precisely by the works with which (as I see it) Deutsch's philosophy of art collides. I suppose that if my definition is right, the magnificence, the glory, the radiance, the splendor drop out of the essence of art, however central to certain works of art like the Taj Mahal or the stained glasses of Chartres or the Sistine ceiling or the interior of Chartres San Carlo or *Las Meninas*—or, or, or—the works we make pilgrimages to be in the presence of.

I think I can understand why Deutsch especially prizes such works and the experiences with which they furnish us. It is because those experiences are close to mystical experiences: "The 'mystical' is just that level of essential spirituality where religion and art most closely meet, interrelate, and separate" (p. 99). "The religious mystic," he adds, "is able to dispense with artworks entirely." The mystic's goal is more the overcoming of the self in the mystical object than the realization of the self through the work of art. On Deutsch's view, art takes us to the last step before the mystic's flight, and perhaps the last step of which Deutsch perhaps thinks himself capable. Small wonder, then, that he seeks to build into the concept of art as much of mysticism as he can manage. In art we find some intimations of mysticism's reality.

Eliot Deutsch's biographers will be able to trace the itinerary from his study of Sri Aurobindo to his latest book on the philosophy art. Perhaps somewhere along that path he pondered whether he was up to the mystic's calling. I cannot helpfully speculate. But judging by the way the book on art ends, it has been the constant preoccupation of his philosophical career. I believe, to invert a famous sentence in the *Tractatus*, that *Das Mystische* is not that the world is, but how the world is. So my biographer will want to understand my hunger for the commonplace. What rather fascinates me is that we are as different from one another as we ever were, but different in the same way that we were at the beginning of our relationship.

References

Danto, Arthur C. (1981). *The Transfiguration of the Commonplace: A Philosophy of Art.* Cambridge Mass: Harvard University Press.

Deutsch, Eliot (1975). *Studies in Comparative Aesthetics.* Honolulu: University of Hawaii Press.

————. (1996). *Essays on the Nature of Art.* Albany: State University of New York Press.

Leonard, George (1994). *Into the Light of Things: The Art of the Commonplace from Wordsworth to Cage.* Chicago: University of Chicago Press.

Vett, Spark (1997). Interview with John Armleder. In *Parkett* (50/51).

Further Reflections on the Rock Garden of Ryōanji: From *Yūgen* to *Kire-tsuzuki*

Graham Parkes

Without a speck of dust's being raised,
the mountains tower up;
without a single drop's falling,
the streams plunge into the valley.
— Musō Soseki

I am grateful to Eliot Deutsch for providing the initial stimulus, through his essay "An Invitation to Contemplation: The Rock Garden of Ryōanji and the Concept of *Yūgen*," for my visiting a place that I have since come to consider as one of the most profoundly beautiful spaces on the planet.[1] It is indeed a site conducive to contemplation, and to give an adequate account of its aesthetic impact one does have to move beyond traditional Western conceptions of beauty to Japanese ideas such as *yūgen*.

1

Approaching the Zen temple that bears the name "Dragon Peace" (*Ryōan*), and which nestles at the foot of the luxuriantly wooded hills that border Kyoto on the northwest, one gradually leaves behind a commotion of traffic and urban activity that increases with every year. Walking up the cobblestone pathway leading from the main road, one enters an area of relative peace and quiet (depending on how many other visitors—and especially from bus or school tours—are there at the same time). Not only does Ryōanji enjoy a magnificent natural setting, but the grounds of the temple as a whole are among the most beautiful in Japan. So much so that the visitor who enjoys gardens with ponds, rocks, trees, and other vegetation could easily spend a day admiring the immediate environs of the famous rock garden. Kyōyōchi, the expansive "Mirror Pond" at the south end of the temple precincts which dates from the twelfth century, is a delight in any season, reflecting as it does a variety of splendid trees and containing several exquisite islets and rocks.

In order to experience the rock garden most fully in its context (and Buddhist philosophy consistently emphasizes the experience of things in contexts), it is better not to follow the signs indicating the "Usual Route," which leads directly to the rock garden, but to spend time contemplating the rich profusion of natural— though also arranged—beauty that surrounds it. In numerous sub-gardens a multitude of handsome rocks stand among elegant trees and bushes, while some lie, apparently slumbering, in sun-illumined moss that glows green around them. Majestic stands of bamboo sway in the breeze, mysteriously inviting into shadowy backgrounds. Exotic palms thrust sharply skyward among trees blossoming delicately in the spring. Even if the heart of these gardens were empty (in the sense of void), rather than occupied by what the keepers of the temple like to call "the garden of emptiness," the grounds of Ryōanji would still be well worth visiting.

Getting back to the "Usual Route" and climbing the broad and gradual gradient of the steps that lead up to the buildings surrounding the rock garden, one might notice underfoot a variety of exquisitely colored cobblestones. And if the leisurely visitor happens to stop in at the men's *otearai* before viewing the garden, he can enjoy a unique preliminary perspective on the group of rocks nearest the far end. (The view from within the women's facilities appears not to afford a similar partial perspective.) This is the time, too, for the returning visitor to prepare to be astonished, on first stepping onto the wooden walkway that runs along the north side of the garden—which is the only place from which to view it—at how small it is in area. Although it measures less than thirty meters from east to west and ten from north to south, the vast spaces it opens up in the mind tend to make one remember it as being much larger than it really is. (At least in my own case, in spite of mental preparation each time, I never fail to be breathtaken by first seeing it again: its image in memory remains persistently vast.)

But it is well to step back before going on, for a brief consideration of the historical background to this remarkable garden.

2

Under the influence of Chinese gardens, the Japanese garden traditionally contained ponds, rocks, and waterfalls as well as trees and other vegetation. It was the Shingon School that first introduced, after its establishment in the ninth century, a specifically Buddhist element into gardens in Japan, which were at that time primarily pleasure gardens for royalty and aristocracy, even though they often incorporated various kinds of cosmic or religious symbolism as well. The specific innovation deriving from Zen Buddhist influence was the style known as *karesansui*, or "dry landscape." The first mention of this style of creating a garden "without ponds or streams," occurs in the oldest known treatise on Japanese gardens, the *Sakuteiki* (Manual of garden making), which dates from the eleventh century.[2] This type from the Heian Period was the ancestor of the characteristically Zen rock garden, but the immediate precursors of the garden at Ryōanji are attributed to the Zen monk who is regarded by many as Japan's greatest maker of landscape gardens, Musō Soseki (1275–1351).

The first of his two masterworks dates from around 1340 and is at Saihōji, popularly known as the "Moss Temple" (*Kokedera*), which lies in the foothills to the west of Kyoto. On being commissioned to renovate the grounds of the temple, which had fallen into disrepair, Musō Soseki performed a number of bold innovations on the main garden, which had been centered around a large pond. But on the hillside to the north he created a new, smaller and radically different garden. Using around fifty largish rocks taken from an ancient necropolis nearby, he created a kind of "dry waterfall" by arranging them in three tiers coming down the hillside.[3] Surprisingly, only a few of these rocks, which are covered with lichen and are now surrounded by "pools" of moss, look as if they have been fashioned: most of them appear totally "natural," as if they were the site of a cascade deep in the mountains. But the more one contemplates them, the more impressed one becomes by the absolute *rightness* of the way they have been arranged. From the various perspectives adoptable by standing or sitting at the foot of this "rockfall" in front of its broadest tier—the tiers become narrower, and the size of the rocks

larger, as they ascend—the composition looks perfect. Even Cézanne, that consummate positioner of rocks in relation to trees (albeit in two dimensions), could
not have arranged the elements more expertly.

Vertical bands of lichen on some of the larger rocks give the illusion of water
flowing over them. (Some water does, of course, run down them in heavy rain,
but the surrounding ground absorbs it so that no actual streams develop to spoil
the effect.) After a while one is reminded, as perhaps Musō Soseki was, of Zen
master Dōgen's talk of "mountains flowing" and "moving on water"—even
though the only movement perceivable is the play on the rocks of the sunlight
filtering through the trees that arch over the rockfall from either side.[4] But perhaps the most powerful effect is auditory: if one can arrange to contemplate the
garden alone, on a windless day the almost total silence is occasionally interrupted
by the deafening roar of a waterfall that is not there.

Whereas in the time of destitution when the mosses took over the temple in
the nineteenth century the garden around the pool symbolized the Pure Land of
Amida, the more "natural" garden on the rough hillside above represented *this*
world, into which Zen practice aims to effect a total integration. Musō Soseki rep-
licated this kind of contrast when he was given the task of transforming a former
imperial villa (situated midway between Saihōji and Ryōanji) into the Zen temple
that now flourishes under the name Tenryūji ("Heaven Dragon Temple"). In this
case, however, the garden and pond, for which Musō apparently took his inspiration from Song dynasty landscape paintings exemplifying ancient ideas of
paradise, and the dry landscape (again in the form of a waterfall) are directly jux-
taposed in the same site. Whereas the *karesansui* at Saihōji is situated in such a way
as to make it self-contained, the garden of Tenryūji is a consummate example of
the principle of *shakkei*, or "borrowing the landscape." The dry waterfall, which
nowadays can be seen only from across the pond, is the centerpiece of a larger
composition of rocks placed mainly around the pond's edge, which in turn is surrounded by a "frame" of trees and bushes, which then shades imperceptibly into
the surrounding landscape backed by the magnificent hills of Arashiyama.

Although consisting of fewer elements than its precursor at Saihōji, the dry
waterfall of Tenryūji again comprises rocks of exquisite shape which have weathered with bands of lichen that suggest downflowing water. Here, in contrast to the
predominantly vertical orientation of the larger rocks, there are three thin slabs

laid end-to-end over an inlet of the pond at the foot of the rockfall which give the impression of a bridge. (This is the earliest example of what would become a common configuration of rocks in Japanese ponds.) Because they are more visibly surrounded by exuberant vegetation than their counterparts at Saihōji, the inorganic nature of the rocks at Tenryūji impresses the viewer by more powerful contrast. Nevertheless, it would be inapt to call them lifeless; nor is what animates them so magnificently the minimal accommodation, on the part of these beings that have never known life or death, of only the simplest life forms of lichen and moss. The longer one devotes one's attention to them, the more alive they appear with a life of their own. One comes to appreciate why Dōgen repeatedly emphasizes that rocks and pebbles are "Buddha-nature" (*busshō*) just as much as so-called "sentient" beings.[5]

But the significant feature of the dry waterfall of Tenryūji is the way it is mirrored in the pond—as are the other rocks that border it, all of which merit prolonged attention. Only on an unusually windy day can one contemplate the rockfall without being aware of its being "doubled" by the reflections in the pool at its base. The substantial rocks that seem to descend majestically down the hillside, harboring an invisible cascade, are mirrored by insubstantial inverted counterparts beneath them. But rather than suggesting a contrast between the real (*nirvāṇa*) and the illusory (*saṃsāra*), the juxtaposition of rocks and reflections suggests an interplay on the *same* ontological level. The natural world and its image, the substantial and its opposite, are both there, or here, at the same time. They are both necessary, belonging together: the thing is simply to distinguish between them—which one cannot do unless one is aware of the insubstantial counterpart even when it is not directly presented in a mirror image.

3

Back at Ryōanji, on stepping out onto the smooth wooden walkway, we come upon the space that is the heart of the temple's gardens. "A garden of just stone and gravel,"—so begins "An Invitation to Contemplation"—"a piece of physical nature, and yet it invites one to participate in contemplative being. . . . The Rock Garden of Ryōanji is at once precise and natural" (25). As with the *karesansui* of Musō Soseki, this garden is a synthesis of art and nature in that it consists of natural elements arranged with consummate precision. At Saihōji and Tenryūji the compositions of rocks could conceivably be natural, in the sense that one can imagine encountering such groupings occurring spontaneously in nature. Indeed, an effect of seeing these dry landscapes is precisely to sensitize the viewer to the beauty of the relationships exhibited by "natural" dispositions of rocks—even though in the field, as it were, it is often necessary to experiment with various standpoints before coming upon the optimal position from which to appreciate such beauty. (Musō Soseki has, in a sense, done this moving around for us, so that his compositions look perfect from almost any standpoint within the garden.) But at Ryōanji the rocks have been placed within a rectangular "sea" of carefully raked gravel, so that it is quite impossible to imagine the ensemble as natural.

But there is a little more there than just stone and gravel: in each of the five groups of rocks in the garden (from east to west: 5, 2, 3, 2, 3, making a total of fifteen) there is also *moss,* as well as a thin layer of lichen on the larger rocks. In two of the groups the rocks are surrounded by a bed of green, while in the others some of the rocks lie outside the moss. These touches of life provide a striking contrast to the unremittingly inorganic nature of the rest of the garden, while at the same time corresponding with the trees that are visible beyond the garden wall. In summer the bright green of the moss echoes the lush colors of the trees, while in winter its color matches that of the evergreens beyond, and the mauve hues the moss assumes in that season mirror the tones of the bare branches of the deciduous trees that border the wall. Being surrounded by a sea of gray gravel the moss emphasizes the effect created by the elements of the garden being "cut off" from the nature outside (about which more will be said in section 5). The point is that without these touches of green life the garden would look very different, just as the "seed" of white within the black part of the yin-yang figure, and vice versa, is indispensable to the effect.

"The Rock Garden suggests this paradox, that the juxtaposition of elements which constitute it is at once arbitrary and necessary. One can imagine that the elements could be changed and exchanged without doing violence to the quality of the whole" (25). The term "arbitrary" here, I must admit, throws me off. The rocks in the garden are surely natural, in the sense that it is unlikely that its creator fashioned them much, if at all. But the more one contemplates them, the more their positioning appears perfect; and to change or exchange any of the elements would surely detract from the aesthetic impact of the whole. One could no more change the composition and retain the masterpiece than with the highest achievements of a Beethoven or a Cézanne. In Buddhist terms, the arrangement of the rocks is a consummate exemplification of the principle of interdependent arising (Jpn. *engi*, Skt. *pratītya samutpāda*), the idea that each particular is what it is only in relation to everything else. A different configuration of rocks in the garden could still exemplify this point, but nowhere near as effectively.

Another source of puzzlement for me in Eliot Deutsch's essay is this:

> One cannot apprehend a garden in the same manner as a painting or a piece of sculpture, for a garden makes available too many perspectives. (The fifteen stones of the Rock Garden cannot, in fact, be grasped all at once from any horizontal perspective.) One can stand in front of a painting from many positions, but it is the 'same' painting that one sees in a stronger sense than when seeing a garden from different locations. (26)

The parenthesis makes the important point that it is impossible to see all fifteen rocks at once: something is constantly withheld or hidden, and if one wants to talk of the work's aesthetic effect in terms of *yūgen*, this withholding would be a major contributing factor. But because the rock garden at Ryōanji can be viewed only from the platform that runs along (the larger part of) its northern side—or is at least intended to be viewed only from points on this platform—the number of available perspectives on it is actually quite restricted. Most gardens afford the possibility of the viewer's entering them, and thus of being able to adopt a vast number of perspectives on their contents. But the fact that this rock garden, as a typical "contemplation garden" of the Muromachi period, has to be viewed from outside—and from only one of its sides as well as from a restricted range of vertical elevation—actually brings it closer to a painting than most gardens. It is more like a sculpture, of course, in that by changing one's viewpoint one sees relations between constituent elements differently; but whereas one can view most sculptures from a 360-degree field around them and thereby see most of them, parts of the larger rocks in the garden at Ryōanji remain permanently invisible to the viewer. This circumstance would further enhance the atmosphere of *yūgen*.

4

> Unlike most works of art, no amount of familiarity with this Zen Rock Garden can provide one with any very solid assurance as to what it is that one will meet when experiencing it; for the work drives one into oneself. . . The Rock Garden of Ryōanji is not a finished thing: it manifests *yūgen* and is thus an open invitation to contemplative being. (27)

I must again admit to some puzzlement here, perhaps because my own experience has been rather different. Revisiting the garden, and after getting over the initial surprise at its size, I find that the experience is rather like that of seeing an old friend again—except that this one exhibits no perceptible changes over the years. It is, of course, a joy to visit the garden in different seasons, though more for the alterations in its context, and especially in the trees around it, than for the minimal changes that take place within the garden itself (different hues in the moss, a layer of snow, and so on). But I find the experience is less one of being driven into oneself than of being drawn out of oneself: once one settles down to contemplation, it is again a matter of these fifteen rocks, the moss, this gravel, that incomparable wall, and the manifold relations among them. (And, of course, further reflections and ideas concerning the powerful impact of the ensemble.) So in this respect I fail to see how the garden is significantly different, any less "a finished thing," than most works of art that do not require performance—than a masterpiece of architecture, sculpture, or painting.

The concept of *yūgen* seems appropriate here in its connotations of "supreme attainment" and "the subtle" (27, 28), but as developed by Zeami (who took it to profounder levels of subtlety than anyone) only the feature of "half-revealed or suggested beauty" (29) seems apposite to the rock garden at Ryōanji. Zeami uses the term—the best single-word translation of which may be "grace"—almost exclusively of performers and performances. The *locus classicus* is section 12 of *Kakyō* (Mirror held to the flower), where he speaks of "the grace of speech" or "words," and of "the grace of music," of "the dance," of "roles," and of "physical appearance."[6] The highest achievement of the actor—and he emphasizes that "very few" are capable of this—is "to enter the realm of grace." It is thus hard to see how the idea of *yūgen* as developed by Zeami helps us understand the aesthetic effect of the rock garden aside from the way, mentioned above, in which its beauty seems to derive from something's remaining unrevealed.

We need to invoke some other notions from Japanese discourse about art, which are more numerous than Eliot Deutsch seems prepared to allow, in order better to understand what is going on in the rock garden at Ryōanji.[7] "The old wall enclosing the rear of the garden is heaped with time" (25)—and thus exemplifies the virtue of *sabi*, for example. The wall is indeed a work of art in itself, though quasi inadvertently: thanks to its having been made of clay boiled in oil, fantastic patterns have emerged over the centuries, as the oil has gradually seeped out. Throughout most of the length of the old wall, which encloses the south and west sides of the garden, mysterious landscapes have appeared on its vertical face suggesting infinite depths, its exquisitely weathered hues complementing the colors of the rocks and moss in front of it. The "skies" of these landscapes are cut off horizontally by a shingled roof running along the wall's length, the angle of which (at around 45°) mediates perfectly between the interior space of the garden and the world outside. This leads us to what may be in this context the most helpful idea from the Japanese aesthetic lexicon: *kire-tsuzuki*, or "cut-continuance."[8]

5

A basic exemplification of this notion is to be found in haiku poetry, which often employs what is called the *kireji*, or "cutting syllable," which effects a cut at the end of a line—and at the same time links it to the next. A consummate example occurs in one of Bashō's best known poems:

Furuike ya	An ancient pond —
kawazu tobikomu	a frog plops in,
mizu no oto	sound of the water.

The *ya* at the end of the first line, rendered in the translation by the dash, is a syllable that "cuts" to the next line in much the same way as a director "cuts" from one scene to the next in a film, breaking and yet maintaining continuity at the same time.[9] Hence the idea of the "cut-continuance." There is also a connection here with the idea of *yūgen*, insofar as cut-continuance characterizes the unique style (*kata*) of walking used in Nō drama. The gait involves the actor's raising the toes, sliding the foot noiselessly forward, and then "cutting off" the movement by lowering the toes—just as the toes of the other foot are raised in order to maintain a continuity, within which each step is nevertheless cut off.

At Ryōanji the major cut is effected by the wall, which cuts the rock garden off from the outside, and yet is low enough to permit a view of that outside from the viewing platform: a paradigm case of cut-continuance. The trees beyond the wall now block the view, and stand in, as it were, for the larger world of nature that used to be visible beyond the garden. Originally the situation exemplified the principle of *shakkei*, since Ryōanji was far enough outside the city as to afford the visitor to the garden a view of unspoiled landscape beyond. Today the trees beyond the wall cut off the sight, thankfully, of urban encroachments, while the wall still cuts off the garden from the trees outside.

This latter cut (which is itself double because of the roof that runs along the top of the wall) is most evident in the contrast between movement and stillness. Above the wall one sees nature in movement: branches wave and sway, clouds float by, and the occasional bird flies past—though hardly ever, it seems, *over* the garden proper. Within the garden a perpetual stillness reigns, and the only movement visible is shadowed or illusory, unless rain or snow is falling. Otherwise, in winter when the sun is low, shadows of branches move across the sea of gravel. The garden is cut off on the near-side, too, by a border of large, round, and dark pebbles reduce the size of space which runs along the east and north edges. Each group of rocks is cut off from the others by the expanse of gravel, the separation being enhanced by the "ripple" patterns in the raking that surrounds each group (and some individuals). And yet the overall effect is to intensify the invisible lines of connection among the rocks.

There is a more radical aspect to the cut, however, which mirrors the distinctively Japanese art of flower arrangement called *ikebana*. The term means literally "making flowers live"—a strange name, on first impression at least, for an art that begins by killing them. There is a gem of an essay by the Kyoto School philosopher Nishitani Keiji on this marvelous art, in which the natural life of one of the most beautiful kinds of natural being is cut off, precisely in order to let the true nature of that being come to the fore. There is something curiously deceptive, from the Buddhist viewpoint of the impermanence of all things, about plants, which sink roots into the earth. In severing the flowers from their roots, Nishitani argues, and placing them in an alcove, one lets them show themselves as they really are: as absolutely rootless as every other being in this world of radical impermanence (*mujō*).[10]

A corresponding cut is operative in the rock garden, insofar as the cutting off from the surrounding nature has the effect of *drying up* its organic life. *Karesansui* means, literally, "dried up" or "withered mountains and waters," but in the title of his poem of that name (cited as the epigraph to the present essay), Musō Soseki uses another character for *kare* that is usually read *kari* and means "temporary." The rock garden contains mountains and waters that are dried up, and so may appear less temporary than their counterparts outside, even though they too will eventually pass away with time. The rocks and gravel are not real mountains and waters: they are just rocks and gravel, even though they are arranged *like* (*nyo*) a landscape. Nishitani has shown the significance of this "likeness" (*nyojitsu*; Skt. *tathatā*) in Zen Buddhism, where each thing, thanks to its oneness with emptiness (*kū*; Skt. *śūnyatā*), is an image without an original, and thus "like" itself.[11] The last stanza of a poem by Dōgen called "The Point of Zazen" reads:

The water is clean, right down to the ground,
Fishes are swimming like [*nyo*] fishes.
The sky is wide, clear through to the heavens,
And birds are flying like birds.[12]

The *nyo* here also means "suchness": in its oneness with emptiness, a being is what it is in being *like* what it is, in its suchness. The rocks and gravel at Ryōanji, in being like mountains and waters, but cut off from nature and dried up, are such that by concealing the outward form of natural phenomena they reveal their true form: suchness, as being one with emptiness.

These ideas take us to the heart of Zen thinking, though it is not possible to pursue them further here. Instead let me finish by taking a step back to a brief consideration of the broader philosophical context of the ideas behind the rock garden at Ryōanji, in the hope that this will help us better understand the feeling that there is some sort of message there, that these rocks and gravel are speaking to us in some way. Just how does the garden issue what Deutsch calls "an invitation to contemplation"?

6

As mentioned earlier, the Shingon esoteric School was the first form of Buddhism to influence the development of the Japanese garden, which it did by introducing mandala and other kinds of symbolism into their construction. The founder of the Shingon School was Kūkai (744–835), who along with Dōgen (1200–1253) is one of the profoundest thinkers of the Japanese philosophical tradition. In a number of different writings Kūkai boldly extends Mahāyāna Buddhist thinking by arguing that the Dharmakāya (*hosshin*), or "reality embodiment," of the cosmic Buddha Dainichi Nyorai (Mahāvairocana) is nothing other than the physical universe. This means that not only vegetation but also rocks and stone—indeed all of "the four great elements" (earth, water, fire, and wind)—are to be included in the realm of sentient beings and revered as constituting the highest body of the *Tathāgata*.[13]

Moreover, with his idea of *hosshin seppō* ("the Dharmakāya expounds the Dharma") Kūkai claims that the physical world, as the Buddha's reality embodiment and in the person of Dainichi Nyorai (the same *nyo* again: Dainichi is the one "thus come"), proclaims the true teachings of Buddhism.[14] But since rocks do not speak human language—speech is for Kūkai one of the "three mysteries," or "intimacies" (*sanmitsu*), of Dainichi—it takes considerable practice for human beings to be able to hear and understand their teachings. As well as hearing the cosmos as a sermon, Kūkai sees, or reads, the natural world as scripture. As he writes in one of his poems:

> Being painted by brushes of mountains, by ink of oceans,
> Heaven and earth are the bindings of a sūtra revealing the truth.[15]

But again, for Kūkai, it takes time and effort to be able to read this sūtra. I think we can better understand the powerful effect of the rocks and gravel at Ryōanji if we take them as proclaiming Buddhist teachings and read them as a sūtra disclosing truths about the world.

Dōgen develops some very similar ideas to Kūkai's, though in terms of the Sōtō Zen tradition, of which he is regarded as the founder. Just as Kūkai identifies the Dharmakāya with the phenomenal world, so Dōgen endorses the Zen verses:

The voices of the river valley are the Buddha's tongue,

The form of the mountains is nothing other than his pure Body.[16]

Philosophically speaking, he asserts the nonduality of the world of impermanence and the totality of "Buddha-nature" (*busshō*): arguing vehemently against the more biocentric standpoint of earlier Buddhism, he claims that Buddha-nature is not just sentient beings but also "fences, walls, tiles, and pebbles" (all of which are much in evidence at Ryōanji).[17] Elsewhere Dōgen writes that "rocks and stones, large and small, are the Buddha's own possessions." Corresponding to Kūkai's notion of *hosshin seppō*, he develops the idea of *mujō-seppō*, which emphasizes that even *insentient* beings expound the true teachings, though in a different way from the sentient. "At the time of right practice," he writes, "the voices and form of river valleys, as well as the form and voices of mountains, generously bestow their eighty-four thousand hymns of praise." And again as with Kūkai, for Dōgen the natural world can be read as sacred scripture: "The sūtras are the entire universe, mountains and rivers and the great earth, plants and trees."[18] No wonder, then, that prolonged contemplation of the rocks and gravel at Ryōanji appears to enrich one's understanding of oneself and the world.

The authorship of this dry landscape garden is uncertain, but whoever the maker was, he clearly stood in the same tradition of seeing the natural world as sacred and a source of wisdom. But by cutting nature out from the rock garden, and arranging withered elements of it within, he carried that tradition a significant step further.

On leaving the rock garden and continuing along the walkway, which leads around the back of the main building, one passes a famous *tsukubai* (a stone water basin of the type used before attending a tea ceremony) bearing an inscription of four Chinese characters that mean: "All I know is how much is enough."[19] Even though the basin was placed in Ryōanji a century or two after the rock garden was laid out there, the dictum seems apposite. Yet on leaving that magnificent site of emptiness I can never resist looking at the south wall of the garden from the outside—and marveling at its understated aura. Deviating only slightly from the "Usual Route" out, one could again spend many hours delighting in the natural attractions along the way, which look significantly different now that the afterimage of the dry garden lingers in the memory. One wonders whether such beauty is something of which it may be impossible to have more than enough.

Notes

Some of the material in this chapter is drawn from my essay " The Role of Rock in the Japanese Dry Landscape Garden," in François Berthier, Reading Zen in the Rocks: The Japanese Dry Landscape Garden *(Chicago: University of Chicago Press, 1999). My gratitude to the University of Chicago Press for permission to reprint that material here.*

1. Deutsch (1975):24–36. I shall refer to passages in this essay simply by the page number.

2. Shimoyama (1976).

3. Berthier (1997): 19.

4. Dōgen (1969–70). *Shōbōgenzō*, "Sansuigyō" (Mountains and waters as sūtras). Further references to Dōgen will be made simply by the title of the relevant chapter/fascicle of his major work, *Shōbōgenzō*.

5. Dōgen, "Busshō" (Buddha-nature).

6. Zeami (1984):92–95.

7. "It is, in some ways, unfortunate that the 'vocabulary' of traditional Japanese aesthetics is limited to so few basic concepts. . . . The few aesthetic concepts . . . were called upon to cover a wide range of experience and were seldom given any very precise articulation" (Deutsch [1975]:36n8). It is true that Japanese aesthetic vocabulary may lack precision in comparison to its Western counterpart (though before condemning this lack we should appreciate William James's praise of the virtues of vagueness), but it is not as limited as all that—especially when one considers that in the East-Asian traditions aesthetic and "ethical" vocabularies tend to overlap. See, for example, the varieties of aesthetic experience discussed in the essays in Hume (1995).

8. The discussion in this section is much indebted to the work of Ōhashi Ryōsuke (1986), who has elaborated the aesthetic implications of the cut-continuance in his book *Kire no kōzō* (Structures of the cut). This work is available in an excellent German translation in Elberfeld (1994), which was approved and expanded by the author in the course of the translation, and also furnished with numerous fine photographs.

9. For a brief account of this idea (though without reference to cinema), see Ōhashi Ryōsuke (1998) 2:553–55.

10. Nishitani Keiji (1995):23–27.

11. See Nishitani Keiji (1982):137–40 and 157–59. Ōhashi (1986) discusses the rock garden at Ryōanji in terms of "likeness" in chapter two.

12. Dōgen, "Zazenshi" (The point of *zazen*).

13. For a more detailed treatment of this topic, see my essay "Voices of Mountains, Trees, and Rivers: Kūkai, Dōgen, and a Deeper Ecology"; Parkes (1997):111–28.

14. For a fine explication of this idea, see Kasulis (1995):166–85.

15. Kūkai (1972):91.

16. Dōgen, "Keisei-sanshoku" (Voices of river valleys, forms of mountains).

17. Dōgen, "Busshō" (Buddha-nature). It is significant that the term *garyaku* in *shōheki garyaku* (fences, walls, tiles, pebbles) also has the connotation of useless, insignificant things.

18. Dōgen, "Sangai-yuishin" (The triple world is mind only); "Mujō-seppō" (Nonsentient beings expound the Dharma); "Keisei-sanshoku"; "Jishō zammai" (The samādhi of self-enlightenment).

19. See James Heisig's sagacious reflections on this dictum in Heisig (1990) and (1994).

References

Berthier, François (1997). *Le jardin du Ryōanji: lire le zen dans les pierres.* Paris: Adam Biro.

Deutsch, Eliot (1975). *Studies in Comparative Aesthetics.* Honolulu: University of Hawaii Press.

Dōgen (1969-70). *Shōbōgenzō.* In *Dōgen zenji zenshū* Vol. I. Edited by Ōkubo Dōshū. Tokyo: Chikuma Shobō.

Elberfeld, Rolf (trans.) (1995). *Kire: Das Schöne in Japan.* Cologne: Dumont.

Heisig, James (1990). "Towards a Principle of Sufficiency." In *Zen Buddhism Today* 8:152–64.

———. (1994). "Sufficiency and Satisfaction: Recovering an Ancient Symbolon." In *Dialogue (NS)* XXI:69–90.

Hume, Nancy G. (ed.) (1995). *Japanese Aesthetics and Culture: A Sourcebook.* Albany: State University of New York Press.

Kasulis, Thomas P. (1995). "Reality as Embodiment: An Analysis of Kūkai's *Sokushinjōbutsu* and *Hosshin Seppō.*" In Jane Marie Law, editor. *Religious Reflections on the Human Body.* Bloomington: Indiana University Press.

Kūkai (1972). *Kūkai: Major Works.* Trans. Yoshito S. Hakeda. New York: Columbia University Press.

Nishitani Keiji (1982). *Religion and Nothingness.* Trans. Jan Van Bragt. Berkeley: University of California Press.

——— (1995). "The Japanese Art of Arranged Flowers." Trans. Jeff Shore. In Robert C. Solomon and Kathleen M. Higgins, editors. *World Philosophy: A Text with Readings.* New York: McGraw Hill.

Ōhashi Ryōsuke (1986). *Kire no kōzō* (Structures of the cut) Tokyo: Chūōkōson.

——— (1998). "Kire and Iki." In Michael Kelly, editor. *The Encyclopedia of Aesthetics* Vol. 2. Oxford: Oxford University Press.

Parkes, Graham (1997). "Voices of Mountains, Trees, and Rivers: Kūkai, Dōgen, and a Deeper Ecology." In Mary Evelyn Tucker and Duncan Ryūken Williams, editors. *Buddhism and Ecology: The Interconnection between Dharma and Deeds.* Cambridge, Mass.: Harvard University Press.

Shimoyama Shigemaru (trans.) (1976). *Sakuteiki: The Book of [the] Garden.* Tokyo: Town and City Planners, Inc.

Zeami (1984). *On the Art of the Nō Drama: The Major Treatises of Zeami.* Trans. J. Thomas Rimer and Yamazaki Maskazu. Princeton: Princeton University Press.

Eliot Deutsch on Truth

J. N. Mohanty

Eliot Deutsch's remarkable little book, *On Truth: An Ontological Theory,*[1] advances a theory of truth that is notable at least for two reasons. For one thing, he gives a theory that claims to take into account ascriptions of "truth" to assertions or propositions, to religious language, and to works of art. For another, in developing this unified theory, he begins with "truth" as applied to works of art, and then extends that theory to the other two domains, namely, the religious and the cognitive. An examination of Deutsch's theory requires that we examine it in both these aspects.

It may be—and I believe most philosophers would regard it as the commonplace point of view—that there is no unified concept of truth. When we speak of a work of art that is true, of a religious discourse as true, and of a proposition that it is true, we are not using "true," in these three cases, *in the same sense.* If this is the case, then one may proceed to regard one of these senses to be the originary sense, and the others to be rather misleading uses of "true." For most philosophers, the predicate "true" *originarily* applies to propositions, in which case "propositional truth" must be the original sense of "truth." Any attempt at a unified theory like the one Deutsch gives us would then be misconceived. But this would amount to dismissing Deutsch's project too summarily, and possibly in a rather question-begging manner.

In this essay I will begin at the opposite end to Deutsch's, and develop a Vedāntic theory of truth with regard to cognitions, and then, at the end, I will suggest, without arguing in detail, how the theory I arrive at fares in the case of works of art and religious discourse.

Propositional Truth

A few terminological comments on Deutsch's theory, to begin with. (These are not essential either to his or to my account.)

On Deutsch's usage:

A proposition *presents* a fact. ("Presenting" = "to communicate a report of a state of affairs")

A fact *reports* a state of affairs or what is the case. ("reporting" = "bringing one's consciousness to the state of affairs" or making it a content of one's consciousness)

A state of affairs is a possible content of consciousness.

Then, on his theory: A proposition is true iff it articulates adequately its *intentionality* to present a fact (p. 84, my italics).

What does Deutsch mean by "a proposition's own intentionality"? The context shows (esp. p. 86) that a proposition has a meaning. This meaning, we are told, is a fact. The intentionality of a proposition is to articulate its meaning by successfully presenting, that is, communicating, the fact. A true proposition succeeds in doing this. A false proposition does not (p. 89).

I find the vocabulary rather muddled. So let me clean it up and restate the central thesis in a more perspicuous manner.

By *uttering* a *sentence* "p" in an assertional manner, I would say, one asserts (or denies) the proposition p. The proposition p is the thought expressed by "p" as well as by all sentences that are synonymous with "p." The sentence *expresses* the proposition. By asserting the proposition, one *states* a fact. In the communicative mode, by asserting the proposition, one also *reports* (to the auditor) the fact, namely *that p*.

So I would not say, a proposition itself presents a fact. As I here said, by asserting a proposition, one *states* a fact. Or, one may say, a proposition is the *sense* of a declarative sentence; a fact is its referent.

The problem about introducing "fact" is that—as is well known—one is led to admit false facts, a rather embarrassing consequence. So one may either stipulate that only true propositions refer to facts and false ones do not, or get rid of the supposed fact altogether, and do so by appealing to Fregean "truth values," or introduce a notion of fact such that a fact is what makes one proposition true and its negation false (as Wittgenstein does in the *Tractatus*).

The next step would be to determine what precisely is the bearer of truth. I would prefer the following locution: a sentence "p" is true (or false) if the proposition it expresses is true (or false). A belief is true (or false) if it is belief in a true proposition to be true, or a false proposition to be false; a belief is false in case it is belief in a true proposition to be false, or in a false proposition to be true. Basic, then, is the proposition as bearer of truth (and falsity).

What about the alleged intentionality of a proposition? There are two ways this locution can be understood, and both are admissible. If a proposition is the *Sinn* of a sentence, and through the *Sinn*, the sentence, or its utterance, or the utterer, refers to a fact, then by "intentionality" of the proposition may be understood either the intentionality of the speaker's consciousness (what the speaker intends to refer to) or the reference of the *Sinn* itself. Deutsch is right in bringing the idea of intentionality into his theory of truth, but we still have to see how best to describe its role in theory of truth.

Correspondence Theory of Truth

Correspondence theory of truth has been severely criticized ever since it was proposed by Aristotle in the West and the Nyāya in India. (The critics have been lately rather harsh, imputing to this theory all sorts of ruinous consequences.) There are, I think, three kinds of serious criticism of the theory. According to one line of criticism, the correspondence theory does not capture the *original* experience of truth, it already presupposes that entities are disclosed to humans as belonging to their world: this original disclosure can be captured in a theory such as Heidegger's early interpretation of "truth" as *unconcealment*. The latter is then claimed to be an ontological theory in contradistinction from truth as correspondence which is concerned only with the adequacy of a derived cognitive structure, namely, of a proposition. Since at present, I am asking what constitutes propositional truth, I cannot simply say that propositional truth itself should be displaced to make room for a more original experience of truth. To say that the correspondence theory is derived, and so presupposes a prior unconcealment of entities (of a hammer as a tool), is not to entail that propositional truths (with regard to the same hammer) do not consist in adequacy of some sort—unless, of course, one rejects "correspondence" *even at the propositional level.*

On the second line of criticism, pressed certainly by Kant, one concedes that adequacy is the *nominal* meaning of "truth," but not more than this. As Kant put it, it cannot give a sufficient and at the same time general criterion of truth, for what truth shall consist in is agreement with the content of one's cognitions, and since that content varies from case to case no general criterion is possible.[2] Kant, however, goes on to present such a criterion in terms of his transcendental logic, according to which truth will consist in agreement with "possible experience." What this means is that the truth of a proposition cannot be measured by this proposition alone as isolated from the totality of one's experience, but rather by its belonging to that open-ended totality—determined by the "Analogies of Experience" which Kant calls 'possible experience.' What Kant then puts forth may be called a "coherentist reconstruction of the idea of correspondence." It is not a rejection of correspondence outright.

A more radical criticism would be along the following lines: it calls into question the very idea of a "proposition"—as a rigid, fixed entity that either is a sentence or is a class of "synonymous" sentences, or a fixed, rigid abstract entity expressed by the sentence, to which is supposed to correspond (in case the proportion is true) a fact. Leaving aside for the present the question that the idea of "fact" is then redundant, and also unhelpful (for we can understand it only with the help of the thought of a true proposition), one may want to argue that looking for the putative fact presupposes that we know what to look for, and the latter presupposes that we have an understanding of the meaning of the sentence under consideration in such a manner that that meaning "tells us" not only what sort of entity it intends to be true of but also *the sort of correspondence* that is to obtain in the case under consideration. Consider a musical score that is to "correspond" to the musical sound, or a mathematical representation of a physical phenomenon. In such cases, there is no "similarity" that simply can be read off the two that are to "correspond." It is only a person who "reads" the score who can recognize the music that is being played as being the music that is represented by the written score, and it is only the physicist who understands the mathematics who can recognize which physical phenomena it represents. There is thus no one idea of correspondence, agreement, adequacy, or even of "picturing." Even the formal notion of "picturing" from the *Tractatus* won't apply to all cases, for it all depends upon how you cut up the representation and the represented into elements among whom the one-to-one correlation is to obtain.

Moreover—injecting a little Hegelian bias into the thoughts expressed in the preceding paragraph—it is plausible to argue that what a sentence expresses is not just a rigid proposition, but a thought that "grows" with the "apperceptive" background against which the sentence is understood. Consider a mathematical sentence "7 + 5 = 12," or a historical sentence "The first Battle of Panipat was fought in 1526": in each case, the meaning, the thought expressed, grows with the knowledge one has of the number system in one case and of Indian history (for example, the founding of the Mogul Empire) in the other, and does not remain the same as what one grasped when, as a child, one first learnt arithmetic or, a little later, Indian history. If the "thought" develops, so does that to which it "corresponds." The nominal explanation of truth—to borrow Kant's words—remains the same, but—as Joachim, from whom this part of the argument is taken, showed, we are approaching a sort of *coherence* theory.[3]

I think the central problem of "correspondence" theory is that when "ascertaining" correspondence between knowledge and reality, you compare your knowledge, not with the putative reality but with other, or other persons', knowledge. One may escape this problem by distinguishing between the nature of truth and the tests of truth, but the idea of "nature" of truth then is reduced to none other than what Kant called "nominal explanation." The other problem, possibly more serious, is that what the true proposition corresponds to cannot be unambiguously fixed and can at best be described as the real, ultimately the Universe, or Reality as a whole. Recall Frege's thesis that the referent of a true proposition is The True, and F.H. Bradley's idea that the subject in all propositions is Reality as Whole.[4]

Two Sorts of Truth Theory: Can They Be Reconciled?

Davidson distinguishes between two types of theory of truth: epistemic and non-epistemic. Epistemic theories—coherence, pragmatic, anti-realistic, or even internal-realistic—understand 'truth' in terms of our knowledge and our theories, in terms of evidence available to us. Non-epistemic theories explain 'truth' as "evi-

which a non-veridical perception leads to frustration while a veridical perception leads to successful practice, similarly applies to many non-veridical cognitions. The dream-water satisfies dream-thirst.

The Vedāntin, therefore, concludes that "truth" (*prāmāṇyam*) has no criterion. But falsity has: a cognition is false in case it is contradicted by a subsequent experience of the same object (as belongs to the cognition that is contradicted). A cognition, then, is true in case it is not false, that is, is not contradicted. But in that case every empirical cognition when it is had by a knower, is taken to be true independently of successfully applying a test, and this taking to be true continues unless and until the cognition stands contradicted by new experience and is rejected as false. Epistemic truth, then, would always be provisional, open to revision; metaphysically truth will remain uncontradicted forever. Now, let me briefly bring out the implications of such a theory.

Recall the enormous controversy that went on, in this country, as regards what more should be added to the "justified true belief" account of knowledge in order to avoid the Gettier type paradoxes. P. K. Sen has maintained, in an unpublished paper, that one avoids the paradoxes by giving up the requirement that p be true (in the analysis of "S knows that p"). That would be in line with the Vedāntins. The predicate "true" has no use in the analysis of empirical knowledge claims. The pragmatist's "working well" is good enough, but don't take it as an analysis of "is true." When the Vedāntin subscribes to the theory of "intrinsic validity," he does not mean by it "intrinsic truth," but that a cognizer, by saying he knows that p, also accepts or rather advances, a claim which, for all practical purposes, is a claim to truth*. If this claim is not falsified, it continues. Ideally, "truth*" becomes "truth" if the claim cannot be falsified. The predicate truth, therefore, has no use in analysis of empirical knowledge. "Falsity" has, for we all abandon some of our beliefs, along the way. On this theory, then, p is true* if it is not known to be false. Note that you do not need another correlative notion of false*. "False" is within the range of our empirical cognitions, "true" is not. But true* is. "True*" is epistemological, true is not (unless you can know a priori that some belief of ours just cannot be falsified). For the Vedāntin, "consciousness is" is such. To deny it, is to affirm it.

Back to Deutsch's Theory of Propositional Truth

In Deutsch's locution, only a true proposition presents a fact. If this means that only true propositions have "corresponding" facts, then the thesis is uncontroversial but trivial. But, then, we are told that "A proposition is true, then, when it articulates its intentionality to present a fact. A proposition is false when it fails to articulate its intentionality." If by "articulating its intentionality" is meant "saying what it means and meaning what it says" (to use Hegel's words), then I can think of only two possibilities. Either a false proposition can also, as much as a true one, say what it means and mean what it says (both can be muddled to an equal degree), or—if you subscribe to a Hegelian theory of meaning and truth, no proposition can fully express what it means and mean what it says, so that meaning, the large network of concepts, will always exceed what is being said. Rightly, therefore, Deutsch speaks of complete meaning. While I would accept this, I still cannot agree that a false proposition such as "There are living beings on the moon" cannot be completely articulated, that its meaning cannot be clarified. If it is false, that is because of either how things are in the world or because empirical verification would reject it, or for some such reason which relates the proposition to some structure that exceeds the proposition's own internal intentionality. It is therefore apt that using the language of intentionality, we follow Husserl to say that a proposition is true if its intentionality is fulfilled, false if its intentionality is frustrated. The talk of fulfillment and frustration seems to covertly introduce verificationism, but the defects of verificationism can be removed by introducing a phrase from Deutsch's: "to the degree and dimension appropriate for the occasion" (87). This would entail that there is no uniform concept of verification that applies to all propositions. As we noted earlier, in connection with a critique of the correspondence theory, what sort of adequacy is required in case of a proposition for it to be true cannot be pre-legislated, but is rather determined by your understanding of its meaning. We should perhaps speak of different levels of fulfillment. If you want to introduce the pragmatic dimension, you have to say that the kind of success or "working well" that is relevant in a particular case is also pre-determined by the intentionality of the proposition. When truth happens to a proposition, its aim is fulfilled, we then see it to be true (p. 90). When Husserl held that truth is evidence, what he meant is that truth is experienced in the experience of fulfillment of a meaning-intention. I think this comes very close to Deutsch's view.

Deutsch says two more things about propositional truth which I will recall. First, he writes, "A proposition is seen by someone to be true when he recognizes ... that there is no correct alternative to the proposition within the matrix of its presentation" (90). Secondly, he concedes, "With the true proposition, however, it should be noted, definitive verification has not taken place, there is an absence of falsification, of contradiction.... With the false proposition, there is falsification" (91). A little later, he adds, "The test for truth in proposition language is ... one of non-contradictoriness" (91).

But these characterizations are important, if correctly understood. The second clearly is Vedānta-like, as Deutsch recognizes in a footnote (p. 120 n.57). But what could the first mean?

There is an obvious sense in which if "It is raining" is true, there is no correct alternative to it. Such alternative as "It is snowing," "It is dry," are just ruled out as "correct" alternatives "within the matrix of its presentation" to "It is raining." But this by itself is not terribly informative. So let us look at this claim a little closer. When "It is raining here and now" is true, "It is not raining here and now" (the indexicals referring to the same spatio-temporal location) is, of course, logically possible, but really excluded from reality. If the actual world may be defined as the set of all true propositions, any one of the many sets of alternatives to those true propositions would generate a possible world. (A re-distribution of truth-values even of one proposition that is true in the actual world would generate a partial possible world.) So what we have is that a proposition that is true in the actual world, allows for no alternatives to it in this world, but does allow for alternatives in other possible worlds. It alone fits into, or as Deutsch puts it, is "right" for, this world.

But since other alternatives may be actualized, contrary to what is seemingly the case when the truth-claim of "This is a snake" yields place to "this is a rope and never was a snake," "This is a snake" is false, it was, even when it was entertained, never an alternative in the real world. Here the Vedāntin's claim comes in. The Vedāntin obviously starts with the "This is a snake" where the latter articulates (perfectly in language as well as in behavioral responses, its intentionality is clear, unambiguous, and definite) a non-veridical perception. It is rejected as false when subsequent experience contradicts it. Up until then it provided adequate basis for sound belief, cognitive claim, and practical response, that is, for what I have called truth*, which is then rejected. What the Vedāntin may be construed as doing is extending this pattern to all empirical propositions.

Truth in Art and Religion

How to test these ideas in the case of art and religious discourse? As I said at the beginning of this essay, I can only indicate the lines I would like to follow. First of all, I want to make sure the nature of ascribing "truth" to works of art. It would seem that the predicates "great," "genuine," and "authentic" can do the same job as "true" in the case of works of art, and also that, in this context, "true" has no significant opposite. A false work of art is not a work of art at all, it only pretends to be one (while a false proposition is a proposition). Secondly, in the case of the empirical propositions, as I have mentioned, the best we get is "truth*," and to be set aside as false is a destiny they all are open towards. A great, genuine, and authentic—in these senses true—work of art is not "fallible," open to revision and possible falsification. Changes of taste, in theory of art and of the life world, do not simply cast aside great works of art as having been pretensions. What happens to them is different. They are neglected, treated as irrelevant, as not "speaking" to us any more, but they continue to exist in their intrinsic splendor. What, in effect, I am drawing attention to, is a significant difference between "true work of art" and "true proposition." A true proposition is really a true* proposition, "truth" in the cognitive domain is an ideal upon whose realization "true*" passes over into "true." With regard to the work of art, if a work of art is true, it is true: here epistemic and non-epistemic truths coincide. For, in the case of a work of art, truth is not, even as a nominal explanation, agreement with reality, it does not pretend to be "correspondence" in any sense. Its truth lies within itself. Nor does history supersede a work of art. Shakespeare's work is not improved upon by Goethe, or Goethe's by Hölderlin. Each is "true" in itself, by its own right. History comes, as it were, to a standstill. As Deutsch emphasizes, its intrinsic intentionality is fulfilled within its own bounds. Schelling puts it nicely when he says that

while the cognitive and the practical are never-ending approximations, in a work
of art (that is, a genuine great and true work of art) the infinite is fully reconciled
with the finite. You cannot improve upon a Kalidas or a Shakespeare. Each one is
unique, in itself and by itself, and is as such true. I believe these remarks are consistent with Deutsch's remarks on truth in art.

To briefly touch upon religious language, I find Deutsch's distinction between
three kinds of religious language—"language of," "language for," and "language
about"—most interesting, as also his remarks on each. But for the present, I will
restrict myself to the most basic layer of religious experience—analogous to perception in the cognitive domain—namely, to the experience of sacredness. My
question is, is experience of sacredness, no matter in what context, where, and on
what occasion, a merely subjective feeling or is it objectively true?

When one devalues an experience as being "merely subjective," one wants to
say, amongst other things, that the thing one experiences as being ϕ is not really ϕ
but only seems to be ϕ. The devaluation presupposes that conceptually the distinction between "is really ϕ" and "only seems to be ϕ" is available in the case of
the predicate "ϕ." I want to contend that that distinction in the case of "sacred"—
the distinction, namely between "is really sacred" and "only seems to be sacred"—
is not available as it is in the case of "red". It would follow then that if one experiences a thing, a space, a time, and idol, a life, as sacred, then it *is* sacred. Such
religious experience, then, presents truth, not merely a claim to truth, it presents
the thing-over-there-being-sacred.

Art and religious experience, then, have objective truth in the strongest senses
available. Propositional cognition aims at such truth, without ever reaching it.

Notes

1. Deutsch (1979). Page numbers within parentheses in the body of the essay are from
this book.

2. Kant (1787) B:82–83. The text referred to runs as follows: ". . . the question: What is
truth? The nominal definition of truth, that it is the agreement of knowledge with its
object, is assumed as granted; the question asked is as to what is the general and sure criterion of the truth of any and every knowledge."

Then Kant proceeds to write: ". . . it is quite impossible, and indeed absurd, to ask for
a general test of truth. . . ." Again, "of the truth of knowledge, so far as its matter is
concerned, no general criterion can be demanded. Such a criterion would by its very nature
be self-contradictiory."

3. Joachim (1906).
4. Davidson (1990):303–4.
5. Davidson (1990):298.
6. Davidson (1990):295.
7. Mohanty (1989).

References

Davidson, Donald (1990) LXXXVII. "The Structure of Content of Truth." *Journal of Philosophy* 87, no. 6 (June).

Deutsch, Eliot (1979). *On Truth: An Ontological Theory.* Honolulu: University of Hawaii Press.

Joachim, H. (1906). *The Nature of Truth.* Oxford: Clarendon Press.

Kant, Immanuel (1787). *Critique of Pure Reason,* second edition, trans. N. K. Smith, New York: St. Martins' Press, 1933.

Mohanty, J. N. (1989). *Gageṅśa's Theory of Truth.* Second edition. Delhi: Motilal Banarsidass.

The Truth: Eliot Deutsch's Ontological Theory

Thomas P. Kasulis

A philosopher plays a variety of roles: teacher, university citizen, writer, evaluator of others' works, and public intellectual. Over the past quarter century I have had the privilege of benefiting from Eliot Deutsch's contributions in all these areas. I knew him first, however, as my professor in a graduate seminar in comparative philosophy at the University of Hawai'i. It was the winter semester of 1973 and I had been studying Asian philosophies at UH intensively for several months. Until arriving in Honolulu, my graduate work in philosophy had been almost exclusively Western. I had gone to UH for an eighteen-month interlude during which I would study Asian thought and get a good start on learning Japanese. My seminar with Deutsch was at a critical point in my education. Through the seminar I hoped to learn how to relate the two phases of my philosophical training. Depending in part on how things went in that seminar, I would proceed from that point to be (a) a specialist in Western philosophy with some expertise in Asian thought or (b) a scholar of Asian philosophy with a strong background in Western ideas and methods, or (c) some third as yet inchoate option in my mind that would let me draw equally on both the Asian and Western traditions. That third option seemed to be called "comparative philosophy" and there was a consensus that Eliot Deutsch exemplified the best in that field. So I went into the seminar to find out not only what Eliot Deutsch did, but also what he was.

The most provocative aspect of Deutsch's approach was the way he exemplified comparative philosophy as an act of constructive thought rather than scholarship. We did, of course, exercise our scholarly skills in analyzing the texts, contexts, and ideas of several philosophers, both Western and Asian. But that was not the point of the seminar. The point was to study philosophies only insofar as they helped us to philosophize better ourselves.

The topic of the seminar in comparative philosophy that semester was "truth." Deutsch had devised a provocative list of philosophers, both Asian and Western, as readings for each meeting in the first several weeks of the course. Befitting the global context of philosophy at the University of Hawaii, we read Śaṃkara as well as Bertrand Russell and Heidegger, Confucius as well as Aristotle and Thomas Aquinas. He also assigned each of us to research and give a short presentation on the meaning of the term for "truth" in a variety of languages and cultures (given my background, I was assigned to research Japanese contexts).

The course was no mere survey, however. Through the careful design of the seminar, we had reached by the midway point of the semester a broad representation of the approaches taken by a variety of philosophers throughout human history. More importantly, Deutsch had also taught us a way of reading and evaluating a philosophical text. He encouraged us not to get so bogged down in the details of each position that we would miss the bigger picture of what was going on. Before we looked too deeply into what was right or wrong in the particular theory of truth we were studying, Deutsch wanted us to get at broader questions. What in the issue of truth was most important to each of the philosophers? How was that dimension of the issue emphasized and analyzed? In doing so, what other dimensions of truth were marginalized, ignored, or even rejected? In each case Deutsch challenged us to find the philosophical motivation driving the analysis and development of the theory. Through this line of inquiry we got, if nothing else, a strong sense of what was at stake in philosophizing about truth and how a theory of truth both reflected and enhanced a particular view of self and reality. We were then prepared for the last phase of the seminar: our own constructive philosophizing.

Although Deutsch had let us develop our own thinking in whatever direction important to us, the thrust of his own thought gradually became clear to us as the course progressed. He seemed to be primarily concerned with two issues. First, he was concerned with how truth could be defined in a general manner so that it would be equally applicable to a variety of philosophical concerns including aesthetics and religion. In our survey of theories of truth, it seemed that most Western philosophers had primarily understood truth as a characteristics of judgments or propositions. Truth, in other words, was about how well we correlated our judgments with an external reality. This assumed that truth was related to reality only insofar as we tried to represent reality in our own concepts. Deutsch, on the other hand, preferred to turn us to look at the traditions East and West where the term for "truth" was intrinsically related to the word for "reality" or "being" (as in the Sanskrit word *satya*, for example). Once we did so, we could see the broader context for the so-called "ontological theories of truth" developed by such philosophers as G. W. F. Hegel, Martin Heidegger, and Albert Hofstadter. In such cases truth emerged out of, rather than externally referred to, being.

Secondly, and this was not surprising considering his own previous work in aesthetics and the philosophy of religion, Deutsch was convinced that truth had something to do with "rightness." To his way of thinking, the proposition- or judgment-based theories of truth that emphasized "getting it right," where "it" referred to the statement or judgment, were derivative rather than primary. That is, by crafting an ontological theory of his own, he had hoped to develop an understanding of truth that would be more general than that of the Western epistemologists, but yet also be applicable to epistemological issues. More concretely, he hoped to develop a theory in which "rightness" would apply to art works and religious statements as well as to propositions. In our 1973 seminar Deutsch had not yet fully worked out his theory, but I found the very project exciting and philosophically satisfying. If nothing else, Eliot Deutsch had hooked me on pursuing a career as a comparative philosopher.

I was eager to see what Deutsch would finally do with his theory and it was with great pleasure that I read his *On Truth: An Ontological Theory* when it appeared in print in 1979.[1] I was also touched to read the following in his Acknowledgments:

> My greatest debt, however, for the theory of truth elaborated here is to my students in a graduate seminar on the problem of truth held at the University of Hawaii. What the students in the seminar taught me on the subject is I hope evident in this work. (ix)

That passage was no token, *pro forma,* statement of gratitude. Instead, it revealed something fundamental about Deutsch's relation to his students—he treated them as fellow philosophers or at least as apprentice philosophers. As I recall, I was one of those students in the course who raised many critical questions, sometimes challenging Deutsch's own reading of texts or the assumptions he was bringing to his theory. Yet, I never felt he resented me for it. In fact, quite the contrary. He seemed to enjoy the chance to rethink his position, to try to give it a new and better justification or articulation. As we shall see, Deutsch's theory is that even if what one says is not false, it is always at least theoretically possible to better articulate and achieve the truth. He lives and teaches by that philosophy.

In short, when I took the opportunity of the present volume to read *On Truth* once again, Deutsch's insights, his flow of analysis, and his elegant turns of phrase all took me back to that seminar in Honolulu. The man, at least to those of us who know him well, is patently visible in the work. In that book we find Deutsch arguing for some of his most dearly held beliefs. A central one is that we must not let a restrictive philosophy diminish our humanity, to impoverish our capacity for aesthetic appreciation or spiritual power. No philosophy that reduces truth to a simple correspondence between statement and reality will ever be adequate to the task of dealing with the truth we find in art or religion.

That belief of Deutsch's is in marked contrast with two positions commonly held among a certain cohort of Western philosophers. The first is that "truth" in art or religion is not the same as truth in its fundamental meaning—the correspondence between judgment and reality. According to this interpretation, to speak of truth in art or in religious language is more an analogy that suggests the importance to the speaker of certain art works or religious discourse. But it is not really "truth" in its proper sense. The other common option is to think of artifacts like art works as having "meaning" just like that of any propositionally framed utterance. As such, we can evaluate whether that meaning is true or false in much the same way we evaluate statements. Neither of those positions, argues Deutsch, is acceptable. They both share a common error, namely, the premise that propositional truth is the paradigm for all kinds of truth. Deutsch's response is to reject that premise not out of hand, but by formulating a theory of truth that can use artistic or religious expression for its paradigm and yet still account for truth in the propositional, language- or concept-based context.

Where X is "anything that has the capacity to realize rightness" and Y is "a person qualified to perceive that X is true," Deutsch gives the following formulation of his ontological theory:

> X is true when and only when it achieves rightness through the articulation of its own intentionality. X is perceived by Y to be true when Y recognizes that there is no correct alternative to X within the matrix of its presentation. (93)

Using this definition, X could be any number of things, but for the sake of argument in the book, Deutsch concentrates on three critical examples: art, religious language, and propositional language. He begins with his discussion of truth in art.

Deutsch understands such truth to reside in the artistic expression itself, rather than in how it relates to something else. Art does not point beyond itself to some external meaning (or to some externally derived standard of beauty), but rather reveals within the limitations of its presentation its own "intentionality." It presents itself as something and to the extent it realizes that intentionality, it expresses truth. In this respect, we must not ignore the work as an act of artistic creativity that had available to it a variety of possibilities. If the work has a "rightness" to it, its realization of some of those possibilities rather than others fulfills its own internal necessity of self-expression. The truth of the work of art lies in its ability to command our attention so that we recognize what it is getting at, what it is presenting itself to be, and why it had to be exactly the way it is. As Deutsch himself puts it, "a work of art is true when and only when it attains authenticity through the presentation of its own intentionality" (38).

The issue of "intentionality" is central to Deutsch's theory. Because philosophers use that term in many different ways, we need to understand Deutsch's particular understanding. When Deutsch understands the work of art as expressing only one possibility, the one (if the art work is authentic or true) that best realizes the intentionality of the work, there is a suggestion at least of the artist's agency. For Deutsch we are not interested in the artist's intention *per se,* but instead in the intention articulated within the work of art itself. The intention is the way the work presents itself on its own terms, its attempt to fulfill itself in what it presents itself as. Yet, as a human artifact the work of art is necessarily connected to the artist. This point is clarified when Deutsch contrasts the work of art from a natural phenomenon, however beautiful.

> When we speak in formal terms of "necessity" in art, we do so it seems always in the context of our recognizing the work as a created object—one that is open to infinite possibilities, or to put it another way, one whose being is self-determined. In contrast to our experience of the "design" in natural objects, where we recognize that the necessity governing the design is external, . . . in our experience of artworks we discern (quite unconsciously and unthinkingly, no doubt) its freedom precisely as self-determination. The rightness is *inherent*; it does not follow from natural laws but from the dynamic interactions of its elements as controlled by creative intelligence. (40)

It is, according to Deutsch, the "aesthetic force, significance, and beauty" that sets off the "intentionality" of the art work from a design of nature.

Although there is much more to explain about Deutsch's theory of truth in art, we have described the bare bones well enough to raise some issues. First, I have a question about the inclusiveness of Deutsch's definition of art. A good case to consider would be what is commonly called "folk art." We now have museums full of beautiful objects that were originally created not for display, but for everyday use. Can a blanket or a pitcher that was created to be used as a blanket or pitcher be a work of art according to Deutsch's theory? I am not sure. Certainly when put on display in a gallery, the objects are treated as works of art and I think rightly. But what makes it so? In some ways the display itself is what makes the artistic intentionality stand out and call for our aesthetic attention. In its "home" context, the blanket could just as easily stand out as a means of preserving the warmth of a baby. In fact, that would have been its primary frame of reference.

Yet, in talking about such primary and secondary frames of reference, might we not, in Deutsch's terms have slipped into talking about the artist's instead of the art work's intentionality? Let us consider an even more complex and intriguing example, the creation of a tea bowl as a utensil for performing a tea ceremony. In that case I suspect the potter from the start was involved in an artistic act of creation. The usefulness of the tea bowl as part of a tea ceremony might, from that perspective, be part of what Deutsch calls the "matrix of presentation" just as the clay is the medium in that same matrix. Given that matrix, I think it is perfectly intelligible to say the tea bowl has an autonomous artistic intentionality. Yet, from the standpoint of the performative art of the tea ceremony in which the tea bowl is used, that autonomy would have to be part of the autonomy of the performance itself. The tea bowl's individual autonomy would be, as it were, less autonomous. In fact, I think it could be argued that to consider the tea bowl as a work of art separate from the tea ceremony performance as a work of art is similar to the blanket's on display in the museum. The difference in this case is that the blanket has the dual identities of art work and practical utensil, whereas the tea bowl's dual identities are both artistic. The oddity of displaying a tea bowl in a museum is that to do so is to cut off the tea bowl from an intrinsic aspect of its artistic intentionality, to be a tea bowl in the intentionality of the tea ceremony. This may be why some masters never show an exquisite bowl except as part of a tea ceremony, but within that ceremony, it is part of the ritual to admire the tea bowl itself. This seems to be the only right context for fully appreciating what the bowl really and fully is.

To me this suggests that a work of art may have inherently more than one intentionality. In the case of folk art, only one of these inherent intentionalities is artistic. In the case of the tea bowl, however, it would seem that we would have to say the dual intentionalities inherent in the bowl are *both* artistic. I find this consequence of the theory acceptable, but I wonder if Deutsch would do so as well.

In the next chapter of the book, Deutsch turns to the question of truth in religious language. His first move is to distinguish three different kinds of religious language, what he calls "language of," "language for," and "language about." The first kind is the expression of an authoritative sacred source: the sacred reality is, as it were, speaking through the human speaker. In that respect, the truth of the religious "language of" is based not so much in an evaluation of the content of the statements, but rather in a determination of the source of statement. To put it in the vocabulary of one group of religions, we might say that if indeed God is speaking, the issue of the statement's truth is already determined. Such religious "language of" is, therefore, self-veridical and there is not much to be said about it philosophically. Deutsch does note three conditions for its truth, however (51). First, the speaker must believe in the sacred source of the utterance. Second, there must be an "authentic basis for the speaker's self-convincement." In other words, for it to be recognized as true, there must be a basis for trusting that the statement is what it purports to be and is not, for example, an act of chicanery or deception. Third, the situation of the expression as sacred (the sacred as being self-expressive through this particular person at this time and these circumstances) must seem possible to us. That is, we must be able at least to imagine such an event could occur.

Interestingly, Deutsch does not give any examples of true or untrue expressions of religious "language of." He gives two reasons for this silence (49). First, "it is simply not the case that all or even most persons are likely to agree that an alleged example is in fact an example of revelatory language." The one reason he gives for this is that any utterance must be in a particular language and insofar as that language is part of the self-expression of the sacred, it cannot be adequately translated. The second reason is that to accept something as an example of a religious "language of"

> calls for more than a simple recognition of a particular as belonging to a type;
> it calls for direct experience of, and involvement with, the unique, individual
> thing — and for that one must obviously be prepared. (51)

Those two points serve us well in understanding why we will not be able to find
universal agreement as to whether a particular example of religious "language of"
is truly revelatory. Yet, that does not explain why Deutsch does not offer a "phenomenological" or "empirical" example of a particular religious community's taking a specific instance of "language of" as true. That is, although all of us may not
be able to decide unanimously whether a particular utterance of this sort is true,
we should (at least theoretically) be able to agree that "X" serves as such an instance of truth for community "C." Of course, we can all probably think of such
instances (the *Qur'an* for many Muslims, aspects of the writings of Paul for many
Christians, the *Vedas* for some Hindus). So it may not seem examples are really
necessary. When we start trying to analyze the details of such examples, however,
a new series of questions arises. In particular what is the role of what Deutsch calls
a person's "being prepared" so that one might judge the truth of an alleged case of
religious "language of?" Does this entail the participation in some religious praxis
or at least in the religious education of the tradition? Does one have to be attuned
or made sensitive to the revelatory in order to recognize it? Are there grounds for
judging the validity of the education ("brainwashing" as opposed to "being ex-
posed to the tradition)" or the praxis ("hazing" as opposed to "legitimate religious
practices")? If so, how does the judgment of validity of the "being prepared" relate
to the truth of the language? Is it a kind of expert knowledge that comes from
doing rather than a purely intellectual event?

For most philosophers of religion, the focal interest is in discussing and analyzing religious "language about" rather than "language of." Deutsch recognizes
this fact and he himself fits the pattern, giving thirteen pages to the former and
only four to the latter.

Although Deutsch is probably right in saying that there may not be a lot a
philosopher can say about religious "language of," it might be worth the effort to
analyze the phenomenon as fully as possible. Socially, culturally, and spiritually it
is critical to develop philosophical grounds for distinguishing true religions (in
Deutsch's rich sense of "truth") from false religions. It is noteworthy that for the
people involved in the (alleged) religion, the weight of their commitment often

derives mainly from what is considered the "rightness" of some purported revelatory language. In fact, the allegedly revelatory, "religious of" aspect of religions often outweigh for their adherents the importance of doctrinal consistency. In light of that fact, we philosophers should try to make any contribution we can to sorting out the criteria that establish religious "language of" as true. So, when Deutsch says (51), for example, that religious "language of" requires "discernment" and "recognition of spiritual quality," what exactly does he mean by those terms? In discussing truth in art in chapter 1 (37), Deutsch uses the phrases "discern that the work of art is beautiful" and "recognize inherent significance." Are we to understand those terms in the same way when discussing truth in religion? I doubt that Deutsch would want to give us the impression that if we know how we relate to the artistic, we then know how we relate to the religious. Surely there are some differences worth explaining. In fact, why else would Deutsch not hesitate to give examples of rightness (or lack thereof) in specific art works, yet not want to do the same for religious "language of?" Furthermore, without engaging a circularity in which "spiritual" and "religious" are defined in terms of each other, what exactly is meant by "recognition of spiritual quality?" I would suggest that Deutsch needs to give these terms the same kind of nuanced attention he did when discussing truth in art.

Next Deutsch turns his attention to what he calls "religious language for." This is the shortest discussion of the three kinds of religious language (two pages), but I nonetheless found nothing significant to be missing. Basically, he says religious "language for" is for *somebody* and is a "teaching language" (52). Its use is to point out the spiritual path for the sake of another person. As such it must be responsive to the needs of the audience; it must be "*for* him, in openness to his being" (53). Therefore, its truth lies not in its source (as in "language of") nor primarily in its reference (although that is certainly involved). Instead, its truth is judged primarily in relation to its "pragmatic efficacy" (53). Deutsch is particularly insightful when he talks about the "commitment" or "faith" the responder must bring to the exchange. This involves, as Deutsch puts it succinctly, the responder's taking of "the *risk* of at least partial self-surrender to his guide" (53). In my terminology I would say that religious "language of" is the language of reality, whereas religious "language for" is the language of praxis. Again in light of our discussion of religious "language of" and the need for "preparing" a person, because praxis is at the heart of "language for," it might be useful to think more thoroughly about the possible relations between the two.

Lastly, Deutsch turns to the third kind of religious language, "language *about.*" Deutsch correctly points out that this species of religious language is for most philosophers the only kind worth analyzing. Fortunately, Deutsch himself has a much richer understanding of religious language than most philosophers of religion and so it is not surprising that his analysis takes us further. Deutsch explains that religious "language about" is "'public' and 'objective;' that is to say, it is language which appears to be reducible semantically about propositions and statements—to language-units whose truth or falsity can be agreed upon in principle by logical and empirical verifying procedures" (54). Deutsch takes this as his starting point, but quickly moves on to explain some of the ways in which religious "language about" is distinctive from most other kinds of propositional-like statements. He notes, for example, that it is used theologically "to transmit a religious tradition"(57); that it recognizes the "limitations of language in speaking directly about reality"(57); and that it is "expressive and creative of (and not just allegedly descriptive of, or reportive about) the relations between man and the divine" (61). Deutsch's insistence on the limitations of language with reference to the sacred leads him to make the following somewhat radical statement:

> *The further one is from the life of spiritual being, the more one is compelled, it seems, to talk about it. The closer one is to the divine, the less one is capable of even uttering a name. When one inwardly possesses some thing or state of being, one has no need to objectify it. The finite intellect, in the realm of the spirit, works only on absences.* (55, italics in original)

Given all this, what can we say about truth in religious "language about"? First, Deutsch explains that it must always be understood in its own religious (or even metaphysical) context (64). "The more that language is reducible or transposable without loss of meaning to context-neutral propositions (as indeed is the case with much theological writing), the less it comes under the general category of religious language" (62). Deutsch concludes, therefore, that religious "language about" is "less a matter of correspondence between statement and fact" and "more properly a matter of right formation of consciousness" (64–65). Even though such language has a propositional dimension, "it can be seen to have a cognitive richness that goes considerably beyond most propositional language, for it may be creative of relationships (which open the way to further insights) and not just presentative of facts" (65). On all those points I find Deutsch's characterization of religious "language about" to be insightful and convincing. I would like to suggest, however, that insofar as Deutsch claims that religious "language about" is a "matter of the right formation of consciousness" (a point with which I concur), it can also serve a function much like religious "language for." Part of the path in religious traditions (what the religious "language for" points to) typically contains an aspect of "right thinking." In other words I would claim that, properly understood, religious reflection (including some of what is called "theology") may serve a necessary role in not only the formation, but also the expression, of religious consciousness. Deutsch (inadvertently perhaps) is privileging a certain kind of religious form as paradigmatic. His paradigm is not only mystical and translinguistic (as the italicized quote above suggests), but also individual rather than communal. Deutsch recognizes something of the communal dimension when he notes that religious "language about" can be part of the "transmission of religious tradition." Yet, that transmission would seem to be at least in part a function of "language for" as Deutsch has defined it. That is, religious reflection about the nature of reality may be inevitably related to how "language for" points to a particular religious path. The instruction is *for* the next generation as well as *for* those who of this generation who have lost their way.

Furthermore, and on this point there may be little room for agreement with Deutsch, I would argue that religious "language about" may also, in a critical sense, be *for* the religious person expressing the language. Deutsch is right in observing that virtually all religious traditions recognize the limitations of language, especially in its ability to describe the sacred. But I would not want to extrapolate from that to say (as Deutsch does explicitly and in italics), "*The further one is from the life of spiritual being, the more one is compelled, it seems, to talk about it. The closer one is to the divine, the less one is capable of even uttering a name*" (57). This may be true sometimes, but I am wary of the overgeneralization. In point of fact, many religious people would argue that the most intense religious experience, a closeness to the sacred, can be had commonly in communal contexts, contexts that may indeed include the voicing of commonly held doctrines (such as speaking in a Quaker meeting, in enunciating the Nicene or Apostle's Creed during a church service, the chanting of the Heart Sutra, etc.). In such cases the sacred presence is not something other than the religiously infused community at that moment. Furthermore, one can, I believe, think of cases (in certain kinds of preaching, for example) when the preacher is "filled with the spirit" and engages in that form of "language of" that is also "language for." At the same time, however, the truth of such a sermon (if it manifests "rightness") would also seem to fit exactly the type of "formation of consciousness" that Deutsch emphasized in discussing "language about." Such sermons often preach doctrines as well as edify. In fact, the sermon may arise as an intense encounter with the divine that is *necessarily* in language, including some "language about." The "preaching the good news" in such a situation is an act of sharing that is inseparable from the direct experience of divine love. At least it can be. As we noted already, Deutsch claims that to understand "religious language about" as something more than neutral propositional claims, one must pay attention to the distinctively religious "context." Part of that context, I would argue, is religious praxis, especially communal religious praxis, and it is that praxis that connects the three types of religious language.

In short, when there is a spirit-filled expression such as the example of the sermon just described, all three types of religious language are involved. Doctrines are included in a proposition-like form, so we have "language about." Yet, in some respect we also have the divine self-expression manifest in the sermon mouthed by the preacher or in the recording of one kind of sacred text. That "in-spiration," that infusion of spirit, suggests religious "language of." The language is as revelatory, perhaps as much to the human being expressing it as to the audience. Yet, the sermon also "points the way" and in that instructional aspect, it can function also as religious "language for."

How should we understand that multiple nature? We might divide the sermon into its individual sentences and type each one as one of the three kinds of religious language. I doubt that would be successful, however. Even it it could make such a fine distinction in each case, the very process would violate the integrity of sermon as a single religious act. In some respects this brings us back to the case of the Japanese tea bowl discussed earlier. In that case I argued that it might be meaningful to think of the tea bowl as having a dual artistic intentionality, as an art work in itself and also as part of an artistic performance (the tea ceremony). The tea ceremony itself involves a time when the tea bowl is admired as an artistic item in its own right. In considering cases of religious language such as the ones we have been discussing, it might be useful to see them as each involving multiple intentionalities (two and perhaps even three). Importantly, however, these multiple intentionalities are not simply a matter of viewing the same utterance (or textual reading) in different contexts or from different perspectives. Rather it is an intrinsic characteristic of the language usage that it can be simultaneously both or all three. To see it as only one of the religious language types would be to deny the language its own autonomy, its ability to present what it is in its own terms. To recognize this intrinsic character of some instances of religious language, we have to move away from the mystical, individual experience as the paradigm for all religious experience and look at religious language as more fully embedded in communal practices.

The third domain Deutsch analyzes in his book is that of truth in propositional language. As we recall, Deutsch's entire project in this book is to show that by developing an adequate theory of truth that works for the rightness of art works and religious language, we can generalize that theory so that it will also cover the truth of propositional language. If successful, this will undercut the common practice of trying to understand truth in art, for example, by using models developed primarily in the philosophy of language and logic. Up to now, we have seen that there are various areas in Deutsch's application of his theory to works of art and religious language that may need augmentation. However, we have found no reasons to challenge the theory itself. So the real test will simply be whether Deutsch's theory is adequate to understanding propositional truth, the type of truth most other philosophers consider primary. If Deutsch succeeds here, his project succeeds. If not, however well it functions for truth in art or truth in religious language, it will not be, according to Deutsch's own explicit intent, successful.

We need not reiterate Deutsch's argument in detail, especially his detailed comparisons and contrasts with a variety of theories from contemporary language philosophy. We need only review it in the broad strokes. Deutsch starts with meaning. Following the approach he used in his discussion of art and religion, Deutsch looks for meaning as emerging out of the expression itself rather than as something external to it. The key again is intentionality, not the intentionality of the person making the expression, but of the expression itself as it develops out of its own "autochthonous" (as well as regulative and constitutive) rules. That is, the statement presents itself as being something of a certain sort manifesting its own intention on its own terms. The statement achieves meaning only if the utterer crafts it (following the rules, including the self-generated autochthonous sense of "rightness") in such a way that a respondent (using knowledge of the elements of the statement and the rules) can recognize the intentionality of the statement.

So the question now is: what is the intentionality of propositional language? Answer: to present a fact.[2] A fact in turn is "the report of the occurrence or the nature of any content of consciousness" (79). Its domain is "anything of which we can be aware" (79). Any possible content of consciousness is what we call a "state of affairs." Therefore, (if true) propositional language *presents* a state of affairs. Through this ingenious application of the insights achieved by studying the truth of art and of religious language, Deutsch has found a way of avoiding all the traditional problems associated with correspondence theories of truth. In Deutsch's model we do not have the ultimately unexplainable gap between what the proposition is and that to what it corresponds "out there." Instead, in Deutsch's model, the propositional language is presenting its own intentionality of reporting "the occurrence or nature of any content of consciousness." There is here no gap, no correspondence between two different kinds of entities that need explanation. A false proposition, therefore, is one that fails to achieve its own intentionality, that of presenting or reporting a fact.

This leads to an intriguing conclusion. A proposition either presents a fact or it fails to do so. To that extent it is true or false. Yet, insofar as presenting the fact is an achievement, among true propositions we can properly talk about the degree of their success in that presentation. There are, as Deutsch puts it, "degrees of truth-realization" (90). This has important implications for the testing of truth as well. Deutsch articulates the point in this way: "A proposition is seen by someone to be true when he recognizes rightness in such a way that there is no correct alternative to the proposition within the matrix of its presentation" (90). The corollary of this is that in testing for truth, we look not so much for verification as for noncontradictoriness.[3] What is not falsified, which means what is not replaceable by a proposition with more "rightness" in achieving its intention of reporting a state of affairs, is allowed to stand as "true." There is the understanding, however, that this truth (which is not and cannot ever be definitively verified) is subject to later contradiction, to later replacement by a proposition that is more rightly realizing the intention of reporting that state of affairs. As Deutsch puts it, "a true proposition is not contradicted; it is not uncontradictable" (92). Falsification, therefore, has a special meaning in Deutsch's account. It is not necessarily what we think of as negation in formal logic. Deutsch gives the following example: "If someone says, 'The sky is gray today' when in actuality it is clear blue, it is not enough to have 'The sky is not gray today': falsification would call for 'The sky is blue today'" (91). Deutsch is not very detailed in his explanation of why this is so. I assume his argument would be something like this. The intention of the original proposition is to characterize the color of the sky today; it is to "ascribe properties to a subject" as he puts it. Therefore, "The sky is blue today" better succeeds in rightly fulfilling that intention. "The sky is not gray today" would negate the original proposition but would not best report the state of affairs in relation to the intention of the proposition. We need "The sky is blue today" to realize that intention.

There is one aspect of Deutsch's theory of truth in propositional language that I would like to pursue further. For a proposition to be true, it must mean something and meaning occurs, as Deutsch points out, in a communicative context. Let us examine what Deutsch says about this context in relation to truth.

> A true proposition is one that, to the degree and dimension appropriate for the occasion, successfully presents a fact; which is to say, one that rightly articulates its own intentionality so that it calls for response, reaction, and verification by those to whom it is conveyed. (87)

My question refers back to the apparently hard and fast distinction that Deutsch made between religious "language about" and propositional language. Propositional language is "not fundamentally 'formative' in character; . . . its primary function is to tell that something is the case" (76). Yet, as we have just seen, Deutsch describes the true proposition as calling for "response, reaction, and verification by those to whom it is conveyed." That would seem to be quite close to religious "language about" in that such a "call" would seem to move the listener in certain ways to think about certain things and, therefore, in *some* sense to be "formative of consciousness." A true proposition has the intentionality that is the "reporting of the occurrence or the nature of any content of consciousness" and, we now see, also calls for a response from the listener, focusing that listener's consciousness on the report. In that respect a true proposition intends to be not only a report but also a step toward a rapport. So, althought it is true that religious language is more than just propositional in character, it also seems there is something religious about propositional truth. Truth in propositional language is itself spiritually edifying in some ways. That is not (at least to me) a surprising conclusion, but I wonder if Deutsch would accept it.

What then can be conclude about this ontological theory of truth that Deutsch has developed? The intentionality of the book is, I believe, successfully realized. It achieves rightness insofar as I find no ground for falsifying it: I can see no correct alternative to it. Of course, my report of its truth is only that I leave it uncontradicted. It does not mean that it is uncontradictable. An even more successful articulation of the truth is always possible. Eliot Deutsch would want it no other way.

Notes

1. Deutsch (1979). In this essay, all numbers in parentheses in the text refer to the page numbers in this work.

2. Incidentally, as an aside, Deutsch points out that religious language, even "language about," is never just propositional because as religious language, it is formative of consciousness. That is not within the domain of the intentionality of a proposition (76). With that little comment, Deutsch has effectively disarmed much of the language philosophy that has tried to explain or explain away religious language by a propositional analysis.

3. In footnote 57 Deutsch notes the Vendāntin character of this emphasis on noncontradictoriness. He also observes in that note that the self-evidential nature of truth in his theory is also comparable in some ways with Vedānta.

References

Deutsch, Eliot (1979). *On Truth: An Ontological Theory.* Honolulu: University of Hawaii Press.

The 'Tradition Text' in Indian Philosophy for Doing History of Philosophy in India

Gerald James Larson

In a volume of essays that Eliot Deutsch and I coedited some years back, *Interpreting Across Boundaries: New Essays in Comparative Philosophy*, Eliot's own contribution to that volume was an essay entitled "Knowledge and the Tradition Text in Indian Philosophy."[1] In that essay Deutsch argues that the "form" of presentation in Indian philosophy in terms of *sūtra*-s and *kārikā*-s, followed by *bhāṣya*-s, *vārttika*-s, *ṭīkā*-s, and so forth, rather than inhibiting or constricting the development of Indian thought (which is the conventional view regarding the style or form of Indian philosophizing), instead, provides a continuing mechanism for creative development. Says Deutsch:

> My argument will be that this idea of philosophy as "recovery" rather than "discovery" is central to the traditional understanding of a philosophical text. In making this argument I am not claiming that we have some completed original text as such on which diverse commentaries were written, but rather that what constitutes the text in Indian thought is precisely the *sūtra* (or *kārikā*) and/or other authoritative sources, together with the ongoing exegetical work. In Indian philosophy we have as the basic unit what we might call the "tradition text": the philosophical content of a "school," in the best sense of the word.[2]

Deutsch comments further:

> The basic commentary . . . or the shorter commentaries, with the subcommentaries . . . and glosses . . . form, hermeneutically, integral parts of a continuing argument or text. . . . The exegetical material expands, refines, modifies arguments and ideas, and presents new ones, usually with increasing precision . . . , seeking to bring greater systematic coherence to its body of ideas. The philosopher-commentator, in other words, seeks to remain faithful to his authoritative sources, but in his own creative terms. It is thus that we can speak of his work, together with its authoritative sources, as constituting a "tradition text."[3]

What Deutsch intends with his notion of the "tradition text" is that a philosophical perspective cannot be reduced to one collection or book or a single author, but is, rather, a cumulative tradition unfolding over time involving many voices and numerous exegetical interventions.

I have found Deutsch's notion of the "tradition text" helpful in my own work in trying to piece together certain developments in the history of Indian philosophy, specifically, with respect to the traditions of classical Sāṃkhya, classical Yoga, Abhidharma Buddhist thought, and early Vedānta. All four of these represent "tradition texts" in Deutsch's idiom, namely, (1) the *Sāṃhyakārikā* of Īśvarakṛṣṇa, (2) the *Yogasūtra* (hereafter=YS) of Patañjali, (3) the *Abhidharmakośa* of Vasubandhu, and (4) the *Brahmasūtra* of Bādarāyaṇa, the *Gauḍapādīyakārikā* and the *Brahmasūtrabhāṣya* of Śaṃkara—and all of these, of course, with their exegetical traditions.[4] What has particularly interested me is the manner in which these "tradition texts" have tended to overlap in the unfolding of these traditions, not in the sense of the continuing polemics between the "schools" through the centuries, but, rather, in the sense in which the terminology of the "tradition texts" overlaps over time, and I would like to suggest in this article that attending to this overlapping in the development of the "tradition texts" may help us piece together some of the early chapters in the history of Indian philosophy.

I first approached this problem in an earlier paper published in *Studien zur Indologie und Iranistik* entitled "An Old Problem Revisited: The Relation between Sāṃkhya, Yoga and Buddhism," in which I suggested that the classical Yoga philosophy as represented in Patañjali's YS appears to be a hybrid formulation derived from the "tradition text" of the old Sāṃkhya philosophy (or the *Ṣaṣṭitantra*) and the early "tradition text" of Buddhist philosophizing as found primarily in the *Abhidharmakośa* and *Bhāṣya* of Vasubandhu.[5] Moreover, the "tradition text" of classical Yoga philosophizing together with the "tradition text" of Vasubandhu's work appear to feed directly into the "tradition text" of Gauḍapāda and Śaṃkara, or, in other words, appear to be constitutive of the "tradition text" of Advaita Vedānta.

In this present article I want to move the discussion one step further by trying to understand the reasons for the incorporation of what appears to be the Buddhist "tradition text" into the "tradition text" or *sūtrapāṭha* of the YS and what this means for trying to piece together the history of Indian philosophy in the first centuries of the Common Era.

First of all, however, let me offer a quick summary of the extent of Buddhist terminology in the Sāṃkhya, Yoga, and Vedānta traditions. It has been recognized, of course, since Deussen and Dasgupta that there are many Buddhist terms in the YS.[6] Especially the *sūtra*-s in Book IV (the Kaivalya Pāda) have often been cited as being under heavy Buddhist influence, since it appears to be clear that in *sūtra*-s 16–21 of Book IV the compiler of the YS is responding to the consciousness-only notion of Yogācāra Buddhist thought. Beginning with Dasgupta and coming down to Frauwallner, many scholars have therefore dismissed Book IV of the YS as a later appendage or interpolation.

The problem, however, cannot be so easily swept away, for, as Louis de la Vallee Poussin demonstrated years ago, the presence of Buddhist terminology in the YS is not only found in Book IV but extensively in the first three Books as well. La Vallee Poussin has cited well over a hundred terms or notions that appear to be common to both Yoga philosophy and Buddhist philosophy, some fifty of which La Vallee Poussin has traced to the *Abhidharmakośa* and *Bhāṣya*, that is, to Sarvāstivāda, Sautrāntika, and early Yogācāra contexts.[7] Some of the more important of these terms are the following: *śraddhā, vīrya, smṛti, samādhi, prajñā, bīja, vāsanā, āśaya, nirodha, kleśa, dharma, lakṣaṇa, avasthā, bhūmi, dharmamegha, samāpatti, pratipakṣabhāvanā,* and so forth.

Moreover, as a student of classical Sāṃkhya philosophy, I was struck by the curious fact that these Buddhist terms (this Buddhist "tradition text," if you will), or perhaps better, these terms that are jointly shared by the YS and Buddhist textual environments (especially the *Abhidharmakośa* and *Bhāṣya*) are totally absent from the Sāṃkhya textual environment or "tradition text." This led me to the rather obvious conclusion that the *Yogasūtrapāṭha* represents a hybrid formulation, a conflation or, if you will, a new "tradition text" combining the old Sāṃkhya philosophy and the early Buddhist philosophy. I then identified this hybrid formulation with the work of Vindhyavāsin, the Sāṃkhya teacher, thereby agreeing with a suspicion that Frauwallner had expressed in passing in his treatment of the history of Yoga, and suggested that this philosophical conflation becomes the ground upon which much of the later Vedānta philosophizing of Gauḍapāda and Śaṃkara develops.[8]

The first stream in the Yoga conflation, namely, the old Sāṃkhya philosophy or *ṣaṣṭitantra* might well be characterized as "discernment philosophy" (because of its focus on *adhyavasāya* or "reflective discernment" by the *buddhi* and by its focus on *vyakta-avyakta-jña-vijñānāt, cf. Sāṃkhyakārikā*, verse 2, or, in other words, "the reflective discrimination" of *prakṛti* and *puruṣa*). Its principal *pramāṇa* is *anumāna* or inferential reasoning. Its ontology is an eccentric dualism of primordial materiality and contentless consciousness. Its epistemology is a critical realism, based upon its assertion of *prakṛti* as *triguṇa*, and its philosophy of mind is reductive materialist, that is to say, there is no mind-body or thought and extension dualism in Sāṃkhya.

The second stream in the Yoga conflation, namely, the old Buddhist philosophy, might well be characterized as "*nirodha-samādhi*" philosophy (because of its focus on meditation and its pursuit of altered states of awareness). Its principal *pramāṇa* is *pratyakṣa* or perception. Its ontology is pluralist, and its epistemology is naive realism (Sarvāstivāda) or representationism (as, for example, Sautrāntika and the later Yogācāra). In terms of its philosophy of mind, it is also reductive materialism in the sense that it like the Sāṃkhya also affords no special status to the "private life of the mind."

To identify these two streams of philosophizing, however, is not to say that classical Yoga philosophy is nothing more than a combination of Sāṃkhya and Buddhist thought. It is, rather, an updating of the old Sāṃkhya, a creative intervention in the "tradition text" of Sāṃkhya in an attempt to bring the old Sāṃkhya into conversation with many of the issues that were developing in the early classical period, that is, *ca.* the fourth and fifth centuries of the Common Era. The hybrid formulation, or this new and updated "tradition text" is a kind of Neo-Sāṃkhya (hence, my inclination to agree with Frauwallner and others that it is primarily the creative innovation of Vindhyavāsin), and, thus, it is neither a mistake nor an accident that the *Yogasūtrabhāṣya* is entitled *Sāṃkhyapravacana-bhāṣya*, or "A Commentary on an Interpretation of the Sāṃkhya."

It is instructive to see how the Sāṃkhya of the YS differs from the old Sāṃkhya of Īśvarakṛṣṇa, for by seeing the points of difference it becomes clear how the old Sāṃkhya is being upgraded or brought up to speed, as it were, with the philosophical issues being debated in the classical period. The conventional or textbook discussions of the differences between the Yoga philosophy of Patañjali and the Sāṃkhya philosophy of Īśvarakṛṣṇa usually focus on two main differences, namely, (a) that whereas Sāṃkhya represents the theoretical basis for meditation,

Yoga represents the practical implementation or praxis; and (b) that whereas Sāṃkhya is non-theistic (*nirīśvara*), Yoga incorporates the notion of God (*īśvara* or *seśvara*) in its presentation of the classical system of meditation by way of accommodation to popular sentiment. Both characterizations are partially correct, but a careful study of the *Yogasūtrapāṭha*, the relevant Buddhist texts and terminology (especially from Vasubandhu's *Abhidharmakośa* and *Bhāṣya*), and the Sāṃkhya corpus, indicates that the differences are much more thoroughgoing. Six differences are especially salient:

(1) Whereas classical Sāṃkhya speaks of *buddhi*, *ahaṃkāra*, and *manas* as three distinct faculties that make up the *antaḥkaraṇa* or "internal organ," classical Yoga philosophy reduces the three to one all-pervasive *citta* or "mind-stuff" (*cf.* YS I.2, I.37, and II.54). The "thirteenfold instrument" (*trayodaśa-karaṇa*) of Sāṃkhya (made up of intellect, ego, mind, the five sense capacities, and the five action capacities) becomes, then, for Yoga only an elevenfold instrument, or even more simply, the all-pervasive *citta* itself. The term "*citta*," of course, appears variously in the ancient literature, both Brahmaṇical and Buddhist, but it is hard to avoid the parallel with discussions of "*citta*" in Sautrāntika and Vijñānavāda Buddhist contexts in particular. The Yoga view, however, stresses the objectivity or non-sentience of *citta*, thus making *citta* almost synonymous with *prakṛti* (*cf.* YS IV. 19). A pure contentless consciousness (*puruṣa*) is needed to render the *citta* and its modifications capable of self-awareness (*cf.* YS IV.18–25).

(2) Whereas classical Sāṃkhya speaks of the thirteenfold instrument wrapped, as it were, in the five subtle elements, as the "eighteenfold" subtle body (*sūkṣma-śarīra*) that transmigrates at death to a new rebirth body, the simpler and more sophisticated Yoga view is that if the *citta* is all-pervasive, at the moment of death, there is an immediate transference to a new embodiment, hence, obviating a need for a subtle body. Here again the parallel with Buddhist (and Jain) discussions is obvious, with the Theravādins (and classical Jain thought) like the Yoga philosophy arguing that there is no need for a subtle body (*antarābhāva*), and with the Sarvāstivādins and other Buddhist schools arguing for some sort of subtle body. Interestingly, on this point, the *Abhidharmakośa* discussion comes out closer to the old Sāṃkhya view of a need for a subtle body in contrast to the Yoga view which appears to relate to the Theravāda (and Jain) rejection of a subtle body.

(3) Whereas classical Sāṃkhya deals with what can be called the phenomenology of experience in terms of the fifty components of the *pratyayasarga* (the so-
called "intellectual creation" of five misconceptions, twenty-eight incapacities,
nine contentments and eight attainments), which, together with the ten "basic
principles" (*mūlikārtha*-s) make up the group of sixty or the "*ṣaṣṭantra*," Yoga
greatly simplifies the description of phenomenal experience in terms of the
"transformations" (*vṛtti*-s) of "awareness" (*citta*) in terms of *pramāṇa* (correct
awarenesses through the means of knowledge), *viparyaya* (incorrect awarenesses),
vikalpa (verbal constructions or discourse), *nidrā* (sleep), and *smṛti* (memory)(*cf.*
YS I.5–11). Clearly the Yoga idiom is a more sophisticated philosophical account
and closely mirrors the classical Indian philosophical discussions of *pramāṇa*-
theory, theory of error, theory of language and meaning, theory of states of
awareness, and theory of memory that are to be found in, for example, Buddhist,
Nyāya, and philosophy of language environments.

    (4) Whereas classical Sāṃkhya deals with the issue of time and transformation
solely in terms of the theory of *guṇa-pariṇāma*, Yoga philosophy offers a sophisticated account of time and transformation in terms of momentariness (*kṣaṇa, cf.*
YS IV.33) and a theory of the three perspectives on change and temporary transformation (*cf.* YS III.13–14), namely, change in *dharma*, change in *lakṣaṇa* and
change in *avasthā* ("... *dharma-lakṣaṇa-avasthā-pariṇāma* ...," *cf.* YS III.13).
Change in *dharma* is the change of characteristic (a lump of clay becoming a pot),
change in *lakṣaṇa* is the change of past to present and, finally, to future (lump of
clay, pot, eventual broken pieces); and change in *avasthā* is the change in any object as it grows old (the pot newly made, the pot as it ages, and the pot as it becomes old). As is well-known, the Buddhists (Sarvāstivādins, Sautrāntikas, and
Vijñānavādins) all debated the problem of change in precisely these terms.
Whereas the Buddhists chose from among these possibilities (and others as well)
(as discussed presumably in the *Mahāvibhāṣa* and among the Vaibhāṣikas), the
Yoga philosophy accepts all three explanatory modes and relates them to its theory
of the *dharmin* (*cf. Yogasūtra* III.14), or, in other words, the Sāṃkhya theory of
satkāryavāda and the notion of an abiding substance over time (*prakṛti*). Sāṃkhya
philosophy, therefore, is provided with a sophisticated theory of change and
transformation within the developing idiom of classical discussions of change and
transformation, thereby filling a glaring gap in the old Sāṃkhya "tradition text"

and at the same time getting beyond the hopeless Buddhist arguments of trying to salvage a notion of time with a theory of momentariness that consistently undercuts any meaningful notion of temporality.

(5) Whereas classical Sāṃkhya does not mention God and is considered for the most part (at least in its classical formulation) to be *nirīśvara*, in the sense that a creator God is really not necessary given the overall metaphysical account of *puruṣa* and *prakṛti*, the Yoga philosophy develops an interesting theory of God, which, on one level, follows a Sāṃkhya orientation in that God is not a creator but, rather, one among the plurality of *puruṣa*-s (*puruṣa-viśeṣa*, cf. YS I. 23–24), but which, on another level, nicely answers the Buddhist critique of God (as well as the Jain critique) (both of which argue against God as creator) while at the same time putting the Sāṃkhya-Yoga God or Guru or Primal Knower in precisely the same condition as the Buddhist and Jain "omniscient ones" (*sarva-jña*-s)(cf. YS I. 25). The old Sāṃkhya had simply not addressed the issue of God because it was irrelevant from the perspective of the metaphysic and theory of knowledge. With the rise of Buddhist and Jain philosophizing, however, and the emergence at about this same period of Nyāya theistic speculation, the issue of God became much more pressing, and it can be argued that the Yoga philosophy nicely fills in the lacunae from the old Sāṃkhya "tradition text." In this regard, it should be stressed that most of the scholarship on the history of Indian philosophy has missed the importance of the theological discourse in the Yoga "tradition text." From the time of Garbe, Keith, and Dasgupta all the way down to Frauwallner, the Yoga theological "tradition text" has been dismissed as an add-on in response to popular sentiment. It is becoming increasingly clear, however, that the theology of the Yoga "tradition text" is a fundamental creative intervention in the unfolding classical Indian philosophical discussions of theology.

(6) Finally, and perhaps of greatest importance, whereas classical Sāṃkhya had developed its soteriology largely in terms of the simple "discernment" of the difference between *puruṣa* and *prakṛti* (*vyakta-avyakta-jña-vijñānāt*) and arguing for its ultimate principles on the basis of inferences of the *sāmānyato-dṛṣṭa* type (that is, arguing to what is imperceptible in principle on the basis of certain general and necessary features of what is perceptible), the Yoga philosophy develops a much more sophisticated and detailed theory of "discernment" based on *samādhi*-s (altered states of awareness) of the *samprajñāta* type (that is, intentional aware-

nesses) and the *a-samprajñāta* type (that is, non-intentional or "*nir-bīja*" awarenesses)(*cf.* especially all of Book I and Book IV of the YS in this regard as well as major sections of Books II and III as well). The former are what Frauwallner once characterized as the "cognitive intensive," whereas the latter are what might be called the "cognitive restrictive." Frauwallner, being largely an Indologist and not sufficiently attuned to the relevant philosophical issue, made the unfortunate suggestion that, therefore, there are two types of Yoga patched together in the YS, clearly missing the significance of the obvious philosophical issue involved, that is to say, the difference between intentional and non-intentional awarenesses. In any case, in this regard Yoga brings to bear old Indic traditions of meditation that focus on *dhāraṇa, dhyāna, samādhi, nirodha, samāpatti,* and so forth, to be actualized in the *aṣṭāṅga-yoga* (*cf.* YS II. 28ff.) and the *kriyā-yoga* (*cf.* YS II. 1ff. Whether these old practices and notions are originally in Brahmanical or Buddhist environments (or both!) is difficult to determine, but the Yoga philosophy brings these old notions into a masterful synthesis that provides both a theoretical as well as practical account of the old Sāṃkhya discernment of the distinction between *puruṣa* and *prakṛti*. The compiler of the YS is familiar with the discussions of meditation in the older Brahmanical and Buddhist texts, and he nicely adapts them to the structures of Sāṃkhya philosophy. It could well be the case, of course, that there were old Yoga traditions of a pre-philosophical kind from which Brahmanical tradition, classical Yoga philosophy, and Buddhist philosophy drew. What is important to recognize, however, is that these old meditation notions and theories are now updated by the Yoga discourse into a revitalized Sāṃkhya "tradition text" in a manner that provides a sophisticated philosophical psychology for the classical period.

Earlier I stated that these six differences between classical Sāṃkhya and Yoga are especially salient, since they show in each instance an advance in philosophical sophistication on the side of Yoga philosophizing in comparison to the old Sāṃkhya. In other words, it becomes obvious that the Yoga philosophy of Patañjali is a good deal later than the old classical Sāṃkhya of Īśvarakṛṣṇa. Furthermore, the Yoga philosophy is in polemical contact with Buddhist thought, not only of the Sarvāstivāda and Sautrāntika type but of the later Vijñānavāda type as well. It also becomes clear, however, that although the Yoga philosophy is in polemical contact with the Buddhist "tradition text," and, indeed, makes extensive use of the new philosophical discourse coming into use in the classical period, each of the innovations introduced in the Yoga philosophy has for its purpose a clarification and extension of the old Sāṃkhya philosophy. In other words, the Yoga "tradition text" is very much a "Sāṃkhya Pravacana," that is, an interpretation of Sāṃkhya.

By way of conclusion, let me say that Deutsch's notion of the "tradition text" has been helpful to me in two distinct senses. First, from the perspective of doing history of philosophy in India, if one were to ask, whatever happened to the old Sāṃkhya philosophy, one could well give the answer: there it is in the updated and creative innovations of the "tradition text" of Yoga. In other words, there is no such thing as "old Sāṃkhya." There is, rather, a growing, evolving "tradition text." Moreover, this updated and creative innovation of the Sāṃkhya-Yoga "tradition text" feeds directly into the emerging "tradition text" of Gauḍapāda's and Śaṃkara's Advaita Vedānta. It has been said that Western philosophy is a series of footnotes on Plato. I am inclined to say something similar, *mutatis mutandis*, about Sāṃkhya: Buddhist philosophy and terminology, Yoga philosophy, early Vedānta speculation, and the great regional theologies of Śaivism and Vaiṣṇavism are all, in an important sense, footnotes and/or expressions of a living "tradition text" of Sāṃkhya.

Second, and much more important, however, from a philosophical perspective, Deutsch's "tradition text" has put us all on notice that, finally, Indian philosophy is not Indology, Buddhology, Sanskrit or area studies, important as these disciplines are. It is first and foremost creative philosophy. When all of the Indological and Sanskritic work has been done, we are only at the threshold of the truly exciting task, that is, taking up the "tradition text" and "doing" Indian philosophy for our own time!

Notes

1. Larson and Deutsch (1988):165–73.

2. Deutsch (1988):169.

3. Deutsch (1988)170–71.

4. For the *Sāṃhyakārikā* I have used the text and translation as found in my own book, Gerald J. Larson, *Classical Sāṃkhya* (Delhi: Banarsidass,1979; second revised edition):255–77; for text and translation of the YS and the commentaries of Vyāsa and Vācaspatimiśra, I have used Ram Shankar Bhattacharya, editor, *Pātañjala-Yogadarśanam* (Varanasi:

Bharatiya Vidya Prakashan, 1963) and J. H. Woods, trans., *The Yoga-System of Patañjali*
(Cambridge: Harvard University Press, 1914; Harvard Oriental Series 17); for text and
translation of Vasubandhu's work I have used Swami Dwarikadas Sastri, editor,
Abhidharmakośa and Bhāṣya of Ācārya Vasubandhu with Sphutārthā Commentary of
Yaśomittra, 2 volumes (Varanasi: Bauddha Bharati, 1981) and Leo M. Pruden, trans., Louis
de la Vallee Poussin's *Abhidharmakośabhāṣyam*, 4 volumes (Berkeley: Asian Humanities
Press, 1988–90) as well as Stefan Anacker, trans., *Seven Works of Vasubandhu* (Delhi:
Banarsidass, 1984); for the Sanskrit text of Gauḍapāda and Śaṃkara, I have used the *Works*
of Śankarācārya, Volumes I, II, and III (Delhi: Banarsidass, 1964; Government of India
Project for Important Sanskrit Books) and Vidhushekhara Bhattacharya, trans., *The*
Āgamaśāstra of Gauḍapāda (Delhi: Banarsidass, 1989 reprint of 1943 edition), and George
Thibaut, trans., *The Vedānta Sūtras of Bādarāyaṇa*, 2 volumes (New York: Dover Reprint,
1962; Sacred Books of the East, XXXIV and XXXVIII).

5. Larson (1989). An expanded version of this original article was presented at the Xth
World Sanskrit Conference, Bangalore, India, in January 1997. Yet another version appears
in *Asiatische Studien* (1999), pp. 5–14.

6. Cf. Dasgupta (1963):229–30. Cf. also Frauwallner (1953):408ff., for Frauwallner's
discussion of the YS and its composite structure with at least two distinct kinds of Yoga,
namely, the Yoga of Insight (or "cognitive intensive" Yoga)(Books II and III) versus the Yoga
of Suppression (or "cognitive restrictive" Yoga)(Book I).

7. La Vallee Poussin (1936–37):223–42.

8. Frauwallner (1953):408ff.

References

Anacker, Stefan (trans.) (1984). *Seven Works of Vasubandhu.* Delhi: Banarsidass.

Bhattacharya, Ram Shankar (ed.) (1963). *Pātañjala-Yogadarśanam.* Varanasi:
Bharatiya Vidya Prakashan.

Bhattacharya, Vidhushekhara (trans.) (1989). *The Āgamaśāstra of Gauḍapāda.*
Delhi: Banarsidass, reprint of 1943 edition.

Dasgupta, S. N. (1963). *A History of Indian Philosophy.* Volume I. Cambridge:
Cambridge University Press.

Deutsch, Eliot (1988). "Knowledge and the Tradition Text in Indian Philosophy."
In *Interpreting Across Boundaries: New Essays in Comparative Philosophy.* Edited by Gerald James Larson and Eliot Deutsch. Princeton: Princeton University Press.

Frauwallner, E. (1953). *Geschichte der indischen Philosophie.* Volume I. Salzburg: Otto Muller Verlag.

Larson, Gerald J. (1979). *Classical Sāṃkhya.* Second revised edition. Delhi: Banarsidass.

———— (1989). "An Old Problem Revisited: The Relation between Sāṃkhya, Yoga and Buddhism." In *Studien zur Indologie und Iranistik,* 15:129–46.

Larson, Gerald James and Eliot Deutsch (eds.) (1988). *Interpreting Across Boundaries: New Essays in Comparative Philosophy.* Princeton: Princeton University Press.

La Vallee Poussin, Louis de (1936–37). "Le Bouddhisme et le Yoga de Patañjali." In *Melanges Chinois et Bouddhiques,* 5.

Pruden, Leo M. (trans.) (1988–90). Louis de la Vallee Poussin's *Abhidharmakośabhāṣyam.* 4 volumes. Berkeley: Asian Humanities Press.

Śaṅkara (1964). *Works of Śaṅkarācārya.* Volumes I, II, and III. Delhi: Banarsidass; Government of India Project for Important Sanskrit Books.

Sastri, Swami Dwarikadas (ed.) (1981). *Abhidharmakośa and Bhāṣya of Ācārya Vasubandhu with Sphutārthā Commentary of Yaśomittra.* 2 volumes. Varanasi: Bauddha Bharati.

Thibaut, George (trans.) (1962). *The Vedānta Sūtras of Bādarāyaṇa.* 2 volumes. New York: Dover Reprint; Sacred Books of the East, XXXIV and XXXVIII.

Woods, J.H. (trans.) (1914). *The Yoga-System of Patañjali.* Cambridge: Harvard University Press; Harvard Oriental Series 17.

The Spiritual Value of Suffering

6

Herbert Fingarette

"The problem," says Eliot Deutsch "is to determine the spiritual value of suffering."[1] That is the problem I propose to address in the following remarks.

In his recent work, *Religion and Spirituality*, Professor Deutsch addresses in highly original ways many facets of these two deeply problematic aspects of human experience. Appropriately (to my mind) he does so not by elaborating theoretical positions but through the medium of provocative epigram, story, dialogue, and crisply succinct commentary. His lifelong concern to probe the human spirit in humanly meaningful terms is reflected at a new level in this recent and evocative new book.

I want to take up here the problem of suffering that he poses. Although it is not explicitly pursued in his book, he does in another context present comments that bear substantively on the topic. I will come to these in the latter part of my own remarks.

The very phrasing of the question—"the spiritual value of suffering"—already suggests the paradoxical and puzzling truth: Suffering does have, or at least can have, spiritual value. Yet, given what seems to be the inherently negative connotation of the concept of suffering, and indeed what appears to be the intrinsically undesirable nature of the experience, how could suffering, in and of itself, have positive value, whether spiritual or not?

To my mind, the path to understanding the spiritual value of suffering lies in this: It is the only way to achieve anything of spiritual value. In asserting this I do not mean to say suffering is one thing and these spiritual values are, independently, the effects of suffering. The spiritual value of suffering lies within the experience of suffering. To suffer is in and of itself to experience what is of spiritual value.

The principle obstacle to understanding the nature of suffering and what it entails is that for most of us there is a nearly ineradicable association between the notion of suffering and that of pain or at least distress or malaise of some kind. Nevertheless in the root meaning of suffering this is wrong, however much it may seem on its face to be self-evidently true.

The first step toward enlightenment here—but only the first step—is to see that "to suffer" is a deeply ambiguous verb. The older, more fundamental, and still viable meaning of "suffer" does not necessarily convey the idea of pain or distress.

The Oxford English Dictionary gives some twenty separate meanings for the English word "suffer." The linguistic roots of the word are Latin. The first root is *sub*, meaning "under." The second root is *ferre*, meaning "to bear." Cognate versions of the word, with the same Latin roots, exist in Spanish, French, and Italian.[2]

The first principal set of meanings in English is given as "to undergo, to endure." The second principal set of meanings is given as "to tolerate, to allow." While many (but not all) of the other meanings in the first set are said to imply that what is undergone is painful, this is not true for the definitions in the second set. The various meanings in the latter set are primarily explained as "allowing or permitting something or someone to be or to act without interference." The latter set is characterized as reflecting principally older usages which have become literary or even archaic or obsolete. Essentially the same points are made in the Unabridged Webster's International Dictionary, second edition. The same ambiguity exists in Spanish, French, and Italian. All these languages use cognates of "suffer" to mean simply "allow."

In its sense as "to tolerate," "to allow," "to permit," "not to interfere," we find it in a classic instance of English. The King James version of the New Testament has Jesus saying: "Suffer the little children to come unto me . . ."[3] Here "suffer" clearly means "do not interfere," "do not forbid," "let it be," and implies nothing in the way of pain or distress.

A closely related term—with cognates in all these languages[4]—is "patient." It is no mere coincidence that we read of "the patience of Job." This will puzzle anyone who examines the Old Testament text of *Job* and who takes "patience" to be used in the predominantly modern usage. Today "patient" generally implies one who bears *quietly*, without raising a fuss. But Job was not mild, not deferential, and not quiet. Quite the contrary. He rants and roars, page after page, unceasingly challenging (blasphemously) the Lord Himself, with being injust. He was patient, however, in the sense that he suffered: he endured, he bore the pain and the grief of a man who no matter what the cost refused to try to manipulate the pain away by confessing hypocritically to sins he never committed, and begging forgiveness. His enduring—in this case his honesty in preference to evading the reality of an unjust God—opened the way for the Divine revelation of Reality to him.

"Patience" has as its root "passive." In modern colloquial usage, the "patient" in the doctor's office may in fact be impatient—agitated and unwilling to wait. But the use of the term "patient" to characterize the physician's client comes out of the earlier, primary meaning of "patient." The patient is "the one who is acted upon," the one who is passive and endures without interfering, the one who suffers the physician to act. This need not entail pain, indeed it may entail relief and comfort.

What I have been saying may seem to be merely a thesis about words. It is indeed about words, but it is also a thesis about human existence. It is true that the linguistic cognates of "suffer" that I have mentioned up to this point all belong to much the same family of languages. So it may seem that I am taking advantage of an accident of linguistic history. But many centuries have passed since these languages—and their respective societies—have gone their different ways. Yet the underlying *concept* has remained stable through time. That is because there is at work here not just a word but a fundamental human concept. It is notable that within European civilization, but in a different major language family, and in connection with an entirely different linguistic root, we see the same concept. The word is the German "*leiden*." This, too, carries the meaning of suffering pain, and also the more general concept of simply allowing or tolerating and not interfering.

Still more fundamental proof of the ubiquity of this ambiguous concept emerges when we turn to entirely different civilizations. It should be no surprise that once one clearly defines the fundamental meaning of suffering and appreciates its central spiritual role, it becomes apparent that the idea plays a key role in Asian civilizations. Thus it becomes clear that we are dealing with a universal, substantive human experience, not a mere linguistic coincidence. Unfortunately, translations of texts from other cultures into Western languages have generally missed the point.

In effect, suffering is the central theme of the ancient, enormously influential Chinese work, *Daodejing* [Tao Te Ching]. Laozi [Lao Tzu], the putative author, speaks of a wondrous power, the *de* 德, that arises from following the Way. In turn, the Way is repeatedly characterized as the way of *wuwei* 無爲, of no-action, of letting things be, of letting-go, letting things happen, of going *with* them instead of acting *on* them. The core of Laozi's teaching is expressed in the paradoxical epigram "*wei wuwei* 爲無爲 "[5]—act through non-action. In other words, even in acting one is to suffer the Way to have its way. Don't impose your own way. The imagery of passivity dominates the language of Laozi.

Laozi's book of the Way and of its marvelous Power is replete with evocative, typically paradoxical admonitions. They teach not only the power but also the *fulfillment* that comes from authentic suffering. He regularly refers to the one who suffers the Way to go its way as the wise one, the sage. The sage, says Laozi, relies on actionless activity, wordless teaching.[6] The sage stays back, and so is ahead.[7] Laozi asks, Which of you can make yourself inert, to become in the end full of life?[8] Banish wisdom, discard cleverness . . . diminish the self and curb the desires.[9] To become straight, let yourself be bent; to become full, be hollow. The sage does not strive, therefore no one can contend with him.[10] I know, says the sage, the value of action that is actionless.[11]

The translational problems of rendering classical Chinese terms into the European languages can easily obscure the relationships among the ideas. The absence of the word "suffering" or its cognates in the European language translations of Laozi is notable. The modern translators are dominated by the modern narrow sense of the word "suffering"—that is, suffering pain. Nevertheless, in spite of the word's absence in the translations, I would maintain that once one fixes clearly in mind the generic meaning of "suffering," and ceases to subsume it under the specific meaning of "suffering pain," it becomes clear that the concept is central to the *Daodejing*. Suffer the Way to be. Do not interfere. Be like water—passive, and yet in the end powerful.

In a much later Chinese perspective—that of Chan [Zen] Buddhism—the same basic theme emerges. For example, the great Sixth Patriarch, Hui Neng, in his seminal teachings known as the *Platform Scripture*, characterized the supreme enlightenment as utter openness, utter abandonment of the imposition of ego. Thus for example, he composed the following verses:

> Perversity at work—affliction;
> Correctness at work—no affliction;

Neither perversity nor correctness at work—Purity;
Perverse views lead into the world.
Correct views lead beyond the world.
Throw both away—Wisdom emerges.[12]

In yet another great civilization, that of ancient India, the *Bhagavad Gītā* centers once again on the same basic theme. Here Professor Deutsch's own translation, and his writings in this area, provide rich sources of insight.

The doctrine of *karman* (action) embodies as a central paradox the idea of the "action in inaction," and "the inaction in action" (*karmani akarma/akarmani ca karma*). The *Gītā* says that he who understands this karmic concept is wise.[13] Such a person has "abandoned attachment to the fruits of action"[14]—so that, even when engaging in action, one "does nothing."[15] Constant in success or non-success, even when he is acting [the yogin] is not bound.[16]

Once again we see that, amidst all the complexities of the *Gītā*'s teachings, a central theme is the "discipline" (*yoga*) of complete openness, of openness to what is, openness to what "has to be done."[17] This implies one is not dominated by the questions: What do I want? What do I get out of this?

This inaction-in-action is what liberates spiritually. It is the passivity that liberates. It does not necessarily bring pleasure or joy, though it may perfectly well do so. It is a form of fundamental indifference to pleasure and pain.[18] It is what in the words of European languages can be described as authentic suffering.

It may be well to note that, once again, translational problems obscure the identity (and universality) of the concept that lies behind the differing words and linguistic traditions. The Sanskrit word often translated into European languages as "suffering" is the word *duḥkha*. Indeed it is in the context of "defining" *duḥkha* that Professor Deutsch poses the problem that I take up in this essay: the problem of determining the spiritual value of suffering.[19]

In this context Professor Deutsch implies that *duḥkha* can mean suffering, and that suffering is inherently a form of distress or malaise. It is just this combination of ideas, however, that generates the "problem" of the spiritual value of suffering.

I believe that in the *Gītā* the notion of *duḥkha* is not well translated as "suffering." The term is appropriately translated into English as "pain," or "misery," or "sorrow," or in any case as a generalized form of distress or malaise. However, what is distinctive about the yogin is not that he is freed from suffering, but is freed from the attachment to pleasure which makes pain a form of *duḥkha*. The yogin suffers pain and pleasure to be—they are for him "the same."[20] Liberation from *duḥkha*, or as the *Gītā* says, "this disconnection from union with *duḥkha*,"[21] is not an absence of pain but a spiritual condition of which it is said, "by no [*duḥkha*], however heavy, is he moved"[22]—which implies that the yogin can experience intense *duḥkha* but is not moved by it. That pleasure and *duḥkha* are "alike" to the yogin does not mean, of course, that he cannot distinguish between them. It means he suffers both with equal openness, equal readiness to bear them for what they are, and does not try to make the world go his way, to seize pleasure and avoid pain.[23]

Analysis of *duḥkha* brings to the fore the fact that even the specific notion of suffering pain is itself crucially ambiguous. Built into our usage is often a special philosophical assumption, and an associated specific spiritual bias, namely that pain and distress are our enemies. But there is a dramatic and objectively verifiable difference between suffering pain as a fact, and making pain into an enemy.

It is a well-established medical fact that the physical pain people experience is commonly 30 to 40 percent anxiety-generated—the "enemy" aspect—rather than physically caused by the initial ailment.[24] That is why the placebo effect is so powerful in ameliorating pain. Give a person in pain an inactive placebo that is labeled *Morphine*, for example, and the consequent expectation of relief results in a marked diminution of experienced pain. In short, one's attitude to pain makes a marked difference in the nature of the experience of pain.[25]

The concept of suffering is manifest not only in the Western languages. It is central to certain Western philosophical-religious lines of thought as well as Eastern ones. Not only is patience, openness to reality, a central theme of the Old Testament Book of Job, it is also the core of the New Testament teaching of humility and *caritas*, acceptance of all creatures, sinners as well as the pious. Christian humility is deeper than, and different from, meekness. Jesus was not meek.

In Western mystical tradition we see the same concept, for example in such a teacher as Meister Eckhart. Eckhart spoke of the enlightened one's disinterested engagement in the world of joys and sorrows as a condition akin to that of a swinging door. The door swings back and forth, while all the time the hinge at the center remains fixed and solid. God, said Eckhart, "is love"; but he also said that God is "immovably disinterested." To understand how these two assertions express a single coherent thesis is to understand authentic suffering.[26]

The question remains, however: Why should it be that "suffering"—letting be, being open—should have come to take on in modern times the significance of implying distress, unhappiness, pain? ("Passivity" has come to have negative connotations, too, and for analogous reasons, as will be seen.) Why has the aspect of joy been lost from sight in the experience of suffering? Indeed, why does the idea of joy in suffering seem a contradiction in terms, or, at most, the definition of masochistic perversion?

In the modern age, self-assertion is a fundamental value. To be patient is to be frustrated, whereas to act and to shape the course of events to one's liking is to be gratified. It follows that where this attitude of self-assertion predominates, to suffer, to be passive is in its very nature to be defeated. Passivity against one's will signifies debility, and brings pain, distress, humiliation. Is it any wonder that the notion of suffering has come to imply distress in one form or another?

Although there is much truth in saying, as I have, that our age more than most is an age of self-assertion, it is also true that in many ways we are characteristically patient, and do suffer authentically. Some of the clearest examples of this can be seen in the area of the arts. I think particularly of music and literature because I happen to be most familiar with these.

Listening to music can, of course, be adulterated by the intrusion of one's own ego, one's personal thoughts, feelings, wishes. As a young man I used to listen to Tschaikovsky's *Romeo and Juliet* overture, and part of my intense reaction was due to the projection into it of my own romantic thoughts and sentiments. I made the music serve my purposes. Even now, when listening to music I sometimes try to identify in it examples of performance technique or of compositional style that are of interest to me. Here again my own purposes are imposed on the musical situation. I play the violin in a Mozart string quartet, wondering as I play whether I'll be able to avoid embarrassment when I attempt that upcoming sudden leap from low G to the G three octaves above. Ego intrudes.

On the other hand, whether listening or performing, there quite often are stretches of time where there is only the music present to me. I am totally absent. I let the music live its life. I listen or play in a way such that what is happening in the music is all that is happening so far as my consciousness or activity goes. When playing the violin I am, of course, actively moving my fingers and my bowing arm, yet it is in a way misleading to say at such moments that I am doing this.

This is inaction-in action, *wuwei*. That is, it is the demands of the music that elicit and control the finger and bow action. I simply do, as the *Gītā* says, what "has-to-be-done." And when my ego does interject itself, that is just the point where I am likely to falter. There is no time or place for ego here. The music must be in total control if the music is to be played successfully.

In short, I have to forego asserting myself, and let myself be the medium, not the master; I must patiently suffer the music to perform itself, to live through me. When this happens perfectly, the meaning and impact of the music become most perfectly (and wonderfully) revealed to me, undistorted by ego. What results is not some technical information about the music—the sort of thing I could get from a book. Nor is it even knowledge about those features of the music that are crucial to its beauty—I could get this information by reading a piece of analytical and sensitive music criticism. It is not *information* that is at issue. What is at issue is the direct perception, the living of the musical reality itself.

Such suffering is by no means restricted to the context of the arts. It is to be seen—or, sadly, not seen—in the way we experience our emotions and feelings. In the realm of emotions, of feelings, of attitudes, of relationships to others, we often speak of wisdom as the condition of true and deep and realistic understanding. That we are so often not wise is the evidence of our inability to open ourselves to our feelings.

Here lies the source of the problem raised by Professor Deutsch. That problem initially arises on those occasions when we see that someone's suffering has engendered spiritual values such as wisdom and humility. This fact can in turn cause one to suspect that spiritual value of some kind may always be engendered by suffering. This in turn leads us to ask why it should be that suffering always, or at least characteristically, engenders spiritual values. It is this concatenation of circumstances that in my opinion elicits Professor Deutsch's question.

The first stage of the answer lies in noting the facts already mentioned. *Duḥkha* can engender spiritual values in a particular instance if it compels us to surrender our ego-motivated myths of control, and to perceive (in frustration) the reality that exposes these myths. Spiritual values such as wisdom and humility can then arise.

Writers, poets, and psychologists have brought to our attention, however, that even in the most inward realm of feelings we often misperceive or, worse yet, self-deceive. Generally speaking, most of us ascribe to ourselves—impose on ourselves—the feelings and emotions and attitudes that our culture defines as proper for the occasion. Moved by feelings that are not "proper," acting in ways that evoke disapproval or that result in frustration, the choice is often avoidance or cover-up rather than the openness that engenders wisdom.

Drink, drugs, self-deception, scapegoating—the ways of evasion are many. Those unwilling to suffer are unable to gain insight into this aspect of their inner world.

The more fundamental answer to Professor Deutsch's problem, however, lies in the fact, as I argue here, that the concept of suffering has ever had a deeper and more general meaning. Beyond the suffering that is *duḥkha*, the frustration of the self and its will, there is the fundamental condition of suffering. To suffer in this sense is simply to allow, to be open, not to impose the ego-will or interfere, to suffer reality to be and to show forth.

It is this latter suffering which at times results from confronting rather than evading the meaning of one's *duḥkha*, but at times, at least for some, is simply the natural condition of the person in the setting.

If what I've been saying is on track, then suffering—in its fundamental and generic sense—may be a time of pain, but so too may it be a time of joy. To be open to music, to be open to one's feelings, to be open to one's relation to another person may be joy if such is the nature of the music, the emotion, the relationship. The quality of what is suffered is not solely determined by the stance of the sufferer. Also crucial is the actual objective quality of that which is suffered. That quality may be of any kind—joy, sadness, frustration, pleasure, pain. . . . There is no limit, no guarantee of happiness here, only of dignity.

Against this background I can now turn specifically to Professor Deutsch's remarks, early in his book, about the concept of "spiritual passivity." "Spiritual passivity," he says, "is the death of the restrictive ego and the birth of true awareness."[27] Later he says, "Spiritual passivity is a state of blessed forgetfulness,"[28] which is to say forgetfulness of the ego.[29] The mind becomes a mirror of the "sacred harmony of being."[30] (Calling to one from within this condition, spiritual passivity becomes love, even "divine love.")[31]

I believe that what Professor Deutsch calls spiritual passivity is essentially the same as suffering when that word is taken in its fundamental and most general sense. True, Professor Deutsch's language, unlike mine, is perfused with religious—or as he might prefer to say—spiritual overtones. Words such as "blessed," "sacred," and "divine" are used by him to characterize "spiritual passivity." Nevertheless he does say that the reference is not to a personal being. The subject of these adjectives is "a state of being realized in human consciousness."[32]

That the condition of spiritual passivity is the condition of suffering becomes evident in remarks about spiritual passivity such as, "a simple letting go," [33] "a kind of contemplative attentiveness. . . ."[34] "Clearing the mind of anticipations, one becomes as a mirror reflecting a sacred harmony of being." [35] "Spiritual passivity is a retrieving of one's nothingness."[36] It is the "death of the restrictive ego, . . ."[37]

Aside from these broad affinities between spiritual passivity and suffering, there are certain specific elements in Professor Deutsch's remarks about spiritual passivity that call for comment.

I might say at once that my comments do not imply any general objection to the use of "religious" language such as I've cited, so long as they carry (as in Professor Deutsch's usage) no theological meaning. On the contrary, such language is often eloquently and aptly used by Professor Deutsch, along with equally eloquent and apt but non-religious language characterizing spiritual passivity.

On the other hand, the spiritually passive consciousness is always cast in his text in radiantly positive, indeed ecstatic, terms. But how can true openness to what-is, openness to the reality of this world, be always a beatific experience? This, to me, is simply not the case. Openness to reality must include the entrance into one's consciousness of horrors as well as beauty. Openness to reality reveals not only one's own pains, but more generally, human cruelty, torture, greed, corruption, hate, disease, failure, frustration, misery—as well as heroism, joy, love, honor, compassion, and sublime beauties. It is difficult to assess which of these two dimensions, the dark or the light, is the more dominant overall.

I believe that the one-sidedness of Professor Deutsch's report reflects an activity rather than spiritual passivity. "Contemplative listening," he says, "is a gathering up, a bringing together of what is otherwise scattered and disjointed."[38] Therein lies a refusal to be open to what-is, that is, disorder, and the intent to impose one's own conceptions and desires.

This bringing together of what is scattered is, as I see it, the imposition of one's ego; it reflects the hunger to find unity and beauty in a reality which is by the hypothesis "disjointed," "scattered," and very possibly unbeautiful as such.

Has Professor Deutsch actually found reality to be as he describes it when he is spiritually passive? Or is it, rather, as I have to think it is, a promise and a hope based on the tacit presumption that somehow, in the end, Reality is Good? That presumption reflects the wishful thinking and hoping that underlies the Judeo-Christian-Islamic religions. It is not a necessary presumption. In Job, in mysticisms, in much of Eastern thought, good and bad are finite qualities, neither one being ultimate.

On the other hand, Professor Deutsch's comments on how we achieve the condition of spiritual passivity (or suffering, in its fundamental sense) seem to me to be exactly right. There is no "technique" by which one can achieve this state of openness.[39] One does not achieve it by taking its achievement to be a task. The attempt to make one's way to some sort of special "experience" can lead at best to a kind of ego-satisfaction that is not spiritual passivity at all.

For spiritual passivity is a form of passivity, not a purposefully produced condition. Thus we have the paradoxical demand upon us: We are to reach the condition of spiritual passivity, but not by active effort. As Professor Deutsch so truly says, we are "called" to it; it is the receipt of grace.

If, as Eliot Deutsch says, the problem is to determine the spiritual value of suffering, he has already laid the ground for the solution. To suffer is to be spiritually passive, and thus it leads to the only true wisdom, to reality, and thus to the only true appreciation of our existence. In the end, this must "happen"—grace, if you will—but it cannot be made to happen.[40]

Notes

1. Deutsch (1995):146.
2. Spanish: *sufrir.* Italian: *sofirre.* French: *soufrir.*
3. Mark 10:14.
4. Spanish: *paciente.* Italian: *paziente.* French: *patient.*
5. *Daodejing* 3.
6. *Daodejing* 2.
7. *Daodejing* 7.

8. *Daodejing* 15.

9. *Daodejing* 19.

10. *Daodejing* 22.

11. *Daodejing* 43.

12. *The Platform Scripture*, St. John's University Press, (1963): ch. 36.

13. Deutsch (1968):4.18.

14. Deutsch (1968):4.20.

15. Deutsch (1968):4.20.

16. Deutsch (1968):4.22.

17. Deutsch (1968):3.19.

18. Deutsch (1968):12.17–18. See also: 14.24–25; 18.10.

19. Deutsch (1995):146.

20. Deutsch (1968):6.32. See also: 14.24.

21. Deutsch (1968):6.23.

22. Deutsch (1968):6.22.

23. There are, indeed, some passages that may seem inconsistent with this oft-repeated theme in the *Gītā*. Thus the Lord says at one point: ". . . one comes to the end of *duḥkha*" (18.36). Read in context, however, this is a tautology rather than a substantive comment: In this passage the Lord is not speaking of the state of the yogin but is describing the respective kinds of happiness associated with each of the three *guṇas*. Of course, when one is experiencing the form of happiness that is specific to one of the *guṇas*, one is insofar not experiencing the relevant *duḥkha*. Each of the *guṇas* is associated with its specific form of *duḥkha*, (18.37–39) for the *guṇas* are associated with body (14.20). Only when the *guṇas* are transcended is the body transcended, along with birth, death, old age, and *duḥkha*, and thus immortality achieved (14.20).

24. "Review articles have generally found placebo effectiveness rates to be from 30% to 40%." Leven (1991):1753.

25. I myself was once subject to a series of intense ("cluster") headaches that at first more or less immobilized me. Eventually I adopted a different attitude. Instead of fearing and fighting the pain, I simply let it be—it was *there*, but it was something toward which I took no stand. It was just a fact. Thereafter I could carry on, even when the pain was there, the very same pain as before.

26. Eckhart (1957):87, 246.

27. Deutsch (1995):5.

28. Deutsch (1995):6.

29. Deutsch (1995):6.

30. Deutsch (1995):7.

31. Deutsch (1995):7.

32. Deutsch (1995):5.

33. Deutsch (1995):5.
34. Deutsch (1995):5.
35. Deutsch (1995):6.
36. Deutsch (1995):6.
37. Deutsch (1995):5.
38. Deutsch (1995):5.
39. Deutsch (1995):6.
40. Some of the material in this essay, substantially revised, is taken from the author's essay, "Sufrimiento," in Fingarette (1996):11–21.

References

Blakney, Raymond Bernard (ed. and trans.) (1957). *Meister Eckhart.* New York: Harper & Bros.

Chan, Wing-tsit (trans.) (1963). *The Platform Scripture.* Asian Institute Translation Series, No. 3. New York: St. John's University Press.

Deutsch, Eliot (trans.) (1968). *Bhagavad Gītā.* New York: Holt, Rinehart, & Winston.

———— (1995). *Religion and Spirituality.* Albany: State University of New York Press.

Fingarette, Herbert (1996). "Sufrimiento." In *Religion y Sufrimiento.* Edited by Isabel Cabrera and Elia Nathan. Mexico City: Universidad Nacional Autónoma de México.

Levin, Michael R. (1991). "Placebo Effects on Mind & Body." In *Journal of the American Medical Association* 265, no. 13.

Reconciling the Irreconcilable: Some Critical Reflections on Deutsch's *Humanity and Divinity* and *Creative Being*

Daya Krishna

Eliot Deutsch's philosophical enterprise has, in many ways, been a sustained challenge to the current fashions of the day. In the philosophical climate of the decades in which Deutsch has written, who would take seriously a philosopher who undertakes an ontological enquiry into truth when it has been long shown by Tarski, and agreed to by everyone, that "truth" is a quality not of being but exclusively of sentences or propositions? Truth cannot meaningfully be asserted of "white snow," though the sentence "snow is white" can be regarded as true in most circumstances. Who would care to read about humanity and divinity when everyone knows that God had been proclaimed dead long ago and that there are no such things as "essences" and hence there can be no serious talk about "humanity" either?

And yet on reading *Humanity and Divinity: An Essay in Comparative Metaphysics*, I was personally startled by its stunning originality. On almost every page there is something insightful to say, with perceptive comments on the history of philosophy as it developed both in India and the West. It is with this provocative early Eliot that I begin.

In this work, Deutsch starts his discussion with the well-known injunction "Know thyself" and asserts that the Self which one is enjoined to seek and realize is not the self which can be known as an object, or even the self that one experiences as the one which knows or feels or wills. The Self, then, which one is asked to "know" or discover or realize is neither the self that is an object to oneself or

even the "subject" that is the source of all that appears as it will have to be characterized in some way or other and that will necessarily falsify its character as Pure
Subject. It obviously is the pure *ātman* of the Advaita Vedānta which not only has
no predicates whatsoever but cannot have them in principle, and thus is identical
with the Absolute or the Brahman which shares the same "predicament," as it also
is bereft of all possibility of predication, characterization, and relation. The statement of the identity between the Self and the Absolute, or the Atman and the
Brahman, is thus not a genuine statement as these are merely names of that which
is one and the same, and cannot be characterized in any way whatsoever. The assertion of identity cannot even be based on some prior ignorance as in the case of
the "morning star is the evening star," as the term *ātman* or the Self can never be
correctly used for either the empirical self, or that which is the source of that empirical self (which alone can be the possible "referent" of the term in case it is ever
used at all). There is thus "THAT" alone which may be spoken of either as *Ātman*
or as *Brahman* or by any other name, as all names are bound to be arbitrary. Perhaps it might be better to call it just "X," as the usual names are heavily loaded
with associations that are rooted in different philosophical and cultural traditions,
themselves conditioned by space and time.

Yet, who would be excited by such an assertion? The term "X" arouses no
emotions, has no mystical penumbra attached to it, and invites no one to make
any effort at its realization. Thus, all thinkers who have asserted that reality can be
affirmed only in this way and no other, have taken recourse to the notion of "experience" which, according to them, itself points to such a reality and in fact presupposes it in both a logical and existential manner. The way to the Self or the
Absolute, or the *Ātman* or the Brahman, is thus made more exciting and concrete
as it is supposed to be rooted in that which "appears" to be most real, that is, the
fact of consciousness itself. Yet, consciousness is the most slippery foundation to
build anything upon, even though thinker after thinker, both in the East and
West, has taken recourse to it to build a firm foundation for their thought, and
present it as if it were the most self-evident, indubitable truth. Descartes's
"Cogito" is well known, and so is Śaṃkara's "witness consciousness" which alone
remains constant amongst all that appears to it which invariably varies every
moment. Deutsch also takes recourse to this and writes of spiritual experience as
providing a firm foundation for all that he says about the Self and the Absolute

and their total identity. Yet, nowhere does there appear to be the slightest attempt to indicate what exactly is meant by the adjective "spiritual" which qualifies "experience;" thus making a dichotomous division in "experience" itself between that which is "spiritual" and that which is "non-spiritual." It will be difficult to maintain that "experience" *qua* experience can be distinguished in this way, as normally "experience" can only be distinguished in terms of the types of "objects" which are experienced.

Perhaps what Deutsch wants to convey by the term "spiritual" is that it is not experience of any "object" at all, but rather a state of "experience" which has no "object" whatsoever. In case this understanding of the term "spiritual" is correct, then it will have to be understood in a purely negative way, and thus would necessarily refer to that which it denies, as without that it would not be understood at all. There would also be the problem as to whether the terms "experience" and "consciousness" mean the same thing or are different. In the former case, the terms "spiritual experience" and "spiritual consciousness" would be interchangeable, while in the latter case, they would not be so. But whether identical or different, both the terms raise problems which have not been reflected upon by all those who have taken recourse to them to build their imposing structures of thought.

"Consciousness" inevitably raises the question as to whether it admits of qualitative and quantitative differences within it and whether it can possibly admit of its own complete cessation. Consciousness, as we all know, can be clear or confused, intense or dull, tired or awake, focussed or wandering. It can also be lost or gained, as when one says "I lost consciousness" or "I have gained it once more." There may be some problems regarding the first person use of such a phrase, but there can be none about their use in the case of others. Not only this, one may desire or want to become "unconscious" as when one wants to go to sleep. Not to be able to sleep is one of the worst things that can happen to a person and, if this is so, then one cannot accept that "consciousness" or "experience" is always intrinsically desirable *per se*. It is, of course, true that even in sleep, one may dream and, if one dreams, one may be said to be having an experience and if one is having an experience, then one is conscious, at least in some sense of the term. Would then one make a distinction between experiences which occur when one is awake as when one dreams? But then would one also make a distinction between these two states—the waking and the dreaming? Shall we then have to postulate radically different states of consciousness which again are distinguished not intrinsically but by "something" which is, at least *prima facie,* external to consciousness?

The Advaitins, as is well known, have talked of dreamless sleep and have made much of the fact that when one wakes up one says that one had a very sound sleep. But they have not asked the simple question as to whether there is a continuity between the dreaming and the dreamless state, or if there is a radical break between the two, just as there seems to be between the waking and the dreaming consciousness. Not only this, they have not reflected on the situation where one, on being asked whether one had a dreamless sleep or not, says "I do not know." For, if one were conscious, then one could not make such a statement. Similarly, there is the problem of what has been called, in physiological psychology, the threshold of consciousness where a stimulus has to reach a certain intensity in order to become an object of awareness or consciousness. There is, as experiments have revealed, a shifting margin between intensities where it is difficult to say whether one is aware or not of the stimulus that is being conveyed to the sensory organs. The notions of "sub-conscious" and "sub-liminal" present the same kind of questions, especially for those who treat "consciousness" as some sort of substantive entity or an absolute which knows no diminishing or "limits" as, in principle, it can have none.

The dependence of consciousness on external conditions is a problem which has hardly been faced by all those who have argued for its ontological primacy. Nor have the variations and experience due to both "external" and "internal" conditions been either the subject of critical reflection or seen as raising almost insuperable difficulties for the views propounded by idealists in general and Advaitins in particular. The effect of drugs on states of consciousness is well known, but besides this there is the everyday experience of fluctuations in the state of consciousness by fleeting ideas, images, personal relationships, aesthetic objects, apprehension of meanings, and a host of other such things which seem to find no place in the literature that deals with the subject. There is also the faculty of attention by which one attempts to focus consciousness on certain aspects so that one may change one's state of consciousness for the better. The whole range of meditative techniques developed in different traditions try to do this in one form or another. Along with this, there is the problem relating to "levels" of consciousness, particularly the one where the second-level consciousness observes the first-level consciousness and achieves a certain detachment from it.

Ultimately, all the questions relating to "experience" or "consciousness" encounter a foundational difficulty arising from the fact that what we "know" is only about the consciousness or experience of one who is human, that is, one who has a body, a mind and faculties which are usually designated by terms such as reason, imagination, memory, attention, and so on, and who has a capacity for self-consciousness and who can engage in a conceptual activity which symbolizes thought in some objective medium which itself can be deciphered giving rise to fresh thoughts which are not merely a replica of the old, but always add something to it. A person, about whose "experiences" we are talking is not only a "knowing being," but also one who feels and acts and changes his consciousness and experiences through such an activity. Besides this, human beings are surrounded not only by nature consisting of the stars, sun, moon, and plant and animal life but also by other human beings with whom one is in constant interaction and whom one affects not merely in terms of pleasure and pain, happiness and suffering, but also in terms of meaningful living. We do not know what the term experience would mean in the case of most living beings, even though we know that most of them feel pleasure and pain as that is perhaps involved in the very definition of what a "living being" means. There seems to be a little exception in the case of those who have entered the human world such as pets or domestic animals with whom one has a close interaction, but it is only in the case of human beings that we not only consider them as having "experiences" like ours, but also try to induce those which we consider desirable in them through such efforts as we think would most likely produce them. The traditional relation between the spiritual master and the disciple is a paradigmatic example of such a situation, though it obtains in almost all other fields as well. This is as true of the so-called Advaitic experience in the spiritual realm as of others which are also usually described as belonging to that realm.

"Spiritual" experiences, thus, are not of one type only and there has always been a dispute about their classification, and the hierarchy between them. There has also been the problem of the relationship between these different kinds of spiritual experiences and whether they should be regarded as stages in the realization of some one ultimate spiritual experience which is considered to be the highest or whether they are seen as coordinate, complementary, or even as different formulations of one and the same experience which intrinsically is incapable of any formulation at all. The Advaitins, of course, have held that theirs is the highest, almost by definition. Deutsch appears to subscribe to this view also as he contends that because reality is non-dual in terms of the phenomenology of experience, it denies, by definition, the possibility of there being anything other than itself which could possibly replace it in any way whatsoever.[1] But, definitions, even if they happen to be existential or phenomenological are only tautologies and do not prove anything. It just is not the case that all spiritual experiences necessarily are of ultimate oneness or non-duality, as the records of such experiences in all traditions testify to the contrary. There is, of course, the non-Advaitic experience of oneness, but so also there are experiences which deny the ultimacy of such an experience. The non-Advaitic Vedāntins, from Yāmunācārya to Vallabhācārya in the Indian tradition, attest to this and the controversy between them and the Advaitins is based on this very fact. It is also true that one finds Advaitic strains in the profound spiritual experiences recorded in the Jewish, Christian, and Islamic traditions, but they have generally been considered as not articulating correctly the truth of the experience if it is interpreted as controverting the accepted "orthodox" position as sanctioned by their holy texts.

Even those modern mystics such as Sri Aurobindo, who have acknowledged the Advaitic spiritual experience as one of the highest that man can possibly attain, have urged that there are other experiences which are coordinate with it in authority and some which may even be regarded as conveying the truth of ultimate reality better than it. There have been others like Ramakrishna who, in modern times, have personally attested to the validity of Advaitic experience and yet have continued to lead an intense life of devotion to Kāli, the Mother Goddess.

The history of spiritual experiences thus shows not only that there is no such thing as one single spiritual experience, but also that there is no unanimity about either the hierarchy or the interrelationships between them. Deutsch has taken recourse to the well-known idea of sublation in the Advaitic tradition to provide a firm foundation for the assertion that the spiritual experience of ultimate identity between the Self and the Absolute is the highest that there can possibly be as it is the experience of undifferentiated reality that has no "other" to itself. He has made an original use of the concept and urged that the experience is both noetic and axiological at the same time and has coined a new word, "subration," to convey this simultaneous relegation of one experience by another which unequivocally declares it to be both less real and less valuational. In his own words, by "subration" is meant "the process whereby we disvalue a previously valued content of consciousness," and "When something is subrated, it is believed by us to have a lesser degree of reality than that which takes its place."[2] But however intense and overpowering the feeling of the new experience being more real and valuational may be, there is no guarantee that one would never revise such a judgement and think oneself to have been mistaken. The experience of love is a classic instance of such a phenomenon which, when it occurs, is felt by everyone to possess a kind of reality and value in comparison with which everything else seems to be meaningless. Yet, as everybody knows, such a feeling does not last and, many a time one feels that one was mistaken in one's judgment, if not deluded altogether. The experience with respect to many works of art shares some of the same characteristics. Many a time, one returns to work which had aroused joy and wonder along with a sense of reality that far transcended the ordinary world in which one lived, only to discover that the magic is no more. Deutsch has used the word "judgment" in the context of his notion of "subration," but judgments are always subject to revision and there is never any finality about them. Not only this, if the experience is a human experience, one has to "return" from it to ordinary day-to-day levels of experience and even if one "feels" that the latter are less real, they have a compelling necessity about them and can be regarded as unreal only at the risk of becoming "mad" or "insane" in the sense that one will not "know" how to handle them properly. The fading memory of the luminous self-authenticating experience of the transcendent oneness can hardly help one in dealing with the multiple problems that arise at each of these levels to which one has to "return" because one happens to be an "embodied" human being. One may, if one is a spiritual genius, withdraw from all these levels and return again and again to the transcendent experience, but one cannot build any bridges between them, particularly if the experience of the transcendent is conceived in strictly Advaitic terms. There can be, strictly speaking no "crafting of person" about which Deutsch has written so eloquently in his book entitled *Creative Being: The Crafting of Person and World,*[3] written some thirty years after *Humanity and Divinity.*

There is no way down from the Absolute to either the world or the embodied self at any of its levels, and thus, the whole world of human experience of which

Deutsch and others build their contention is left hanging without any relationship to that which they consider alone as real. This relegation of the whole realm of experience not only to complete "unreality" but, utter "valuelessness" makes not only all human enterprise "meaningless" but also renders completely "unintelligible" the relation of the Absolute to the self and the world. The difficulties which the Advaitins have had with regard to the interpretation of the *Brahma Sūtra* 1.1.2 is evidence of this. For Deutsch, the difficulty should be even greater as he bases his case on "experience" itself and not on any scriptural authority or argument, and though he talks of the "phenomenology of experience,"[4] he forgets that, strictly speaking, "phenomenology" starts with a bracketing of reality and, hence, cannot make any metaphysical pronouncements.

It is, of course, true that Husserlian phenomenology took a turn to what has been called "constitutive foundationalism," but this obviously was a suicidal turn as it forgot the "bracketing" which was the necessary prerequisite for the "original" phenomenological enterprise.

The recourse to the idea of subration, as we have already pointed out, cannot help as experience *qua* experience always claims reality and it is only "external" considerations that make one pronounce or judge that what was or is experienced is not real. The past experience which is declared to be unreal on any grounds whatsoever has still to be remembered for what it was because, unless this is done, no pronouncement can be made about it. The same, surprisingly is the case, with an experience that is being "experienced," which at the moment when it is being experienced is judged to be "unreal." For example, the movement of the sun across the skies, though actually experienced as "moving" is still judged to be "illusory" or "unreal" due to theoretical considerations that do not make any difference to the experience *qua* experience. Here the grounds are theoretical and consist in considerations of consistency and coherence. Also, normally an experience cannot be said to contradict another experience as Deutsch says and even a judgmental contradiction can arise only when the subject of the judgment remains the same. No "judgment" can occur in principle at the level of the spiritual experience of the Absolute about which Deutsch has written because there the very possibility of any reflective consciousness being present is denied. Nor can there be any "memory" of the past experience of plurality and multiplicity which could be declared as "unreal" on axio-noetic grounds.

The only way to save the situation is to suggest that the memory of the Advaitic experience of the Absolute renders the experience of the plurality and multiplicity when one returns to it, seemingly unreal and valueless. But, then, it will be a remembered experience, and it is not necessary that the comparative judgment would necessarily continue to remain the same with the lapse of time. There is, of course, the deeper objection that as the subject of the judgment is different in the two cases, one cannot meaningfully talk of any contradiction between them. A comparison between experiences is, in any case, a difficult thing, as not only can the memory paint the past experience in colors that it did not have when it occurred, but also because the actual experience with which it is compared may undergo radical transformation in axio-noetic terms. There is little reason to believe that the experience of multiplicity and difference has always necessarily to be disvaluational in nature just because it is an experience of multiplicity and difference.

The judgment about an experience, whether in terms of reality or value, is never so indubitable as Deutsch seems to assume. It is a commonplace fact with regard to aesthetic experience that when someone differs from our judgment, particularly when the other is supposed to know more about the realm than we do, we begin to doubt our own valuation of the object concerned. Similarly, what is apprehended in perceptual experience, particularly in scientific contexts, is hardly intelligible without the whole paraphernalia of interpretation that is based on theoretical considerations. The analogy is not entirely irrelevant as, even in the case of experiences which are considered to be spiritual, one is advised many a time by the spiritual preceptor not to understand them in the way one has understood them.

The issue of the primacy of the experience in the spiritual realm has perhaps been most thoroughly discussed by Wilhelm Halbfass in his chapter entitled "The Concept of Experience in the Encounter between India and the West" in his well-known work *India and Europe*,[5] where he has argued that the overriding emphasis on spiritual experience in neo-Vedāntism is hardly corroborated by the way the issue was considered in traditional Advaitic texts. He suggests that though the words *anubhūti, anubhāva, saksatkara, darśana,* and so on, are used in the Advaitic texts, ultimately they are not treated as an independent ground for the assertion of either the truth or validity or value of that experience. Instead, it is the

Veda which is treated as the touchstone by reference to which the experience itself
is to be judged, as it alone contains "an objective structure which guides, controls
and gives room to legitimate experience as well as legitimate argumentation."[6] In
fact, if the *apauruṣeyatva* ("authorlessness") of the Veda is accepted, as the "orthodox" Advaitins from Śaṃkara onwards are supposed to do, then the "experience"
of the identity between the Self and the Absolute cannot be that of any human
being.

The situation, of course, is not as simple as the above quotation from Halbfass
may seem to imply, and Halbfass himself is aware of this. But, as the non-Advaitic
Vedāntic *ācārya*-s from Yāmunācārya to Vallabha also appeal both to the spiritual
experience on the one hand, and the Vedāntic texts on the other, it is clear that
neither the texts nor the experience can be interpreted or understood only in one
way and not in another. The giving up of the authority of the so-called
Prasthānatrayi texts by Caitanya and his absolute reliance on the experience of
bhakti alone confirms this further as, according to him, the ultimate spiritual experience is that of *Acintyabhedābheda* and not that of *Advaita* or *abheda* as the
orthodox Advaitins have always contended.

Deutsch ignores this long discussion between the Advaitins and the non-
Advaitins which has had a long history in India not only from Śaṃkara onwards,
but even before him. Samantabhadra, for example, had argued against the notion
of Advaita which was obviously known to the philosophical world of India before
Śaṃkara, as he is supposed to have lived earlier. According to him:

> If the principle of Advaita should be established by means of reason (*hetu*),
> there must exist a duality (*dvaita*) between reason and what is proved
> (*sadhya*). If the principle of Advaita should be established without reason,
> why should not dualism too be established from mere words alone"?[7]

Besides the controversy between the Advaitins and the other schools of Vedānta,
there was also the parallel discussion with the Naiyāyikas, particularly after
Śaṃkara Miśra (1430 A.D.) had written his work entitled *Bhedāratnam.*

Deutsch perhaps feels justified in bypassing this many-sided debate as, according to him, the logic of thought is not identical with the logic of reality[8] and
hence the former is not only incapable of grasping the latter but is also completely
irrelevant to our understanding of it. But, then reality could not be a subject of
understanding either, at least in the usual sense of "understanding." The desire to

understand it would, according to this view, be completely mistaken as perhaps would be all other attempts to relate oneself to whatever is real through any other faculty that one might possess. But, if this is accepted, then it would be impossible, in principle, to understand either the human being or reality for we can only relate to whatever is real as human beings. If human beings are "diverted beings" as Deutsch calls them, then how can one hope for any understanding of either humanity or reality, for a being which is essentially flawed in its very nature can, in principle, do neither?

Surprisingly, Deutsch along with many others, has also talked of the Absolute as creative being. But, if the "Absolute" has essentially a creative side to it, then how can that which it has created be "diverted" or "flawed"? And, if it is so, in any sense of the term, then it can only be seen as a reflection on the creative power of the Absolute itself. This is, of course, the old problem of "evil" to which there is, and can be, no solution. But if one accepts that the Absolute has a dynamic, creative side to it, then neither man nor the world can be seen in such completely "negative" terms as all Advaitins, including Deutsch, do. Deutsch, of course, has not only accepted the essential creativity in the Absolute, but also given a detailed description of the categories in which, and through which, this creativity unfolds in the realms of feeling, mind, and understanding.

The use of the term "categories" is puzzling as it normally denotes the forms which "Being" or "thinking about Being" has necessarily to take and thus involves the notions of ontological or epistemological necessity which, when used in the context of the Absolute, seems, at least *prima facie,* to deny its absoluteness. Not only this, the detailed delineation of the categories seems arbitrary. The categories of feeling, for example, have been given as *rhythm, proportion,* and *integrity.* It is difficult to see how these may be said to characterize exclusively what are generally understood as feelings and their relation, if any, to the dimensions of pleasure and pain, joy and sorrow, suffering and happiness, which normally are supposed to belong to the realm to which the term "feeling" is supposed to refer. Similarly, the categories of *purpose, memory, the ideal, equilibrium,* and *continuity* which are supposed to belong to the mind do not seem to be all of a piece. How *memory* is to be considered as a category seems baffling indeed. The relation between *purpose* and *the ideal* is not very clear; nor does one understand why *equilibrium* should not be considered as a category of feeling rather than that of the mind, and does not *memory* involve *continuity?* And in case it does so, why should the two be mentioned separately?

The categories of understanding present the same problem, as they include besides *space-time* and *causality, universal* and *relation.* The first two have been combined as one, and remind one of Kant who had, however, treated them as *a priori* forms of sensibility. To treat *causality* and *relation* as separate categories seems anomalous, as *causality* presumably is itself a relation between events.

However, what is perhaps even more disturbing is the complete absence of what may be called categories of action or will or that which is designated by the terms, "good" and "bad," "right" and "wrong," "virtuous" and "vicious" or "evil." Perhaps, the categories of *purpose* and *the ideal* under the categories of mind and the category of *integrity* under that of feeling are supposed to perform this function. But, the "moral" dimension seems to be missing in the discussion of the categories; presumably as in the Advaitic framework, there is no room for the reality of the "other" in relation to whom the whole realm of obligatoriness arises. The "self-enclosed" and the "self-sufficient" Self of the Advaitin appears to have no place either for the "starry heavens above," or "the moral law within." In fact, the realm of morality and action are conspicuously absent from Deutsch's framework, as they are found nowhere in the index to the book. Even the mention of "goodness" is in the context of a "loving being" and has little to do with the real conflicts of the diverse obligations which one has towards others. This is inevitable if the human being is not considered a socio-political being or embedded in nature, society, and culture. The moment one denies temporality, the realm of action vanishes and all the problems that it poses vanish into this air. The conflict between *dharma* and *mokṣa* is well known in the Indian tradition, just as the relationship between knowledge (*jñāna*) and action (*karma*). But Deutsch's thought knows of no conflict, as he has "situated" himself firmly in the Absolute where all duality and conflict ceases.

The problem perhaps lies with treating the Absolute as an ontological necessity, and that, too, as completely undifferentiated, as if any "difference" would contaminate its purity, forgetting that such a way of conceiving the "real" can only be a necessity of human thought, having little to do with whatever is "real-in-itself." Deutsch, of course, has grounded his notion in an axio-noetic experience which, according to him, is intrinsically incapable of being "subrated" by any other experience. The only reason for this intrinsic impossibility seems to be that it is implied by and strictly follows from, the very nature of the experience as defined by him. But the Absolute in any of its forms is a "demand" of human experience when it is self-consciously reflected upon. The duality of subject and object within experience appears to be unresolvable unless it is completely overcome within consciousness itself. The Absolute, as K. C. Bhattacharyya argued long ago, is needed to resolve the "existential unintelligibility" revealed in all experience to a self-consciousness that reflects on it. But, as Bhattacharyya observed, this resolution can be attempted in diverse ways, as the existential unintelligibility revealed appears to be different at the level of "knowing," "feeling," and "willing." Thus "experience" itself, according to him, reveals the alternative directions in which the resolution may be sought through a spiritual praxis, which, in the Indian tradition is called *sadhana*. From this arises the notion of alternative absolutes which equally perform the function for which they are postulated, that is, the experiential resolution of the paradox found in experience itself.

One may not accept Bhattacharyya's formulation, but one would expect that any serious reformulation of the Advaitic position would take into account what he has to say on the issue. Deutsch has done nothing of the kind. He has chosen to attempt a major reformulation of the Advaitic position without taking into account the radical reformulation of this position by one of the most original thinkers in the Indian tradition in recent times. The lapse is not understandable, particularly as he himself has made the axio-noetic dimension of experience the central foundation for his reconstruction along with the notion of "subration" that he has used so creatively to render the Advaitic position intelligible.

It may be interesting, in this connection, to see the insoluble problem that Deutsch has set for himself by starting from the self as Absolute, as something already accomplished, at least at the metaphysical level, and not something that is apprehended as an ideal to be actualized and realized by a spiritual praxis which can only hypothetically postulate it as something to be approached. Once one has accepted the identity of the Self and the Absolute as already accomplished, one cannot meaningfully talk of "crafting" a person except in the sense that one tries to actualize on the phenomenological plane what is already realized at the ontological level. Yet, Deutsch tries to suggest other directions for "crafting" both the person and the world that have no relation to this. In his work entitled *Creative Being:*

The Crafting of Person and World, he suggests, for example, that not to acknowledge one's "background, parentage, race, color or whatever . . ." as an inevitable
raw material in terms of which one has to craft oneself would be a piece of "self-
deception." But this goes completely against the Advaitic insight as, according to
it, one has to de-identify oneself with any objectivity whatsoever, including that of
one's body, mind, and intellect, not to talk of background, parentage, race, or
color, and so on. On the other hand, if a person is "a diverted being because life, as
he is born into it, demands it of him" and if "diversion is a natural consequent for
man as a social, material, mental being," then how can one ever hope for any realization of the self as Absolute, while living "in the body" and leading a life in society along with all that it involves? How, then, shall there be even a reconciliation
between the vision that is unfolded in *Humanity and Divinity* and the task that is
envisioned in *Creative Being: The Crafting of Person and World,* only Deutsch can
tell and, perhaps even he cannot as this contradiction lies at the very heart of human reality, and man has not been yet able to resolve it, either in thought or
action.

   Yet, there can be little doubt that these two works of Eliot Deutsch have presented so innovatively and powerfully these two contradictory dimensions of human seeking in a way that challenges each human being to think afresh, and turn
perhaps alternatively, to the twin task of "crafting" oneself and/or "realizing" the
oneness with the ultimate reality that always is present in the depths of one's own
being. Never before has a Western thinker so internalized a non-Western mode of
thought and developed it as creatively as Deutsch has done the Advaitic insights in
his *Humanity and Divinity.* Also, perhaps, no one else has written so well about
the creative challenges that each person faces in the lifelong task of crafting oneself into the "person" that s/he becomes.

   Deutsch has talked of aesthetic necessity in this connection and suggested that
the creation of a personality is analogous to the creation of a work of art and requires
all the imagination and the sensitivity and the coming to terms with the raw materials that one is given, and about which one can do little except to mould
them in the light of imagination and the sensitivity that one possesses. But where
in all this is the fact of mutual interdependence and collective creativity without
which no thinking about the human situation can be complete, whether it be conceived of essentially in terms of total transcendence of whatever man biologically

or socio-culturally happens to be, or in terms of those immanent ideals which accept these and all that goes with them as defining the human situation as we know it?

Perhaps that is the direction which Deutsch's thought may take in the future, or of someone else who might wish to continue what he has thought still further. Yet, there can be little doubt that in any further construction that one may wish to attempt, one would have to take the rich insights which may be found on almost every page of these two books, and for that, one will have to be thankful to Deutsch who has provided them in such rich abundance.

Notes

1. Deutsch (1970):12.
2. Deutsch (1970):10–11.
3. Deutsch (1992).
4. Deutsch (1970):12.
5. Halbfass (1988):378ff.
6. Halbfass (1988):388.
7. *Āptamīmāṁsā,* Verse 26. In Nakamura (1983):283.
8. Deutsch (1970):26.

References

Deutsch, Eliot (1970). *Humanity and Divinity.* Honolulu: University of Hawaii Press.

——— (1992). *Creative Being: The Crafting of Person and World.* Honolulu: University of Hawaii Press.

Halbfass, Wilhelm (1988). *India and Europe.* Delhi: Motilal Banarasidass.

Nakamura, Hajime (1983). *A History of Early Vedānta Philosophy.* Delhi: Motilal Banarasidass.

Two Types of the Philosophy of Religion: Reflections on Eliot Deutsch's Philosophy of Religion

Leroy S. Rouner

Eliot Deutsch is in the front rank of that small handful of influential twentieth-century philosophers who have globalized our understanding of philosophy. As recently as the 1950s, most philosophy courses in European and American universities taught "The History of Philosophy" without any reference to Asian thought. Philosophers such as Sarvepalli Radhakrishnan, Charles Moore, Wing-tsit Chan, William Ernest Hocking, Heinrich Zimmer, Ninian Smart, and Huston Smith—to name only a few—have finally made Western audiences aware of Eastern philosophies, and laid the groundwork for study in comparative philosophy. As Charles Moore's successor at the University of Hawaiʻi, Eliot Deutsch has also contributed to awakening Western thinkers from their dogmatic slumbers through his editorship of the journal *Philosophy East and West,* his work with the East-West Philosophers' Conferences and the Society for Asian and Comparative Philosophy, as well as his writing on Advaita Vedānta philosophy and his translation with commentary of the *Bhagavad Gītā.*

His great contribution, however, is his own distinctive philosophical point of view, a "reconstruction" of Advaita Vedānta which incorporates ideas and insights from various Asian philosophies into his metaphysics, epistemology, ethics, aesthetics, and perhaps especially his philosophy of religion. No contemporary philosopher has made that integration more thoroughly, or more winsomely than Eliot Deutsch. He has moved beyond "comparative philosophy." He is one of the first of a new generation of world philosophers.

My topic is his philosophy of religion. The "two types" to which my title refers are simply "dualism" and "nondualism," and my question is how these have been integrated in his own thought. The title was used some years ago by Paul Tillich to contrast a nondualistic "ontological" type, in which humankind's estrangement from self, world, and the Transcendent was overcome; and a dualistic "cosmological" type, in which the Transcendent was confronted as essentially different from oneself.[1] The ontological type was the healing way of "overcoming estrangement," while the cosmological type was the disjunctive way of "meeting a stranger." Tillich's argument is that the dualistic cosmological type needs grounding in the ontological type in order to do justice to the task of philosophy.

Just how dualism might be "grounded" in nondualism is, of course, another matter. "Grounded in" or "participating in" are philosophical metaphors hallowed by Plato and used ever since to affirm some deep commensurability in the seemingly incommensurable. But is it really possible for nondualism and dualism to be conjoined? Put it crudely: Can there be such a thing as a realistic idealism, or an idealistic realism? Tillich argued that the ontological type is fundamental for every philosophy of religion, since the cosmological type, by itself, creates a radical division between self and God, and between philosophy and religion.

This is a dangerous argument for a Christian theologian, and Tillich's colleagues at Union Theological Seminary in New York in the 1950s often questioned whether his view was authentically Christian. They had a point. In classical Christianity, God, as Person and Actor in history is always, *in some sense,* different from ourselves. On the other hand, Tillich's Union colleagues were also persuaded, on just these grounds, that Luther and Tillich were right to insist that we need a God who is "our friend," and therefore not radically other than ourselves. Hence the emphasis on the Incarnation of God in Christ where Christ, as God become man, was "one of us."

In Tillich's "cosmological" type of undiluted dualism, the fact that God is different from us makes God always "a stranger." Tillich found that view antithetical to the Biblical witness of the Psalmist, that God is nearer to us than breathing, which indeed it is. What is not clear is why, for Tillich, difference had to mean "estrangement," since difference is also fundamental to our experience of love. Not just in the West, but in the visceral depths of normative human experience everywhere, the possibility of someone being beloved by us depends on that person being (once again) *in some sense* different from us. This is true even of same-sex love relationships. Human love is sustained by interest in the other, and interest results from otherness. The beloved is, for us, a window on a different world. Total sameness is either boring or chaotic since it lacks differentiation; and both boredom and chaos kill love.

Tillich's argument did not initially derive from an interest in non-Western philosophy. It came from his German Romantic attraction to mysticism. Nevertheless, it is a good paradigm for some major distinctions between the predominant religious philosophies of the West, which regularly make this dualistic distinction between ourselves and God; and the most influential religious philosophies of the East, which are nondualistic. Tillich's attempt to conjoin dualistic and nondualistic points of view is surely a desirable project. One could even argue that that is what any serious philosophical point of view is all about; how to be an idealistic realist, or a realistic idealist. Eliot Deutsch is a nondualist, with dualistic sympathies. His project differs from Tillich's in many ways, but Tillich's essay helps highlight some critical issues. First, a few working definitions.

Dualism is the metaphysical view that there are two distinctly different kinds of reality in our experienced world. This is a crude way of putting the issue, since there are varieties of both dualism and nondualism, but the definition is basic to all dualisms. Dualism is a necessary point of departure for most Jewish, Christian, and Islamic philosophies of religion since they hold that God is always, *in some sense*, other than ourselves. Put philosophically, it is the view that there are at least *some* external relations in the world of our experience.

Nondualism, on the other hand, is the view that there is ultimately nothing "other" to our deepest inner selves, properly understood, although there is much that "appears" to be other in our ordinary experience, and indeed must be dealt with in terms of this preliminary or seeming otherness if we are to make our way through the daily round successfully. Philosophically put, this is the view that ultimately all relations are internal.

The Jewish/Christian/Islamic view of God as personal and therefore other than ourselves is reflected in the religious life of these traditions. Prayer, for example, in these Western traditions is different from meditation (the characteristic Eastern form of religious reflection) in that it is an appeal for help to Someone who is "out there," and who can help us because they are not us. We are weak, but God is able to do "more than we can ask or think," because He is strong; and so forth.

So, too, ethics in these Western traditions is a response to the *will* of God. The power to do the Good to which God calls us is enabled by the power of God's presence within the life of the believer. In nondualist philosophies of religion, ethics is inevitably a version of stoicism, since the power to do the good is a completely internal resource, there being no external reality to appeal to. Ethical action in nondualist systems of thought is therefore empowered by hitherto undiscovered internal resources of insight and power. Hence the emphasis in these religious traditions on some form of enlightenment. This nondualist experience of understanding the true nature of one's inner self as Transcendent and therefore fraught with potential power contrasts with the dualist experience of Revelation in Western religions, in which insight is given to oneself by God, who is Other.

Revelation is an epistemological category which does not exist in non-Western philosophies of religion, and therefore demands a new category of thought which the West calls Theology. This *logos* of *theos* is grounded in the graceful gift which God presents in our common history, a Transcendent Word which becomes historical for "people of the Book," and especially for Christianity where "the Word became flesh and dwelt among us."

For both traditions "salvation" or "awakening" or "enlightenment" is a radical transformation of the self. There is also broad agreement among the great religions of the West that to know God is, at the same time, to know something definitive about our own individual inwardness. And there is broad agreement among the contemporary advocates of the great religions of the East that philosophical enlightenment is about living a creative historical life among "others." So the issue of differentiation is an exquisitely subtle one.

Tillich stands in the tradition of Augustine, and his "Two Types" helps to illustrate what is at stake here. The "ontological type" defines God as "Being Itself" or "The Ground of Being." In this view everything that is "lives and moves and has its being" *in* God. But Tillich—and Augustine before him—needed to avoid simple pantheism, because it would destroy the distinction between ourselves and God. He does this by recourse to Plato's notion of "participation." Everything that is *participates* in the universal reality of Being Itself. How this participation takes place, however, is unclear. Following Plato, Augustine argued that participation comes through memory. We know that we "belong" to God—or, to use the Biblical metaphor, are "children" of God, or "creatures of the Creator"—because we have a dim psychic memory that we are fashioned in the *imago dei*, the "image of God." But in what critical way does that view differ from Śaṃkara's affirmation that our innermost being is *ātman*, identical with the Holy World Power of Brahman? This, I take it, is the major issue for the comparative philosophy of religion. With this question in mind, we turn to Deutsch's distinctive version of nondualistic philosophy of religion.

His 1969 book on Advaita Vedānta[2] sets the stage for his later work. It is distinctive in that it is a "reconstruction" of Advaita. It is not primarily a work of historical scholarship. He is using Advaita Vedānta as "material for creative thought."[3] In a "reconstruction," questions of historical context, reliance on the authority of the Vedas and Upaniṣads, and traditional interpretation all fall away, leaving the essential core of a philosophical point of view. Deutsch then takes this core view and restates it as a philosophy available to contemporary thought. The result is not a "modern dress" version of classical Advaita. It is Advaita as argued by a contemporary philosopher. And lest what I have called this "essential core" seem abstract, Deutsch retains its classical purpose as a "path of spiritual experience," now made available to any contemporary student of philosophy.

"Spiritual experience" is a difficult notion for most Western philosophers, however, and it is central to Deutsch's view. In the West "spirituality" has usually meant "piety," the deep emotion of one's religious devotion. Deutsch, however, uses the term in the sense characteristic of several nondualistic Eastern philosophical systems. Deutsch's "spirituality" is a way of being-in-the-world, resulting from the "spiritual experience" of reality as ultimately One. His philosophy of religion is therefore democratic. Unlike the esotericism of the classical Indian tradition, where spiritual knowledge was a carefully guarded secret, his is a philosophy of life available to unexceptional folk in our common history. It is not a retreat from the world of ordinary everyday experience into the disciplines of pious religious practice, such as Catholic monasticism, Amish sectarianism, or the world-rejecting wandering of the Hindu *sanyāssin*. It is Advaita for us moderns.

In this subtle sense Deutsch's philosophy of "spiritual experience" is not conventionally "religious," since he is not concerned with religious institutions, ritual practices, or religious piety. He is a philosopher concerned with the ultimate truth about how things are. This truth, while not irrational, is beyond our conceptual grasp, but it can be known through "spiritual experience." Here he has an interest-

ing bond with twentieth-century Protestant Christian Neo-orthodox philosophers who also rejected "religion" with all its trappings in favor of "faith," an essential deep commitment to a view of our relation to a Transcendent God. The
difference between him and them, of course, is that for them this insight comes
through experience in Revelation. It is not inherently *in* experience, as it must be
for nondualists like Deutsch. His view is also consonant with some "New Age"
thought, although his views are rigorously philosophical in ways which much of
that popular movement are not.

What he calls the "religious spirit" has been central to his work, and he has
been critical of those contemporary philosophers who have sought to marginalize
notions of creativity deriving from art and religion. If "spiritual experience" is the
foundational concept of his metaphysics, "creativity" is the central focus for his
philosophy of life. His epistemology does not rest primarily on factuality, meth-
odological technique, and explanatory certainty—the obsessive concerns of so
much contemporary philosophy. He looks rather to the creative underlying spirit
of philosophical enquiry as our fundamental source of understanding. In an essay
on "Knowing Religiously," he puts the matter forcefully:

> If one can begin to understand the deepest, richest and most valuable of our
> experiences, one can then go a long way toward understanding other issues. If
> we can understand creativity, we might then be able to understand causality;
> if we can understand what religious language is, we will then be better able to
> understand what a proposition is; if we can understand what it means to
> achieve freedom of consciousness, we can understand what free will means,
> and so on.[4]

In some of his earlier writings, such as *Advaita Vedānta*, Deutsch presented his
point of view in terms of more or less traditional concepts and arguments. In
more recent writings, however, his growing interest in art is evident in his attempt
to paint a picture of what "spiritual experience" is like. This is not an abandonment of philosophy, any more than his "reconstruction" of Advaita was an abandonment of that philosophical point of view. It is rather a recognition of the limits of traditional philosophical discourse when facing the problem of truth. The
epistemological resources out of which spring arguments for causality, propositional truth, and doctrines of free will are not themselves causal, propositional, or
doctrinal. Deutsch's problem is how to get at them.

This is a brave philosophical adventure. He is seeking out the realm of what William James called "pure experience," that fundamental ground from which all specific and articulate experience comes. For James this was a realm of confusion, with images and impressions tumbling in on one another. In James's view the task of the mind was to grasp and shape this confusion in order to create a "world" for the knowing subject. In this sense, each person's "world of experience" resulted partly from what she or he chose to focus on in this confused ground-world of experience-stuff. For Deutsch, however, James's "buzzing confusion" of "pure experience" is not some metaphysical silly-putty to be shaped by the mind; it is already a world with its own meaning, to which the mind opens itself. So this is not a situation in which an aggressive knowing subject grasps and shapes a known object. It is rather the situation of the Advaitin in which the ordinary notions of "self" are—as we say today—"deconstructed" so that the "pure" passive self sees "pure experience" as the dance of *māyā*, which is itself a frenetic overlay of that Ultimate Divine Truth which is passive silence.

But Deutsch adds a twist to this classical Advaita notion of the *jñāna-yogin's* discovery of that true selfhood which lies beneath body, mind, or even spirit. That addition is care, concern, or—more simply—love. He is very clear about this. "The openness, the insight we have spoken of, must be thoroughly informed by love."[5] The implication, as I read him, is that love is a universal human reality. But the traditional Hindu philosophical notion of love in a nondualistic universe is rather different from say, the Christian notion of love in a world where both God and our neighbor are understood to be different from ourselves. The Hindu notion is one of emotionally detached devotion—a commitment free of the entanglements of desire, as counseled by Lord Krishna to Arjuna in the *Gītā*.

The motivation for this detachment is freedom from pain, the practical goal of virtually all Indian philosophical schools. Attachments of any kind are sources of pain, and must be avoided if the individual *ātman* is to be free from the earthly cycle of *saṃsāra*, and attain *mokṣa* or true spiritual freedom. Ordinary human life is lived in terms of motion: in space, from here to there; in time, from now to then; in relationships, from me to you. And the message of nondualistic Hindu culture is that anything that moves can hurt you. So the traditional goal of life is to minimize motion, both inwardly as emotion, and outwardly as the belief that going from here to there, or now to then, is "getting someplace."

To be sure the culture of India is ambivalent on this issue. The temples at Khajurāho celebrate sexual attachments, and the mythic tale of Rāma and Sītā in the *Rāmāyaṇa* models a passionate commitment of lovers. And in ordinary life, surely Indian lovers have no less care, engagement, and commitment to one another than lovers elsewhere, even though the traditional arranged marriage is a "cool" event, as opposed to the "hot" romanticism of the Western love marriage. But surely care, concern, and love are, indeed, "attachments." How could they not be? If we say that we care about someone we mean that our sense of ourself is somehow tied into their life, and is, in some sense, dependent on their presence for us. To love someone who is suffering is to suffer with them. Love means bearing one another's burdens, sharing their joys and sorrows.

From the point of view of a classical Advaitin, however, the ultimate secret to successful living is ultimately a deep "detachment" from the world. True, this is characteristic only of the latter stages along life's way in the traditional Four Stages of Life. But its significance here is that it is understood as progress toward what life really means. For traditional Advaita, we know the truth of our historical existence only when we have shuffled off those attachments to our near and dear which we had previously thought were the true meaning of our lives, and discovered that there is no ultimate truth to our historical existence *per se*.

Deutsch argues his claim for the centrality of love in the Hindu tradition by quoting the *Gītā*: "Having become Brahman, tranquil in the Self, he neither grieves nor desires. Regarding all beings as equal, he attains supreme devotion to Me" (8.54). But is devotion to Krishna the ordinary "caring" or "love" we have for one another, which Deutsch calls for? When we ordinary folk lose those we love, do we not grieve for them? And is not that grief even a rough measure of the depth of our love? We grieve for them because we wanted and needed them to be part of our world. When they are gone, we are diminished. This detached Hindu/Stoic tranquility, substitutes a passive sense of identity for the agency of our ordinary attachments.

In the tradition of Advaita, the love of "God" is an all-absorbing recognition that Reality is One and that there is no differentiation between Self and Other. In that sense, there is no death, or grief, or loss, but only the rolling, infinite, ongoing reality of things as they are. And that Reality is not the truth of the historical world, or of personal attachments, or of one's "life story." It is the Reality which lies Behind all this; the Reality of the substratum from which all the surface stuff of immediacy and history and personal relationships comes.

The difference between this "ontological" type of the philosophy of religion, and the "cosmological" type is that the cosmological type is historical, so that what happens in history is not a veil of illusion over True Reality, but—rightly understood—that Reality itself. Hence what we know in history is the Truth. Not complete Truth to be sure, for what we know is always seen "through a glass, darkly"; but nevertheless real truth. And, by the same token, what we do in history *is* the Good, and not just a symbol or a metaphor for the Goodness which transcends anything we can think or imagine. Here faithfulness to God is devotion to One who calls us to acts of love, like feeding the hungry, clothing the naked, and "loving the neighbor as oneself." Our souls are saved not by piety toward God, but love toward the neighbor. And in this cosmological or historical scenario, the neighbor is precisely *not* oneself.

At this point, Deutsch's affirmations about the centrality of love and caring strike me as more Jewish or Christian than Hindu. But perhaps not. The Christian lay theologian, C.S. Lewis, wrote about the Joy which each of us seeks and harbors in our inmost heart of hearts. He called it

> the secret signature of each soul, the incommunicable and unappeasable want, the thing we desired before we met our wives or made our friends or chose our work, and which we shall still desire on our deathbeds, when the mind no longer knows wife or friend or work.[6]

Might one argue that this Desire of all desires is comparable to the Hindu desire for *mokṣa*, the freedom of release from a life of pain, which is also a final identification with the Divine?

This brings us to questions about the nature of the Self in Deutsch's view, and the nature of true knowing. As to selfhood, Deutsch first stresses the utter simplicity of being, a non–subject/object-bound view of reality. Advaita argues that we confuse self and world, and that this process of "differentiation" is the source of our difficulty. We "superimpose" aspects of the not-self onto the self, and of the self onto the not-self. The result is a confusion of images. He says that

> we quite naturally misidentify ourselves by wrongly mixing ourselves up as "subjects" with a world taken to be entirely constituted by diverse "objects." We scatter ourselves, as it were, about the world, and then come to believe that its limitations are ours.[7]

As I understand it, this is another way of stating the classical Hindu doctrine of "attachment." We come to believe that those things to which we are attached in this world constitute who we really are: our vocation, our relations (husband, father, son, friend), our particular hopes and our most poignant dreams. But if we are not this—that is, if we are not our historical existence as we experience it here and now—who *are* we, and how do we know that that is who we are?

Deutsch's answer is indirect. When we have "desuperimposed" ourselves from the world, he argues, we realize the world's "profound oneness." For the great Hindu mystics this realization was a profound personal experience. For the rest of us, however, Deutsch admits that it is not part of our experience, and as far as I can tell, it has not been part of his. So what does the claim mean? If not a profound personal experience, why would one choose to substitute another's affirmation of their experience, however impressive, for one's own?

Is this, perhaps, a celebration of William James's "will to believe," where the truth of this metaphysic is confirmed by the fruits of a creative life? Or is the argument that this vision is ethically and morally so compelling that one is ready to adopt it simply on the grounds that it is "lovely, and of good report"?

For Deutsch, this seems to be the point where philosophical argument is no longer relevant. His is not unlike Plato's view in the famous metaphor of the "divided line." When one moves across the "divide" which separates dialectical argument in the world of historical experience to the reality of the Ideas and the ultimate idea of the Good, argument gives way to vision. Here one does not "figure out" that something is true; one "sees" that it is true, although for Deutsch the definitive experience is more one of listening than seeing. In *Religion and Spirituality* (1995) he says that he "does not intend to persuade so much as hopefully to call forth and allow a wide range of responses which may awaken one to various possibilities of spiritual experience."[8] Here are echoes of Gabriel Marcel's *Journal Metaphysique* and William Ernest Hocking's *The Meaning of God in Human Experience*, both of which employed sophisticated argument up to a point, and then turned to a phenomenology of experience, presented as an appeal. In Hocking's fine phrase, "This is my experience. Is it yours also? Does it have something of our common humanity in it?"

Deutsch hopes for a "wide range of responses" and "various possibilities of spiritual experience." But what is crucial for this wide ranging variety? What is the "spirituality" which defines them all? Since the inwardness of Advaita Vedānta is his norm, the opening section of *Religion and Spirituality* on "Solitude" is especially instructive. He defines solitude as "not a state of withdrawal" but "an achieved state of wholeness" which calls for a re-collecting of oneself,

> a bringing home, as it were, of one's thoughts and memories, one's wayward emotionality and unresolved tensions. Gathering these up, letting them be heard and then re-integrating oneself anew with them is the task of this initial solitude.[9]

The next move is to "make an island of oneself." This is not a protective privacy, born of fear, but a "solitude of self-formation" which renders one "invulnerable to any threat from others, for here one no longer has any little interests of one's own to be challenged."[10] And in the following section on "Spiritual Passivity" he goes on to say that this passivity gives one an "attentiveness" which helps one let go of everything in the way of a solitary communion. He adds that

> Spiritual passivity is a state of blessed forgetfulness. Suspending temporality, it opens up an entirely new space for being, every moment becoming a fresh discovery of who one most truly is, for what is received in spiritual passivity is the very truth of spirit; silence divine.[11]

This description fits a very wide range of spiritual experience, from the intensity of Yogic meditation to the moment of quiet in an empty village church when a passer-by stops for a time of reflection, and the in-gathering of her or himself. Deutsch moves then to reflection on Divine Love. He proposes that this contemplative state of spiritual passivity "becomes a loving state of being when it is filled with a radiant power which desiring nothing, encompasses everything."[12] This state will vanish the moment we let our desires take over, but it is essentially "a state of being realized in human consciousness wherein all existence is taken-up and is transfigured and transformed."[13] This Divine Love which is also the Divine Goodness "transvaluates all one's previous values in the light of its Divine Power, rendering them, in comparison to itself, as nothing."[14] So Politics, History, Art, Religion—and more—ultimately turn out to be "as nothing."

This All/Nothing perspective of the nondualist contrasts with the dualistic Greatest/Least view of the Divine Love. God, in Christianity for example, is "That, than which nothing Greater can be conceived," (Anselm). God is to be loved along with the neighbor who is "one of the least of these my brethren."

But in shuffling off the "little interests"—which we all can agree is a good and healthy thing—what is left to be said about the great interests? One possibility is that there are no great interests. Someone proposed two rules for living: Don't sweat the small stuff; and It's all small stuff. This is good classical Advaita doctrine as I understand it; for if history is ultimately *māyā*, then our life in this world really is, comparatively, all "small stuff." "Little interests" are then the only ones there are.

But Deutsch believes in love. Whether we are faithful to one another in friendship and love do matter to him. Whether we acquit ourselves honorably in professional commitments matters to him. Whether we are good citizens in the larger world matters to him. But didn't these things also matter to the saintly Śaṃkara, the great systematic defender of Advaita? Penultimately, probably yes; but ultimately, surely no. Śaṃkara's was a life of religious piety, founding temples, seeking for that freedom from all worldly things which would ultimately incorporate him into the transcendental realm of *sat, cit, ānanda*, "being, intelligence, and bliss." But Deutsch's spirituality does not include conventional religious piety—he is no founder of temples—nor does he say much about any transcendental yearning for a realm of Ultimate Peace.

I conclude with a question: Isn't his "reconstruction" of Advaita a fairly radical revision of the tradition? And radical in this way: it has turned what was essentially a world-and-life renouncing tradition into a world-and-life affirming one. Wasn't the spiritual power of traditional Advaita rooted in its clear, unsentimental response to the problem of pain which motivates the practical side of so much Indian philosophy? Advaita gave an elaborate rationale for why the experiences of ordinary life need not be painful. The price to be paid for freedom from pain, however, was freedom from ordinary attachments. Because the world was ultimately *māyā*, its accompanying pain was also ultimately unreal, and could be realized as such with the appropriate spiritual discipline.

But that spiritually heroic move was deeply anti-humanist. By *identifying* with everything, one was intimately *related* to nothing. Hence, like the *ataraxia* of Roman Stoicism, one did not grieve human losses. Indeed, the whole point of the spiritual discipline was to drain from one the last vestiges of any emotion which might attach itself to any desired "object," since all such attachments are sources of pain.

Deutsch's philosophy of religion, on the other hand, could not be more life-affirming. It is a dynamic philosophy of developing personhood and creativity.

The reflective passivity it advocates is not a final cutting-off of oneself from the world, but a gathering in of one's scattered self in order to be more focussed and creative in personal life. His is a philosophy for the enhancement of ordinary human life. It is a philosophy for those who cultivate their unexplored inner resources in times of quiet reflection; for those who hold fast to what is good and do not sweat the small stuff; and especially for those who would face their world openly, with a heart for love.

Notes

1. Tillich (1959):10–29.
2. Deutsch (1969).
3. Deutsch (1969): Preface, second unnumbered page.
4. Deutsch (1985):22.
5. Deutsch (1985):27.
6. Lewis (1965):146.
7. Deutsch (1985):26.
8. Deutsch (1995):x.
9. Deutsch (1995):3.
10. Deutsch (1995):3–4.
11. Deutsch (1995):6.
12. Deutsch (1995):7.
13. Deutsch (1995):7–8.
14. Deutsch (1995):8.

References

Deutsch, Eliot (1969). *Advaita Vedānta: A Philosophical Reconstruction*. Honolulu: East-West Center Press.

———— (1985). "Knowing Religiously." In *Knowing Religiously*. Edited by Leroy S. Rouner. South Bend: University of Notre Dame Press.

———— (1995). *Religion and Spirituality*. Albany: State University of New York Press.

Lewis, C. S. (1965). *The Problem of Pain*. New York: Macmillan.

Tillich, Paul (1959). "The Two Types of Philosophy of Religion." In *Theology of Culture*. New York: Oxford University Press.

ritings, and one shouldn't criticize people for not solving problems they did not
t out to address. Rather are the arguments designed to prod him into elaborat-
g on his metaphysical, aesthetic, and religious views as they might bear on these
her areas of philosophy, and public affairs.

In contemporary Western moral philosophy, political theory, and jurispru-
nce, the concept of freedom is central. The challenge of the question "Why did
u do that?" has no moral force unless it is presupposed that the interrogated was
ee to have done otherwise. Most political theorizing—even if undertaken bend a veil of ignorance—still begins with the Hobbesian concept that human
ings are fundamentally free (in a "state of nature" or otherwise), and then at-
mpts to justify subservience to a state (government) which restricts that
eedom. And in jurisprudence, the demands of justice can seldom be addressed,
ther in civil or criminal law, without due consideration of the freedom—
uched in the language of rights—of the parties involved.

The concept of freedom is no less central in practice than in theory, as is
early evidenced by all three branches of the U. S. government, where freedom
s achieved almost sacred status, in name if not in fact. At law, felony convictions
sed on confessions are overturned if it can be shown that the convicted were not
ld they were free to remain silent. A legislator promoting a welfare bill defends it
the basis of enhancing the freedom of the poor, which, with respect to woman
d minorities, is also the justification for much anti-discrimination legislation.
ese bills will be opposed by those who see redistributive wealth measures as an
fringement of the freedom of the affluent to dispose of their wealth as they see
, and/or an infringement of the freedom of majorities to act in accordance with
eir beliefs. And a great deal of U. S. foreign policy is regularly justified as fur-
ering freedom (and its cousin, democracy) in different parts of the world, even
hen the instruments of the policies are bombing raids on other countries.

We can see the importance of the concept of freedom in another way: it is an
tegral part of a larger Western concept-cluster, the terms for which—"liberty,"
ights," "democracy," "justice," "choice," "autonomy," "individual," and so
rth—cannot be clearly defined without also using "freedom." Absent this
xicon, it would be virtually impossible for English-speaking people to discuss
orality, politics, or the law today.

On Freedom and Inequality

Henry Rosemont, Jr.

Eliot Deutsch is a *comparative* philosopher, to the extent that virt
parative philosophers share the goal of making philosophy as tru
the future as it has been mistakenly thought to be in the past. But in
he is simply a philosopher, whose many writings have made signal
to such fields as metaphysics, aesthetics, and the philosophy o
spirituality, ranging from his *Humanity and Divinity* (1970) to *Ess
ture of Art* (1996). Informed by knowledge and appreciation of Indi
cal and spiritual traditions, Deutsch has addressed many philosop
they have been traditionally formulated in the West, but has don
original ways. One of these is the concept of freedom, which is
theme in many of his books, the term itself appearing in the title o

The aim of the present essay is to assist Deutsch in a small way t
a signal contribution to other fields as well, by taking the concept of
has developed it with respect to metaphysics, aesthetics, and religion
ing whether his conception might resolve some of the conflicts in
moral philosophy, political theory, and jurisprudence that have g
measure out of differing conceptions of freedom. One major source
be addressed will be the contrasting underlying concepts of freedo
flected in the U. S. Bill of Rights on the one hand, and in the U. N. U
laration of Human Rights on the other. I will argue that while his
freedom—and related concepts of human nature and community—
fair distance in resolving these conflicts, an even more radical visic
societies are to become more equitable and just in the twenty-first
they have been in the twentieth. These arguments are not to be cons
cisms of Deutsch's work; equality and justice have not been focal

Now given that both those who endorse, and those who oppose, any particular judicial decision, piece of legislation, or aspect of foreign policy will do so by invoking freedom, it must be the case that freedom is seen not only as fundamental, but also as an unalloyed good. It is something we *have*, simply in virtue of our being human; we are born free. And differing moral, political, and legal theories are defended and attacked significantly on the basis of the extent to which they do or do not maximize human freedom.

Freedom is not, however, singular; there are many freedoms, and differing rank-orderings of them is what largely distinguishes different moral, political, and legal theories from each other.[1] To fully defend this claim it would be necessary to do a long and detailed comparative analysis of the several theories in all three areas, but for present purposes it may suffice to focus on a single theme which implicates all three, and at the same time is of immediate concern and a major source of conflict in the United States and in the world today[2]: human rights, which are grounded in the concept of freedom as a defining characteristic of human beings.

If I am essentially free—and it is irrelevant here whether this is to be taken descriptively or prescriptively—then it would seem to follow that no one, and especially no government, should curtail my freedom to say whatever I want to say, associate with whomever I wish, accept any set of religious beliefs I hold true, and dispose of any land or material goods I have legally acquired as I see fit. For some, these are the most basic of rights (freedoms), without which I cannot flourish, and therefore I must be secure in their enjoyment, entering only the caveat that I do not infringe these same rights of others.

For Americans, these rights—this freedom—are protected by the Bill of Rights. They are civil and political in nature, and are now commonly referred to as "first-generation" rights. Much of the plausibility of seeing these civil and political rights as the most basic of freedoms is the concomitant view of seeing human beings as basically rational individuals. And if we are indeed such, we must also be capable of self-governance, that is, we must be autonomous. But rational, autonomous individuals must also be free, else they could not realize the potential of that which makes them uniquely human.

The U. N. Universal Declaration of Human Rights, however, goes far beyond civil and political rights. It declares that human beings also have fundamental

economic, social, and cultural rights ("second-generation" rights). First-generation rights are often described as negative, which can be misleading. But they are
surely passive, in that they secure freedom *from* coercion. Second-generation
rights are active: they are intended to obviate social and natural impediments *to*
the full exercise of freedom: the right to an education, a job, health care, and so
on; without these rights, the argument runs, the concept of freedom becomes
hollow. Noam Chomsky has put this point succinctly: "Freedom without opportunity is a devil's gift."[3]

"Freedom from" and "freedom to" are clearly distinct, and "freedom from"
can loom large in our political thinking if our major concern is focused solely on
the threat of authoritarian governments. But if we combine moral and political
considerations, and ask what it means for each of us, not governments, to respect
the rights of others, things look rather different. That first-generation rights are
basically passive can be seen from the fact that 99 percent of the time I can fully
respect your civil and political rights simply by ignoring you; you surely have the
right to speak, but no right to make me listen. Second-generation rights, on the
other hand, are active in the sense that there are things I must do (pay taxes, at the
least) if you are to secure them. Schools, jobs, hospitals, and so on, do not fall
from the sky; they are human creations. And herein lies a fundamental conflict in
differing conceptions of freedom as expressed in the discourse of human rights: to
whatever extent I am obliged to assist in the creation of those goods which accrue
to you by virtue of having second-generation rights, to just that extent I cannot be
an altogether autonomous individual, enjoying first-generation rights, free to rationally decide upon and pursue my own projects rather than having to assist you
with yours.[4]

That I, too, have the second-generation rights to these goods is of no consequence if I believe I can secure them on my own, or in free association with a few
others, and thereby keep secure my civil and political rights. It is equally irrelevant
that I can rationally and freely choose to assist you in securing those goods necessary for the positive exercise of your freedom on my own initiative, for this would
be an act of charity, not an acknowledgment of your rights to them.

Arguments for second-generation rights have a special force in developing
nations, but apply as well to the highly "developed" United States. Of what value is
the right of free speech if, unschooled, it is difficult for me to say anything

intelligent,[5] or I am too sick to say anything at all? What good is the right to freely dispose of what I own if I don't own anything? What good is the right to freely choose a job if there aren't any?

These questions lead to another: What might it take for me to see that you do indeed have positive rights, and that it is not generous feelings but a moral/political responsibility that I must have to assist you in securing them? What is required, I believe, is the rejection of the view of human beings as basically autonomous individuals; rather must we see, feel, and understand each other as co-members of a human community.

No one would insist, of course, that we are either solely autonomous individuals or solely social beings. But if we believe we are fundamentally first and foremost autonomous individuals, then our only specific moral obligations (except for passive respect for the first-generation rights of all others) will be to those we have freely chosen to be responsible for: spouses, children, partners, and so on. If we are first and foremost co-members of a community, on the other hand, then, while each of us is unique, we will all have many and varied obligations to respect the rights of all unique others; both passively and actively.

Autonomous individuals, as noted earlier, must be free; freedom is something they have. Co-members of a community, it would seem, cannot be free in the same way if they bear manifold active responsibilities even toward others they have not freely chosen, and some reflection on our social lives suggests that this may well be the case. We did not choose our parents, freely or otherwise, nor our siblings and other relatives; yet we have obligations to them, and they to us. Except within great constraints, we do not choose our teachers, and if later we elect the teaching profession, do not choose our students. I decide what part of town I may wish to live in, but have no choice of neighbors; I must work where there is employment, not where I wish, and I will have little say about who my supervisors will be. Yet to all these people and many more I stand in a relation of mutual responsibility, to a greater or lesser extent, for the other's well being.

Our basic sociality is evidenced in other ways. A distinguishing feature of *Homo sapiens* is the ability to use language, for which we have appropriate physiological and anatomical mechanisms. But these mechanisms will atrophy fairly quickly unless we are in the presence of other language users, and the more of them who speak and listen to us—the wider, that is, the variety of accents and vocabularies we hear—the greater will be our own ability to creatively express our thoughts, and understand the creative expressions of the thought of others.[6]

Moreover, if freedom is something we have, then all societies more or less repress our exercise of it. It is from the co-members of our cultural community that we develop a world view, a conceptual framework, a concept-cluster of terms with which it is articulated, and it is within this concept-cluster that options are given from among which we may choose. Every world view constrains the number of options, just as, within limits, it strongly influences our notions of what is good and what is bad, what is right and what is wrong, what is beautiful and what is ugly. And this does not merely apply to the process of growing up. The tired, poor, and huddled masses did not become free when they cleared Ellis Island; New World cultural constraints simply replaced the Old.

These reflections are intended to *suggest* why and how it is altogether reasonable to believe that human beings are more basically co-members of human communities than autonomous individuals. But my empirical generalizations surely do not *demonstrate* or *prove* that such is the case, for I don't believe the issue is ultimately an empirical one. Nor do I know of any conclusive *a priori* argument to decide the matter either way. But perhaps we might continue to think about the contrasting views by asking which one more closely accords with our moral intuitions. This is important to do, because each of the views can become self-fulfilling prophecies: the more we believe ourselves to be autonomous individuals, the more inclined we will be to become such.

Certainly reflective persons do not want to be told when and if they can speak out, who to associate with, what religious or other beliefs to hold, how their money should be spent, and what they may and may not do with their possessions. In this light, autonomous individuals will seem more secure than co-members of community, whose obligations at times may well override their inclinations in these matters. I may want to leave my entire estate to my children, but if they are all decently well off and there remains dire poverty in my community, it may be obligatory for the estate to become the community's.

This is a strong argument for first-generation rights being inviolable, variations on it having been invoked for most of this century in the name of anti-communism. The dark side of the argument, however, is not the specter of all individuals becoming featureless figures in a collectivity, but rather that it is detrimental to the promotion—morally, politically, and legally—of equality. An unjust society that gives pride of place to the first-generation rights of autonomous individuals cannot but remain unjust.

What is at issue here is not so much freedom of speech or association, but property rights, especially as they are protected by the U. S. Constitution. Property rights may seem to be economic, and hence second-generation rights, but they are more clearly understood when seen as included in first-generation rights. In 1972, Justice Potter Stewart said:

> [A] fundamental interdependence exists between the personal right to liberty and the personal right in property. Neither could have meaning without the other. That *rights in property are basic civil rights* has long been recognized.[7] [Italics added]

If rights in property are indeed basic civil rights, then it would seem to follow that the more property one has, the more civil rights one can enjoy, suggesting that while everyone should be equal before the law, nevertheless, some—those with much wealth and property—will be more equal than others. This point should not be in dispute, for it has been made by liberals and conservatives alike. Consider the following statements by two constitutional scholars of decidedly different political orientations:

> An economic system resting on private property ownership tends to diffuse political power and to strengthen individual autonomy from government control.[8]

At the same time:

> The federal courts have through most of the country's history been the guardians of wealth and property against the excesses of democracy.[9]

Now the first quote makes explicit the relationship between autonomous individuals and property rights, and the second suggests how government control ("excesses of democracy") can be kept in check by the courts. Why this should be so, and is seen as good, has been stated well by the theoretical economist Mancur Olson:

> A thriving market economy requires, among other things, institutions that provide secure individual rights. The incentives to save, to invest, to produce and to engage in mutually advantageous trade depend particularly upon individual rights to marketable assets—on property rights.[10]

In a world of even a roughly equitable distribution of wealth and property, the protection thereof would be at least politically, if not, morally appropriate. But the actual world is somewhat different. According to a recent U. N. study, for example,

> The richest fifth of the world's people consume 86 percent of all goods and services while the poorest fifth consume just 1.3 percent. Indeed, the richest fifth consumes 45 percent of all meat and fish, 58 percent of all energy used, and 84 percent of all paper, has 74 percent of all telephone lines and owns 87 percent of all vehicles.[11]

And at the pinnacle:

> The world's 225 richest individuals, of whom 60 are Americans with total assets of $311 billion, have a combined wealth of over $1 trillion—equal to the annual income of the poorest 47 percent of the entire world's population.[12]

With statistics like these, it is easy to see why so many U. N. members endorse second-generation rights: 137 countries have ratified the International Covenant on Economic, Social, and Cultural Rights, but the United States is not among them (and is the only developed country not on the list).[13]

To see how starkly the (first-generation) rights of property can conflict with second-generation rights, we do not need to look to very poor countries in Latin America, Africa, or Asia; there are examples aplenty much closer to home. One case involved the transnational oil company British Petroleum, which recently closed a plant in Lima, Ohio, not because it was losing money, but because it wasn't profitable *enough*. Being the town's major employer, BP's decision has obviously been devastating for the entire local community. A spokesperson for the company at the time acknowledged the suffering and dislocation, but defended the decision by claiming that BP's first responsibility was to its shareholders.[14]

If no one can abridge my freedom to do whatever I wish with what is legally mine, then BP has only claimed its legitimate rights in closing the plant. Thus we cannot speak of any "right" the BP workers might have to be secure in their jobs so long as they performed them well and the company made a profit, because obliging BP to keep the plant open would be, harking back to Justice Stewart's opinion, a violation of its civil rights (corporations, too, are autonomous individuals legally).

Co-members of a community, need not, of course, be prevented from owning property and making money—perhaps a fair amount of property, and even money from profits. What they would not be able to do, on moral, political, and legal grounds, would be to dispose of that property and those profits in ways that prevented others from securing necessities (second-generation rights entitlements) needed to flourish as human beings.

Much more needs to be said on this matter to be sure, but we can make a moral case for the view that we are first and foremost co-members of community rather than autonomous individuals, and it will be a strong case to whatever extent our moral intuitions incline us toward equality. Not a perfect equality, but certainly a far greater equality than was described in the *U. N. Human Development Report* cited earlier.

But wait. We seem to have lost our focal point, the concept of freedom. Autonomous individuals are free, and enjoy civil and political rights in virtue of their being free. If co-members of community are very different from autonomous individuals (despite sharing rationality in common), does this mean they are not born free? And if not, what role does the concept of freedom play in their lives? How can they not only claim second-generation rights, but claim as well that they can trump first-generation rights at times?

Enter Eliot Deutsch.

In his commentaries to his translation of the *Bhagavad Gītā*, Deutsch says:

Through a self-transcendence of ego and desire, through an act of love and knowledge, man may overcome all of the sources of that which determines him. The resultant self-determination or "freedom" is not, then, the mere opposite of "bondage." To attain this freedom requires. . . .[15] a path to freedom for the man of action in the world.[16]

In *Personhood, Creativity and Freedom* this theme is developed further:

A person—that integrated, articulated, particular human—is free to the degree to which he realizes the self. 'Freedom' is thus a quality of achieved personhood. It is less a condition which allows for something else (e.g. moral responsibility) than simply a property or feature of what is achieved. I am free just insofar as I am as I ought to be.[17]

And developed still further a decade later in *Creative Being: The Crafting of a Person and World*:

We have said that a person acts freely, and that one is free when one is able to attend to reality and from that attendance to achieve rightness of action. Freedom can thus become a quality inherent in an action itself as well as in the actor, or, to put it more accurately, freedom is an achievement that is always embodied as a quality of an action.[18]

Thus for Deutsch "freedom" is an achievement term, not a stative one. It is not something we are born with, not something we possess, but rather is it something to be attained. Moving from a stative to an achievement concept of freedom will not get us immediately to co-membership in a community, but it is a good beginning. With respect to an individual's freedom, if you have it, I must not inhibit your exercise thereof. But if it is something to be achieved, then it may well be that I have moral obligations to assist you on the path thereto, just as you have obligations to assist me on the path as well.

In connection with his concept of freedom, Deutsch also has a different view of what it is to be a person, for, as earlier quotes show, it is persons who achieve freedom. Persons are very different from individuals, and for the latter he has few kind words: "A person does not seek to dominate another person, although individuals as such indeed often times do."[19] Moreover, for Deutsch:

Persons are social beings. An isolated, totally solitary person would be a contradiction in terms. A person sees another person, however, not just as necessary to oneself, but as that other person—whether man or woman—may be a part of a relationship that can mutually enhance human dignity.[20]

What Deutsch is driving at in these quotes, I believe, is very different from either a "mutual benefit" or "enlightened self-interest" model of human relationships; it is not a model, in other words, of those interpersonal relations that are coming increasingly to the fore in contemporary U.S. society. If I invest in your small enterprise and will share in the profits, then of course I want you to flourish because I will too. On the other (Deutsch's) hand, when a good friend flourishes, I also flourish, but not because I derive some "benefit" therefrom; rather do I flourish simply in virtue of its being a good *friend* who is flourishing, and whose accomplishments I take joy in celebrating.

If freedom is seen as a human goal—and perhaps as the highest human goal—then it can be argued that every human has an obligation to assist others in achieving the goal, or, to return to rights-language, it can be seen why we might genuinely have obligations to assist others in securing those necessities to which they are entitled by virtue of having second-generation rights.

With "persons" in Deutsch's sense thus serving as a first approximation to defining "co-member" as it has been used in this essay, let us now examine what he has to say about community.

> [W]hereas a society is something that everyone . . . is born into and is nurtured by through education and culture, a community is something that is created by persons. . . . A society, then, is a preexistent . . . impersonal structure of socioeconomic, cultural relationship of which a person is simply a part. . . . A community, on the other hand, comes into being by virtue of the voluntary participation of its members. For the individual, a society is a given; a community is an achievement.
>
> Participation [in a community] is thus not so much a relationship between an individual and a group, as it is a mode of being together with others in such a way that something new is engendered.[21]

Society and community are thus very different kinds of human grouping. Whereas the former is probably not greater than the sum of its parts, the latter definitely is. Society is the given, that which makes individuals what they are, and within which they can be, usually are, largely passive in the acceptance of what is given. To become a person in Deutsch's sense, however, requires individuals to be active: active in the first instance by rejecting, modifying, adding to or subtracting from that which society has given, or, at the least, to affirm that given anew as one's own, for which responsibility is then assumed. And activity is also required, as the quote shows, to then gather with other persons to create a community, which, once created, provides a new dimension to the lives of its participants.

This new dimension is not simply assuming the identity of the group by its participants; it is something very different from what boot camp drill instructors aim for with recruits, namely, to get them to see themselves simply as Marines: "Participation in a community does not mean that a person loses himself or herself in a group, or simply turns himself or herself over to another."[22] On the contrary, "In community there is power, but not the coercive power of dominance, rather the creative power that we associate with freedom."[23] And, "A community . . . is not, and can never properly be, hierarchical in the political sense of an unequal distribution of power."[24] Hence equality among and between its members is a defining characteristic of Deutsch's communities. Persons in a community setting are never altogether equal of course, because who does what, and when within a community will be heavily influenced by such factors as age, ability, interest, and so on, on the parts of the persons who comprise that community. But in all morally relevant respects, persons are equal.

All too sketchily, then, we have one vision of what it might mean to be a co-member of a human community who achieves freedom rather than an autonomous individual who possesses it from birth. There is much more in Deutsch's vision that I have not discussed, especially how persons in community will have not only these moral and political dimensions to their lives which have been my focus, but a strong aesthetic dimension as well, along with the possibility of a direct apprehension of divinity. And in achieved personhood (freedom) all of these dimensions are integrated.

I do not know whether Deutsch would approve of the use to which I have put his views, and I am not optimistic that the way I have done so will persuade any autonomous individuals to convert to becoming co-members of community. One major reason for this is that I have contextualized the discussion of freedom in the framework of human rights, and the concept-cluster of rights language terms presupposes the view of human beings as rational autonomous individuals, hence my critique of this view can easily become self-defeating. Civil and political rights were the first to be championed, and they served significantly to counter the concept of the "divine right" of kings—which is why they are referred to as "*first-generation*" rights. This will be clear to any careful reader of the Declaration of Independence, U. S. Constitution, Bill of Rights, the Virginia Declaration of Rights, and the French Declarations of the Rights of Man and the Citizen, and all similar documents (including Locke's *Second Treatise*) from the late seventeenth and eighteenth centuries, when rights language began coming into common usage. The U. N. Universal Declaration of Human Rights (1948), however, goes far beyond the earlier documents in enumerating rights, and, as I have argued, many parts of the U. N. Declaration have been resisted—especially by the United States—because not all of these rights can be secured by autonomous individuals.

For myself, I would do away with rights language, especially as technically employed in moral, political, and legal discourse. While it aids in articulating some of our moral intuitions and concerns, it fails to capture others, and worse, contributes significantly, as I have argued earlier, to insuring that the poor will indeed "always be with us." To my mind, within the conceptual framework of human rights and autonomous individuals, attempts to secure "liberty and justice for all" is of a piece with efforts to square the circle. With respect to language, surely we can condemn despotic governments for incarcerating dissidents without ever invoking human rights terminology. We rightly deplore such treatment of dissidents, but do so on the grounds that the governments have violated the civil rights of autonomous individuals. But assuming that the dissidents are patriots and not simply self-seeking or traitorous, we can equally condemn those governments on the grounds that remonstrance is obligatory in a decent society, and by restricting the physical movements of the dissidents and preventing them from intercourse with their fellows, the governments are hindering them from treading the path to freedom just as surely as if they were being starved to death, or infected with crippling disease. Similarly, we can condemn discrimination based on gender, ethnicity, religion, sexual orientation, and so on, without recourse to rights talk, and so, too, can we applaud the efforts of a Martin Luther King, Jr., and others deserving of our approbation;[25] all within Deutsch's view of freedom as an achievement term.

But the vision of rational autonomous individuals who are essentially free is deeply seated in contemporary capitalist cultures, not least the United States. So much so that even Deutsch, who certainly has no truck for "rugged individualism," seems to have retained a part of that vision. While individuals and persons are very different for him, he uses the same adjective for both: "autonomous."[26] Further, while he claims that his communities are natural, not artificial, it remains that they are human creations, thus artifacts, thus in turn artificial, pejorative connotations of the latter term notwithstanding.

What Deutsch means by "natural" is that it is part of the make-up of persons that they desire to create community.[27] Fair enough; but whence comes this desire? Is it given to individuals by society? Is it given by all societies? In endeavoring to achieve personhood, could one reject or suppress this desire?

These questions suggest that Deutsch may have drawn too stark a distinction between societies and communities, with members of the former more autonomous than he might allow, and members of the latter, while more truly autonomous, as persons, perhaps remaining individuals, too. For mustn't it be the case that the impulse to achieve freedom, to accept, reject, or modify society's "givens," is just another given of a particular society, namely, our own? Worse, how could I even think of coming to terms with my society's givens unless I had the experience of freedom to do so? Mustn't I already be free in some important sense to start along the path of personhood? Is it not, then, that human beings must first understand themselves as free, rational, autonomous individuals before they can strive to be achieved persons?

There is another, related way in which persons seem to remain more rooted in their societies than Deutsch allows. He is far more aware than most philosophers of the importance of history, tradition, and ritual for our all-too-human lives, and he treats these topics skillfully in his writings. He is also aware of the neglect of these features of our lives as a conceit of our own contemporary culture, as when he describes

> the modern Western view of creativity as having to bring something radically new into being. It is as if the artist were called upon to recognize most vividly that there is a lack in history, a void that needs to be filled, all of which implies that the whole of human culture requires his or her creative activity to redress itself.[28]

—and he then goes on to point out how this conceit easily leads us to confuse novelty and originality.

But he does not dwell overlong on history, tradition, or ritual when describing the actions—aesthetic, moral, spiritual—of persons, and this is an important omission for me, especially when it is remembered that for Deutsch, a person's achieved freedom is directly evidenced in just those actions. But how can I distinguish true freedom and creativity in an action from mere random or arbitrary behavior? Surely I perceive the freedom and creativity of a Toscanini, Bernstein, and Rostropovich conducting Beethoven's Fifth Symphony, but that is because I, if you will, know the score; I will not (did not) perceive the freedom and creativity of the actors in the first Noh drama I saw.

Deutsch well knows that the creativity which can flow from freedom can only be expressed within constraints, sometimes great constraints (Kasparov can only freely make his creative moves in chess within the rules of the game, on sixty-four squares). These constraints are given to us by society, especially within its traditions and rituals. True creativity on your part may result in a modification or violation of some of the "rules" of tradition or ritual, but I will only be able to perceive your achieved freedom therein if I, too, know the rules—that is, if we share the traditions and the rituals.

It thus seems to me that in order to achieve Deutsch's personhood, one must first be, *or at least perceive oneself as being,* a free, rational, autonomous individual, and that his societies are not as distinct from his communities as he suggests. To be sure, his persons are far more fully human than his individuals: they are nonegocentric, aesthetically creative and dignified, live in and celebrate community, are deeply moral, and possessed of a spiritual quality. But they must begin by being free, it seems, and thus enjoy the civil and political rights which, if my earlier arguments have force, hinders the achievement of justice and equality, especially in U. S. society, which in turn implies that not everyone in our society, and very few people in developing countries, can have a genuine opportunity to become a person.

Now given how much I have profited from Deutsch's work over the years, I find this conclusion unsettling. And because I know very few people who embody the ideals of achieved personhood that he describes as much as Deutsch himself, I suspect he may find it unsettling, too.

Five options seem available: (1) My logical is faulty (that is, the conclusion does not follow from the premises); (2) One or more of my premises is false (that is, I have misinterpreted Deutsch somewhere); (3) the conflict between first- and second-generation rights can be reconciled within the framework of rights language (that is, it is indeed possible to secure "liberty and justice for all"); (4) the highest aim of moral, political, and legal theorizing must be to secure procedural rather than substantive justice—equality—(that is, liberty takes precedence over justice); or (5) a more radical model of co-members of a human community is needed than Deutsch constructs, one in which personhood, and freedom, are only in part to be seen as achievements of the person; they must equally be seen as being conferred on us by other persons, just as much of what our own actions do is confer personhood and freedom on others; herein, I believe, lies the path not only to moral and political equality, but aesthetic and spiritual nonegocentricity—and thus true freedom—as well.

Only in this latter way, in other words, can we not only achieve greater equality and justice, but approach divinity as well, a theme more central to Deutsch's work, and which he describes in terms of love.[29] Only in this latter way can we fully overcome the empty feeling achingly invoked by the poet A. E. Housman: "And here am I/alone and afraid, In a world/I never made," and replace it with the higher-level love expressed by John Donne: "Any man's death diminishes me, for I am involved in Mankind."

Your turn, Eliot.[30]

Notes

*Not only the content, but the form, structure, and style of this essay were dictated by the context in which it would appear: a volume celebrating the work of Eliot Deutsch, in which each essayist would discuss an issue treated by the honoree in his writings, and to which he would respond in the latter part of the volume. In focusing on a theme—in the present case, freedom—but relating it to other issues, I have followed his own narrative style. In exposition, I have endeavored to understand him aright, because his work has had a significant impact on my own thinking. And my criticisms of that work will be understood, I hope, not as biting a hand that has fed me, but rather as an invitation for him to elaborate upon, or recast some of his views when he sees how they have been construed by sympathetic others.

1. Especially those of the "Harvard Four:" John Rawls, Robert Nozick, Michael Sandel, and Amartya Sen.

2. For the contemporaneous nature of these questions about freedom we can look both to the left and right in U. S. electoral politics. In preparing for a conference on civil society, for example, a fellow of the arch-conservative CATO Institute has said:

> Civil society is a spontaneous order, a complex network of relationships and associations based on the freedom of the individual . . .

And announcing its 1999 Conference, the Socialist Scholars group wrote:

> This year's Conference asks what role freedom has in popular movements and those of the Left, in particular. Philosophers have considered freedom in abstract forms; social movements have shaped it in practice.

3. Chomsky (1997), p. 210. The U. N. Declaration also calls for the rights of indigenous peoples to cultural autonomy, referred to as "third-generation" rights. Those, too, are important rights but the subject of another essay, because they pertain to groups rather than individuals.

4. I have explored this conflict in greater detail in Rosemont (forthcoming).

5. According to a recent report, illiteracy in parts of Appalachia runs as high as 50 percent—at the close of the twentieth century. See Wilson (1999).

6. Following the linguistic views of Noam Chomsky in his many works on the subject. See, for example, Chomsky (1975).

7. Cited in Ely's *The Guardian of Every Other Right* (1992):141. The title of the work is significant in suggesting how the Constitution can be seen by scholars thereof. See also the following two notes.

8. Ely (1992):155.

9. Ely (1992):5.

10. (Olson):000.

11. *U. N. Human Development Report*, 1997. Cited in the *New York Times*, September 27, 1998, p. 16.

12. *U. N. Human Development Report*, 1997.

13. *Human Rights: International Instruments*, The United Nations.

14. Cooper (1997), pp. 13–17. At the time this was said, one of the major stockholders in BP was the government of Kuwait, which shortly thereafter sold many of its shares at a great profit.

15. Deutsch (1968):188.

16. Deutsch (1968):189.

17. Deutsch (1982):24.

18. Deutsch (1992):171.

19. Deutsch (1992):212

20. Deutsch (1992):212.

21. Deutsch (1992):216.

22. Deutsch (1992):217.

23. Deutsch (1992):217.

24. Deutsch (1992):218. I have focused on *Creative Being* because it is the most recent of Deutsch's works that develops these ideas in detail.

25. These are discussed in Rosemont (1998).

26. Deutsch (1992):217.

27. Deutsch (1992):219.

28. Deutsch (1996):116n3.

29. See, for example, Deutsch (1970):13; Deutsch (1995):104–6; Deutsch (1992):199.

30. I am deeply indebted to the Editor of this volume, Roger T. Ames, in many ways. In the first instance for inviting me to participate in it, honoring a person for whom my professional respect as a colleague is matched only by my personal affection for him as a friend. I am also indebted to Roger for providing me with ideas that have contributed significantly to whatever value it might have (but is in no way responsible for its numerous shortcomings.) And he has the patience of a saint.

I hope to have stated the issues at stake between first- and second-generation rights more closely herein than I have done in past writings, for which I give thanks to the comments and criticisms given to me by Professor Jeffrey Reiman of American University in correspondence. I also wish to acknowledge with gratitude the work of Ms. Mary Bloomer of St. Mary's College, Maryland, who has turned my wretchedly scrawled penned pages into an aesthetically pleasing typescript ready for publication, and done so with warmth, efficiency, and humor.

References

Chomsky, Noam (1975). *Reflections on Language.* New York: Pantheon.

——— (1997). "Market Democracy in a Neoliberal Order: Doctrines and Reality." *Z Magazine.* September, 1997.

Cooper, Marc. "A Town Betrayed." *The Nation,* June 14, 1997.

Deutsch, Eliot (trans.) (1968). *Bhagavad Gītā.* New York: Holt, Rinehart and Winston. Reprinted by University Press of America.

——— (1970). *Humanity and Divinity: An Essay in Comparative Metaphysics.* Honolulu: University of Hawaii Press.

——— (1975). *Studies in Comparative Aesthetics.* Monograph of the Society for Asian and Comparative Philosophy, No. 2. Honolulu: University of Hawaii Press.

——— (1982). *Personhood, Creativity and Freedom.* Honolulu: University of Hawaii Press.

——— (1992). *Creative Being: The Crafting of Person and World.* Honolulu: University of Hawaii Press.

——— (1995). *Religion and Spirituality.* Albany: State University of New York Press.

——— (1996). *Essays on the Nature of Art.* Albany: State University of New York Press.

Ely, James W., Jr. (1992). *The Guardian of Every Other Right.* Oxford: Oxford University Press.

Olson, Mancur. From an interview with him in *College Park International,* May 1994, published by the University of Maryland. Olson is best known for the paradox of rational choice theory. See his *The Logic of Collective Action,* Harvard University Press, 1965.

Rosemont, Henry Jr. (forthcoming). "Which Rights?" "Whose Democracy?" In *A Confucian Alternative*. Edited by Henry Rosemont, Jr. Honolulu: University of Hawaii Press.

——— (1998). "Human Rights: A Bill of Worries." *Confucianism and Human Rights*. Edited by William T. de Bary and Tu Weiming. Columbia University Press.

U. N. Human Development Report, 1997.

Wilson, Larry (1999). "Appalachian Focus See Change." *Resist Newsletter*, April.

Self-Cultivation as Education Embodying Humanity

Tu Wei-ming

In his seminal essay, "On Being a Person," Eliot Deutsch defines a person as an achievement:

> A person is grounded in spiritual freedom and becomes a loving being in virtue of this grounding. A person is an articulation, a cultivation, of a unique subjectivity whose rightness is secured through the affirmation and creative transformation of the constraints and conditions of his or her individual being. One realizes oneself as a social being and develops that nonegocentricity that allows one to function in society with integrity, autonomy, and freedom.[1]

In this conception of the person, Deutsch observes that a person as persona is a special kind of masking. "The mask that fits rightly shows itself as continually drawing from the spiritual richness of its being."[2] He further notes:

> Articulation is thus a kind of cultivation or crafting (in the best Confucian sense). It is a reaching into the depth of human being—a sending down of roots, a forming of one's being in an explicit fashion with care and concern. It is the vital state of standing in openness to being."[3]

This mode of thinking, together with his idea of the "appropriated body,"[4] strongly indicates that Deutsch's way of crafting person and world is not only commensurable with the Confucian style of philosophical anthropology but also, in terms of the broad contours, characteristically Confucian in nature. Yet, by acknowledging the "central importance" of "the social dimensions of individuality" in classical Chinese thought,[5] he, perhaps inadvertently, relegates the Confucian ultimate concern—the discourse on human nature (*xing* 性) and destiny (*ming* 命) to the background. To be sure, Deutsch fully recognizes the heuristic value of Confucian philosophy "regarding the social nature of man and especially how the social factors can be seen not so much as constraints but as opportunities for self-cultivation."[6] Nevertheless, if I understand the basic thrust of his meditation on "creative being," it is in "the freedom we recognize as possessing in the shaping of our destiny" and the "acknowledgment of the creative power of being in which we share and participate"[7] that his kindred spirit with Confucian humanism truly lies.

We must explore the Confucian conception of self-cultivation to determine in what ways Deutsch's claim to an affinity with Confucian humanism can be sustained, and in what ways there might be significant divergencies.[8]

The overriding concern of the Confucian tradition is education. The primary purpose of Confucian education is character-building, and the starting point and source of inspiration for character-building is self-cultivation. The *Great Learning* (Daxue), one of the four cardinal texts in Confucian moral education, asserts that "from the emperor to the commoner every person must, without exception, regard self-cultivation as the root."[9] This is a claim about a moral ideal and an articulation of faith. Furthermore, it is the natural expression of a style of moral reasoning: self-cultivation is seen as the basis of family harmony and family harmony in turn serves as the basis for the governance of the state. Indeed, only when states are governed is there peace under Heaven. Therefore, all human beings, from the most powerful to the least influential, are obligated to actively involve themselves in this humanist joint venture of self-realization through their own moral effort of self-cultivation. The *Great Learning* assigns self-cultivation the pivotal position in its comprehensive educational program because of an awareness that human survival, as well as human flourishing, depends precisely on this kind of communal critical self-consciousness. It is more than moral idealism and pedagogical optimism that motivates the Confucians to take self-cultivation as the root of family harmony, state governance, and world peace. It is the faith in the improvability of the human condition through cumulative individual effort that prompts them to ground their moral education on self-cultivation.

This deceptively simple assertion is predicated on the vision of the human as a learner, who is endowed with the authentic possibility of transforming given structural constraints into dynamic processes of self-realization. Learning, in this connection, is the procedure by which our bodies are valorized to become aesthetic expressions of ourselves. The true function of education as character-building is *learning to be human*. Through humanization, we embody the humanity inherent in our nature. By digging a well into our ground of existence, we are empowered to tap into the spiritual resources of our own life water to create, nourish, and sustain an ever-expanding network of human-relatedness as well as to actualize our full potential as feeling, thinking, and willing individuals.[10]

The underlying assumption of this seemingly unbridled Pelagic view of human nature is that all members of the human community possess a heart-mind which is endowed with the capacity for affectivity, cognition, and conativeness. Surely, from an evolutionary perspective, humans, animals, plants, and rocks are consanguineous. We humans share a great deal of our basic instincts with other mammals and our knowledge of ourselves can be substantially enhanced by studying other life forms, not only dogs and horses but bees and ants as well. Yet, there are dimensions of human experience that cannot be meaningfully explained in terms of animal behavior; for example, no matter how ingeniously animal behavior is interpreted, it cannot account for the significance humans find in food and sex. Although it is not necessary to specify the uniqueness of being human as diametrically opposed to or completely separated from the rest of the animal kingdom, to reduce the salient features of the human to merely an example of animal behavior is unjustifiable even in sociobiological terms.

Individual diversity features prominently in the uniqueness of being human. As an ancient Chinese proverb has it, human beings, like their faces, are all different. Each human being, because of ethnicity, gender, place, time, and natural endowment, is constituted in his or her specific particularity. Duplication is impossible, even if one shares identical genes. As soon as a person is born, the individuality that comes into being is absolutely unrepeatable. There is a kernel of truth to the existential observation that we all die a lonely death. Indeed, the path that each of us travels is, in its totality, uniquely personal. The Confucian injunction that *learning is for the sake of the self* [11] fully recognizes the centrality of the specific constellation of one's particular human condition. No external demands, including societal encouragement and parental approbation, take precedence over understanding oneself and developing one's own appropriate sense of direction. Learning for the purpose of character-building is an intrinsic value rather than as a means to an end, no matter how noble and lofty the end purports to be.

While learning is for the sake of the self rather than for the sake of others and while each of us, in the last analysis, needs to pursue the path individually and alone, we are not isolated discrete entities but connected centers of relationships. Learning for the sake of the self encourages, indeed urges, us to be connected with a variety of communities—family, neighborhood, school, society, nation, region, and the global village. Self-cultivation in the Confucian sense entails webs of human-relatedness.[12] Through relationships with others and the wider world, we learn to realize ourselves not as abstract concepts but as concrete persons: mothers, fathers, wives, husbands, daughters, sons, friends, colleagues, teachers, students, patrons, clients, benefactors, and beneficiaries. The self, embedded in social relations, realizes its centeredness in dynamic interaction with other selves. Like a flowing stream, rather than a static structure, the self transforms itself as it encounters other selves. This self-transformation in the process of encountering the other entails a process of humanization. In Confucian terminology, humanization (the way we grow up in the human community) necessarily involves ritualization. Human beings learn to be human in a spirit of togetherness through a ritual (*li* 禮) process.[13]

We may envision the ritual process as a twofold educational program. The first is building a cultural code on biological reality.[14] Despite continuity with all modalities of being in the cosmos, humans learn to fully realize themselves by transforming their instinctual demands into social and, occasionally, aesthetic expressions of the self. As the most sensitive and responsive of all sentient beings, humans actively take part in their socialization. They learn to be civil, polite, and kind by living and working with others. Just as there is no private language, there is no private ritual. Ritualization as a social act requires a continuous interchange between the self and an increasingly complex network of human relationships. The creative activity of person-making and culture-making is communal rather than individualistic. Nevertheless, the dignity of the person should not be subsumed under social utility. The Confucian dictum of "learning for the sake of the self" clearly indicates that autonomy and independence are cherished values in self-cultivation philosophy.

The other aspect of the program involves realizing our distinctive personality in an other-related community. Whether or not our sense of freedom is predicated on an awareness of alienation from society, family harmony and, by implication, social solidarity is paramount. A critical consciousness of independence and autonomy need not be in conflict with the recognition that we must be seasoned in social roles. Unless we continuously reflect on the quality of our relationships, we fall short of a meaningful existence. Since, according to the Socratic tradition, the unexamined life is not worth living, without conscientiously appropriating the value of other-relatedness as an expression of our self-care, we cannot live up to the Confucian idea: "If you want to establish yourself, seek to establish others as well."[15]

The apparently narrow ridge between the Scylla of internal individuation and the Charybdis of external socialization provides an open space for the ritual process informed by self-cultivation to occupy the central stage in Confucian education. In this process, human beings are not conceived as self-sufficient, individual souls or content-less, mechanistically programmed robots, but are feeling, thinking, and willing persons committed to self-transformation and capable of self-transcendence. We can characterize the Confucian ritual process as "humanization," a comprehensive and integrated way of learning to be human. The full meaning of this educational program cannot be accounted for either by care of the self or by other-relatedness. Neither individuation nor socialization is adequate in conveying the dynamic interchange necessary for the actualization of the authentic person.

The idea of humanization presupposes humanity (*ren* 仁) as both substance and function. As substance, humanity is a quality. Like the seed or kernel, it constitutes the core and the most important part of all members of the human community. No human being, no matter how exalted is above humanity and no matter how depraved is beneath humanity. Although it is only when we are deliberately engaged in caring for ourselves that we can be said to be truly in possession of our humanity, as long as we are alive we naturally and spontaneously have access to our humanity. Humanity is that which makes each of us human. Yet, it is the transformative potential of the seed or kernel that makes it a real presence rather than an imagined possibility. If we assume, as most Confucians of the Mencian persuasion do, that the most universalizable defining characteristic of being human is "the feeling of commiseration" (or straightforwardly "sympathy"),[16] humanity, in the most elemental sense, must be understood as affectivity. Only secondarily will it be perceived as rationality or connativeness. The idea of sympathy in the Confucian tradition is compatible with reason and intention; indeed, humanity as sympathy is not only feeling but also willing and thinking.

As function, humanity manifests itself primarily in other-related situations. Being sensitive to and aware of those around us requires, at a minimum, an ability to establish a sympathetic resonance with the other. Our heart-mind (*xin* 心) is such that it is, at least in principle, capable of responding to any aspect of the myriad things in the cosmos—a blade of grass or a distant star. Sensitivity and awareness are innate qualities of the heart-mind. While, in practice, we are often insensitive to the overwhelming majority of things and happenings in the world and unaware of many intimate events around us, the capacity of the heart-mind to be touched and moved is always present. Confucian humanism espouses that the human heart-mind, through its sensitivity and awareness, can form "one body" (*yiti* 一體) with Heaven, Earth, and the myriad things.[17]

Normally, however, the specific others that evoke our sensitivity and awareness are those close to us. It is naturally human to feel discomfort when our beloved ones suffer. According to Mencius, our inability to bear the suffering of others, an exemplification of commiseration or sympathy, is the "beginning" (*duan* 端) of humanity.[18] In practice, the "others" are precisely those who in biological and sociological terms, are closest to us. This childlike attachment to our primary caregiver(s), considered by several major religious traditions as the basis of egoism, is, in the Confucian order of things, not necessarily a hindrance to our self-realization. Indeed, if this relationship is correctly perceived and vigorously cultivated, it provides a rich spiritual resource and abundant supply of energy for personal growth. The focus of Confucian elementary education can be conceived thus: the affectivity between parent and child, one of the most sacred, complex and problematical of human feelings, is taken to be the center of a continuous spiritual exercise enabling us to appreciate human-relatedness in its primordial form. Since the lack of such an affection leads to grave negative consequences for human flourishing, how to develop a proper measure so that the love between parent and child is never lost presents a major challenge.

The Confucians are acutely aware of the cost of an obsessive attention to this particular dimension of the human experience. Still, they insist that since a defining characteristic of the human condition is the necessity and desirability of parental care (or its functional equivalent), it seems natural and logical to consider the parent-child relationship as the basis for educating humanity.

The construction of an ethic, an elaborate cultural code, on the basis of a biological reality seems to be a strategy of making virtue out of necessity. However, the recognition that the parent-child relationship is educationally significant precisely because it is biologically given is predicated on this ethical wisdom: learning to be human begins with an awareness that one is not alone and that one's feeling of attachment is profoundly meaningful for one's moral growth. Indeed, care of the self properly understood is not at all incompatible with other-relatedness. The fruitful interchange between the self and an ever-expanding network of relationships defines the ritual process as humanization. The interplay between individual impulse and the sympathy of the community strongly suggests that our "stream of thought" is not merely an internally generated psychological fact but imagined or real responses to the world around us. Even Ralph Waldo Emerson, who believed in the divine sufficiency of the individual and refused to grant the positive existence of evil, advocated the ethic of responsibility of the scholar as an active member of a community and tradition.

However, there is a major difference between James's pragmatic individualist assertion that religious faith is "true" when it provides emotional satisfaction and the Confucian sense of awe toward Heaven. Although there may be an agreement between James's rejection of idealist metaphysics and critique of pretended absolutes and the Confucian preference for lived concreteness, the behaviorist tonality in James's pragmatism appears too goal-oriented to Confucian ears. Similarly, while Confucians share Emerson's steady optimism about the transformative potential of human nature, they may have difficulty sharing his sentiments about self-reliance.

In the Confucian perspective, as a concrete, living person, each one of us is fated to be a specific human being. We do not choose our parents, our time and place of birth, the particular kind of vital energy that constitutes our bodily existence, and the pattern of socialization available to us. In short, there is a structural limitation to who we are and what we can do; the more we are critically aware of our limitation, the wiser we become. Yet, we are free to the extent that we are capable of taking charge of the educational process and conscientiously shaping our characters according to our aspirations. This, I surmise, is the meaning of "learning for the sake of the self." When Confucius remarked that "at fifteen, I set my heart upon learning"[19] as the first occurrence in his succinct autobiographic reflection, he seems to suggest that the beginning of his examined life took the form of self-education. Before then, his existence had been primarily determined by the structural limitation. His meaningful life began when he realized his procedural freedom by taking an active role in shaping his own growth.

The message implicit in the dichotomy of structural limitation and procedural freedom is misleading, if freedom is merely understood as rejection of and departure from limitation. An important Confucian insight into the human condition is the firm grasp of our fatedness not as a predicament to escape from but as an occasion for self-knowledge and self-realization. Our "embeddedness" in the world here and now is not a figment of the mind, an abstraction, a fixed principle, or a verbal articulation, but an undeniable fact and an experienced reality. Surely, we are constrained in thought and action, but the structural limitation which defines our finality is empowering as well. As an occasion, it provides a unique opportunity for each of us to realize the full potential of our specific constellation of possibilities. Instead of rejecting our limitation, we build our worth upon it; instead of departing from who we are, we return to the inner core of our being by thoroughly familiarizing ourselves with our bodies.

The true freedom of the spirit, in this sense, is neither rejection nor departure, but affirmation and returning. The body is the proper home for the soul and spirit. As the ritual process signifies, the elementary education involving the six arts (exercises in ritual, music, archery, charioteering, calligraphy, and mathematics) intends to discipline and cultivate the body so that it becomes a fitting expression of the self. Actually, we do not own but become our bodies. The misconception that somehow our bodies are our possessions is based on the impoverished idea that we are, in the last analysis, thinking rather than feeling, willing, and sensing selves. As we learn to express ourselves through our bodies, our bodies become vehicles rather than obstructions of spiritual self-transformation. Our spirit is not released from the body as the prison house of the soul. Rather, it realizes its power and actualizes its potency through the body. When Mencius announced that only the sages can fully realize their bodily forms, he celebrated the authentic human possibility of transforming our structural limitation into full expression of freedom. The idea that, through self-cultivation, we can transform our biological reality (body) into an aesthetic expression of the human spirit (self) is realized in the last stage of personal growth in Confucius's autobiographic reflection: "to follow the dictates of my heart without transgressing the boundaries of right."[20] The body, so conceived, is more than a given; it is an attainment.

The attainment of the body entails four dimensions (self, community, nature, and Heaven) of the human experience which, in turn, form three fundamental principles: (1) continuous fruitful interchange between self and community, (2) a sustainable harmonious relationship between the human species and nature, and (3) mutual responsiveness between the human heart-mind and the Way of Heaven.

The self as a center of relationships occupies a pivotal position in a continuously evolving series of concentric circles. Community variously constituted (family, clan, neighborhood, school, company, society, nation, world, and cosmos) is always present in our self-understanding. As we interact with an ever-changing complex pattern of other-relatedness, we cherish the hope that our centeredness is enriched without losing its inner identity. While we maintain the dignity, independence, and autonomy of the self as a center, we endeavor to make it open and flexible enough to constantly benefit from the presence of the other. Undoubtedly, as Jürgen Habermas has persuasively argued, it is communicative rather than instrumental rationality that enables us to engage ourselves in a continuous fruitful interchange in society.[21] The need for civility and overlapping consensus through dialogue, conversation, and negotiation is so obvious that either the neo-classical notion of *Homo economicus* or the Lockean idea of the state of nature seems inadequate to account for the fruitful ambiguity in wholesome human interaction. The ancient wisdom of Socrates and Confucius seems more appropriate for providing the ethical foundation underlying self and community.

There is a subtle but significant difference between the Socratic and Confucian dialogue. While both share a commitment to awakening each and every person to self-cultivation and both express faith in the transformability of ordinary people through self-effort, they differ remarkably in understanding the sort of moral capacity that is required. Socrates's preference for logical analysis and dedication to rational argument prompted him to question everyone and everything. Since he refused to rely on any source of knowledge except the reasoning mind, he was inattentive to, if not outright contemptuous of, established ritual, time-honored convention, and deep-rooted tradition. In addition, he also seriously doubted the usefulness of the authority of sacred books for the attainment of *eudaimonia* (the Aristotelian concept as a generic Greek educational ideal).

Confucius also recognized the value of critical scrutiny of widely accepted ideas, alertness of the mind, and intellectual curiosity, but he believed that education by acculturation to the time-honored values and practices of the ancient civilization was vitally important and that it need not be an uncritical submission to authority. On the contrary, the true transmitter of the Way is, strictly speaking, not a gadfly. To awaken rather than torment the soul requires exemplary teaching which often appeals to common sense, so that those who are seasoned in conventional beliefs may perceive the profound significance of values and practices they merely take for granted.

Far from being tacit acceptance of the status quo, the Confucian faith in the realizability of the ultimate meaning of life in ordinary human existence is a conviction that, in the relationship between self and community, sympathy is both necessary and desirable. Critical reflection is compatible with and complementary to the harmonious flow of feeling that makes us an integral part of the ritual process, but rational analysis in itself, without the prior consent of those involved to become willing participants in dialogue, is unlikely to bring about the anticipated Socratic results. The activation of independent-mindedness and the production of a reasonable discourse community require sympathetic resonance as well as communicative rationality.

In summarizing the newly published collection of essays on *Confucianism and Ecology*, Mary Evelyn Tucker and John Berthrong observe:

> Confucianism may be a rich source for rethinking our own relationships between cosmology and ethics in light of present ecological concerns. Its organic holism and dynamic vitalism give us a special appreciation for the interconnectedness of all life-forms and renews our sense of the inherent value of this intrinsic web of life. The shared psycho-physical entity of *ch'i* (*qi*) becomes the basis for establishing a reciprocity between the human and non-human worlds. In this same vein, the ethics of self-cultivation and the nurturing of virtue in the Confucian tradition provide a broad framework for harmonizing with the natural world and completing one's role in the triad [the interrelation of Heaven, Earth, and humans].[22]

Accordingly, a sustainable harmonious relationship between the human species and nature is an essential aspect of Confucian education.

Of course, it is misleading to assume that Confucius, Mencius, and Xunzi in the classical period or Zhu Xi, Wang Yangming, and Dai Zhen in the imperial age were ecologically aware in the modern sense of the term, but by subscribing to the thesis of "the continuity of being,"[23] the Confucians always considered "forming one body with Heaven, Earth, and the myriad things" not only as an exalted human aspiration but also as an attainable common experience. The assumptive reason is that the human body is an integral part of the natural world; the way we breathe, drink, and eat clearly indicates our connectedness with nature. This fact alone suggests that this connectedness is not merely an imagined possibility but an experienced reality. The celebrated opening line in Zhang Zai's (1020–1077) *Western Inscription* is, consequently, not a romantic assertion about cosmic togetherness but a spiritual articulation of human indebtedness to nature as the moral basis for filial piety:

> Heaven is my father and Earth is my mother, and even such a small creature as I finds an intimate place in their midst. Therefore that which fills the universe I regard as my body and that which directs the universe I consider as my nature. All people are my brothers and sisters, and all things are my companions.[24]

In this view, we are and ought to be filial children of Heaven and Earth as well as indebted sons and daughters of world, country, society, and family.

The Cartesian exclusive dichotomy of the body/mind, spirit/matter, and nature/human is so alien to the Confucian mode of thinking that it appears ill-conceived, a kind of pretended absolute that does not even merit consideration as a rejected possibility. The educational import of Vico's new science and Herder's philosophy of history is certainly more compatible with the Confucian concern for the humanities, but their presumption that culture is definitely separate from, if not diametrically opposed to, nature is highly problematical from the Confucian perspective. Even in Kant's Enlightenment project, the idea of harmony with nature is not at all pronounced. Hegel's phenomenology of the spirit, not to mention Marx's dialectic materialism, is, from the Confucian point of view, thoroughly anthropocentric. Furthermore, the program of self-cultivation, essential for learning to be human in the Confucian tradition, has received little attention in modern Western philosophy since Descartes.

While we human beings are inevitably connected with nature, which is the proper home for our existence, we are not immersed in nature by forming an undifferentiated whole with rocks, trees, and animals. Rather, the sensitivity and awareness of our heart-minds enable us to appreciate our continuity and consanguinity with Heaven, Earth, and myriad things as an integral part of the cosmic process. Through self-cultivation, we learn to become stewards of the natural order. We minister to the sanctity of the Earth by transforming ourselves into guardians of nature. The dictum that "Heaven engenders and humans complete" suggests not only a harmonious relationship but a partnership as well. It may not be farfetched to assume that the secret code of Heaven is implanted in human nature.

Teaching or education, in the opening line of the *Doctrine of the Mean*, is defined as "cultivating the Way" which in turn is defined as "following human nature." Thus, human nature serves as the foundation for the Way and the Way provides the basis for education. This may have been the reason that Confucius confidently remarked, "Human beings can make the Way great; the Way cannot make human beings great."[25] Human nature, the Way, and education are so interconnected in the Mencian tradition of Confucian humanism that education as a form of cultural construction is rooted in what we naturally are.

Indeed, in this view, what we morally ought to become is, in principle, not at all in conflict with what we are biologically given. Yet, it is naive to believe that education is unnecessary, and that if we simply follow our instincts, we will naturally turn out to be good. Even if we do not follow Xunzi's assertion that an artificially designed social program is necessary for "humanist" education, the education that follows the Way and human nature by no means implies that we can build our teaching on instinctual impulses. Although the demands for food and sex are a constitutive part of our nature, it is the feeling of commiseration (the root of sympathy) that makes us uniquely human. Human demands for food and sex are legitimate animal instincts; they form a part of our body, but since they do not in themselves make connections and generate values, we can refer to them as the "small body." By contrast, since the feeling of commiseration can provide an inexhaustible supply of resources for making connections and generating values, it is characterized as the "great body." Paradoxically, the "small body" and the "great body," two classical Mencian conceptions, are intended to designate, on the one hand, a pervasive sense of the human as a member of the animal kingdom (small) and, on the other, the peculiar quality that enables human beings to realize themselves as the most sentient among rocks, plants, and animals in the cosmic process (great).[26]

Specifically, the nature that inspires the Way and, by implication, informs the proper humanist education is the great body rather than the small body. It is vitally important to note, however, that the great body and the small body are not mutually exclusive. Understandably, an important aspect of self-cultivation is to deal with the small body so that its intensity will not overwhelm the great body. Mencius's instruction that, in nourishing the heart-mind, nothing is more effective than making our desires few, clearly indicates that since instinctual demands cannot be fully satisfied, we need to practice moderation in an attempt to bring order and harmony to our otherwise insatiable impulses. Mencius recommended temper-ance; we ought to be constantly in contact and in communication with our sensory perceptions so that we learn that they do not overwhelm our feeling of commiseration. Actually, the greatness of the feeling of commiseration lies in its ability to accommodate the instinctual demands of the small body. On the contrary, sensory perceptions do not automatically give rise to sympathy; for obvious egoistic reasons, they tend to undermine other-related sentiments if they are not properly channeled. Rather than asceticism, moderation is the appropriate and efficacious way of handling desires. The message, then, is to cultivate feelings of commiseration in our nature into fully realized sympathy by focusing on the cultivation of the great body without losing sight of the natural needs of the small body.

Human beings are not only capable of enlarging the Way; they are morally obligated to do so. The path by which this is accomplished is self-knowledge. Mencius believed that if we fully realize the potentiality of heart-mind for sympathy, we will know human nature. By knowing our own nature, we will know Heaven. This may give the impression that Mencius advocated a sort of immanent monism, if not a strong version of secular humanism. Such an impression is grossly mistaken. Instead of anthropocentrism, or the self-sufficiency of the human, what Mencius proposed is mutuality between Heaven and humanity. The most important theme in this connection is that human nature is conferred by

Heaven. Heaven, rather than human nature per se, is the source of the Way and of education. The reason that the human can enlarge the Way is because human nature is Heavenly ordained and thus accessible to the inner reality of Heaven. Furthermore, since the secret code of Heaven is implanted in human nature, our self-knowledge, the kind that is informed by the sympathy of the great body, is tantamount to Heaven's self-disclosure. The mutuality of the Way of Heaven and the human heart-mind is both the highest aspiration of self-realization and the commonest experience of learning to be human.

Paideia originally referred to the pedagogical subjects in ancient Greece comparable to the six arts in Confucian elementary education: gymnastics, grammar, rhetoric, music, mathematics, geography, natural history, and philosophy. The Latin idea of *humanitas*, derived from *paideia*, provided the basic curriculum for medieval Christian education and modern liberal arts education. These subjects, to this date, are the most direct and intimate disciplines for human self-understanding and self-reflexivity. The Confucian approach to this discourse, as exemplified by the centrality of self-cultivation in the *Great Learning* is distinguished by its insistence that paedeia or *humanitas* as a process of learning to be human, must take the concrete living person here and now as its point of departure.

This emphasis on the lived concreteness of the person strongly suggests that embodied knowledge rather than abstract thinking ought to be the foundation of moral education. Through learned reflection on things at hand, we begin to appreciate the fruitful interaction between honesty with ourselves and considerateness toward others. The perception of the self as a center of relationships recognizes that one's dignity as an autonomous and independent individual need not be in conflict with one's integrity as a responsive and responsible member of the community. Indeed, the creative interplay between self-care and other-relatedness generates the dynamic process of learning to be human. While rational argument is necessary for self-knowledge, the rhetoric of assent enlarges and enriches the wellspring of sympathy indispensable for human flourishing. As we learn to extend our feeling of commiseration from the family, school, and community to society, nation, and the world, we appreciate more fully and deeply the meaning of forming one body with Heaven, Earth, and the myriad things. Only then can we truly bear witness to the idea of humanity as an experienced reality rather than an abstract concept. *Paideia* or *humanitas* is, in its core concern, educating the art of embodiment. Through embodiment we realize ourselves (body, mind-heart, soul, and spirit) in community, nature, and Heaven.

In my introductory note, I suggest that Eliot Deutsch's conception of the person, ranging from the "appropriated body" to "human destiny," takes on a shape of meaning quite compatible with the Confucian way of learning to be fully human. That the body as well as the person is seen as an achievement speaks directly to the Confucian idea that the sage, as the most authentic and thorough manifestation of humanity is none other than the "full realization of the bodily form."[27] Indeed, Deutsch's idea of personhood as "attaining a higher unification and identification" reminds us that adulthood, in the Confucian perspective, symbolizes the continuous process of maturing, "not in terms of his achieving some kind of static, lonely independence but of realizing an ongoing, dynamic autonomy."[28]

However, despite my sense of the sympathetic resonance and the natural fit between the contours of Deutsch's philosophical probing and the Confucian humanist project as I understand it, several areas of disagreement cannot and should not be glossed over. After all, as an original thinker, Deutsch charts his own course of thought and action informed by all the symbolic resources he cares to mobilize (Greek, Christian, Indian, Buddhist, Chinese, Japanese, modern Western, contemporary American, and more) without any deliberate attempt to align himself with a school, or even a lineage.

He is quite explicit about this: "To achieve an artful destiny oftentimes requires abrupt discontinuities and dislocations (alienation)—for it is these that present the challenge to imagination to realize a design."[29] Although I am not sure whether or not his situatedness (a combination of the Heideggerian sense of time and Nishida Kitarō's notion of place) as a modern professional philosopher working as an academician in multicultural Honolulu compels him to acknowledge the existential necessity that personal freedom entails an experienced alienation from convention, tradition, culture, and society, the Confucian faith in harmony between self and community does seem impractical, if not too idealistic and naive to the life of the mind that a sophisticated cosmopolitan intellectual, like Deutsch, cherishes and actively cultivates.

Still, while I deeply appreciate Deutsch's insightful suggestion that it is "the aesthetically necessary," as differentiated from the "reasonably necessary," that is "based on a freedom to bring a vital form to realization," I am not fully convinced that this is "the proper ground for the concept of (human) destiny."[30] To be sure,

> It is only when the music, the dance, the drama, the novel, or the poem is happening that we find its meaningful direction and, if it succeeds aesthetically, achieves the awareness of its rightness—its authenticity as the concrete, unique work that it is.[31]

The body and, for that matter, the person as an attainment is, strictly speaking, not a work of art. The idea of crafting, with all of its positive connotations, is too constructivist a view to accommodate the fruitful ambiguities, the hidden opportunities, and the mystery of personal knowledge and self-cultivation. I may produce music, arrange a dance, design a drama, write a novel, or compose a poem, but can I be the producer, choreographer, arranger, designer, writer, or composer of myself? The modernist impulse is to answer the question emphatically in the positive. If we believe that existence precedes essence and that we are entitled and obligated to be the masters of our own fate, we cannot but choose to actively engage ourselves in "the crafting of person and world;"[32] this is the creative task of learning to be human.

However, even if I see clearly the distinction between an habituated destiny and a fully creative one, I am not ready to grant that destiny is "the appropriation of the givens of one's individuality and specific events of one's life in an appropriate way, in a way that has the feel of rightness about it."[33] Deutsch's assertion that "appropriation is more than a resigned acceptance" and that "it involves rather a transcendence of the merely given, in freedom of consciousness and action,"[34] has great appeal to the Confucian ear, but I wonder what happens to the Confucian anthropocosmic vision if the spiritual horizon of the transcendence of the merely given does not rise above anthropocentrism and extend to the Mandate of Heaven. Furthermore, the ethic of responsibility in Confucian humanism demands a critical moral self-reflexivity in freedom of consciousness and action, without which the danger of self-deception motivated by egocentricity is virtually unavoidable. In short, If "[d]estiny ought to be the way a fulfilled life and living appears to be (aesthetically) necessary,"[35] can it afford not to assume a transcendent reference as well as a social dimension?

Notes

1. Deutsch (1992):32.

2. Deutsch (1992):26.

3. Deutsch (1992):26.

4. Deutsch (1992):58–69 has an essay on "The Body."

5. Deutsch (1992):234–235n29.

6. Deutsch (1992):234–235n29.

7. Deutsch (1992):228ff has an essay on "Human Destiny."

8. The following essay presented at the XXth Congress of World Philosophy is in the spirit of what I have in mind.

9. *Great Learning* I.

10. This line of thinking is quite compatible with Deutsch's assertion that "[a] person is a creative articulation, in varying degrees of rightness, of his or her individuality within the matrix of social community and within the enduring reality of the self." See Deutsch (1992):3.

11. *Analects of Confucius* 14.24.

12. *Analects of Confucius* 4.25.

13. See Tu Wei-ming (1998a):17–34.

14. I am indebted to Thomas Berry, the preeminent thinker on ecology and religion, for this insight.

15. *Analects of Confucius* 6.28.

16. *Mencius* 2A6.

17. Although this idea was brought to fruition in the beginning of the Neo-Confucian epoch (eleventh century), it was already well articulated in Mencius. See *Mencius* 7A4.

18. *Mencius* 2A6.

19. *Analects of Confucius* 2.4.

20. *Analects of Confucius* 2.4.

21. Habermas (1990).

22. Tucker and Berthrong (1998): xxxviii.

23. Tu Wei-ming (1998b): 105–21.

24. Zhang Zai (1963):497.

25. *Analects of Confucius* 15.29.

26. *Mencius* 6A15.

27. *Mencius* 7A38.

28. Deutsch (1992):29.

29. Deutsch (1992):225.

30. Deutsch (1992):225.

31. Deutsch (1992):225.

32. The subtitle of Deutsch's *Creative Being*.

33. Deutsch (1992):227.

34. Deutsch (1992):227.

35. Deutsch (1992):227.

References

Deutsch, Eliot (1992). *Creative Being: The Crafting of Person and World*. Honolulu: University of Hawaii Press.

Habermas, Jürgen (1990). *Moral Consciousness and Communicative Action*. Cambridge, Mass.: MIT Press.

Tu Wei-ming (1998a). "*Li* as Process of Humanization." In *Humanity and Self-Cultivation: Essays in Confucian Thought*. Boston: Cheng & Tsui Company reprint.

Tu Wei-ming (1998b). "The Continuity of Being: Chinese Visions of Nature." In *Confucianism and Ecology: The Interrelation of Heaven, Earth, and Human*, edited by Mary Evelyn Tucker and John Berthrong. Cambridge, MA: Harvard University Center for the Study of World Religions.

Tucker, Mary Evelyn, and John Berthrong (eds.) (1998). *Confucianism and Ecology: The Interrelation of Heaven, Earth, and Human*. Cambridge, MA: Harvard University Center for the Study of World Religions.

Zhang Zai (Chang Tsai) (1963). "Western Inscription." In Wing-tsit Chan, trans. and comp. *A Source Book in Chinese Philosophy*. Princeton: Princeton University Press.

The Style of Truth and the Truthfulness of Style

David L. Hall
Roger T. Ames

> *Reason or the ratio of all we have already known*
> *is not the same that it shall be when we know more.*
>
> —William Blake

1. Style is Out of Style

Asking after the style of a thinker or writer has itself gone out of style. Our seemingly obsessive concern for uncovering the ideological impulses motivating every literary or philosophical expression precludes a fair appreciation of what is unique to the particular author. Indeed, there are those who believe texts to be essentially authorless products of complex sets of social vectors. This situation is largely shaped by attempts to discover which texts are "hegemonic" and which are relatively marginalized "counterdiscourses." Such political interests, directed as they are at identifying vested theoretical commitments, have little to do with what makes one author distinct from another. Literary criticism in particular has succumbed to the view that since all thought is socially constructed, there is little to do but to analyze the play of forces behind the political voices shaping social events. These analyses involve bottomless investigations often pursued at the expense of careful readings of the texts themselves. In particular, proponents of so-called marginalized discourses of women, blacks, Chicanos, gays, and so on, have little time to waste on questions of style. There are, after all, battles to be fought, wars to be won.

Perhaps one should be not be overly impatient with this turn of events. There is good reason to combat any suggestion of political dominance in literary and philosophical expression. Certainly the myth of objectivity which led to the bifurcation of philosophy and rhetoric in the first place has been properly discredited, and will not regain any persuasive force for the foreseeable future. Having said this, then, it is problematic to continue distancing ourselves from questions of style, since to do so is to suggest that theoretical and ideological commitments stand independent of the notion of individual personality. This assumption allows that schools may differ from one another; there may indeed be distinct theoretical "styles." But the individual author is then seen to be little more than an excrudescence of social constructions. There is no small irony in the fact that Michel Foucault, and Jacques Derrida, and their epigoni, have made their considerable reputations by denying that there is an agent to own such reputations.

One does not free oneself so easily from the responsibility of addressing "the question of style." For, as we shall argue, this question is central to the understanding of the shape of our Western intellectual culture from its very beginnings.

2. The Question of Style: Historical Origins

The question of style has a peculiar genesis in those cultures influenced by the Hellenic, Hebraic, and Roman sensibilities. Certainly one of the more interesting features of the English language is that, largely due to its mingling of the nuances spun through disparate linguistic shuttles (Greek, Latin, Old French, Anglo-Saxon, Old Norse, and so on), meanings of even the simplest words are often composite and confused. In fact, an investigation of the complex history of a problematic term often leads to the discovery that one of the senses of the term proffered is the very opposite of its currently accepted sense.

There are two distinct and particularly relevant issues here that concern the character of the English language. The complexity of the semantic associations consequent upon a word's passage through a variety of linguistic filters insures that English is a richly vague language of *intensive magnitude*. This is but to say that it is a language in which the words are complexly nuanced by internal semantic associations.

A second peculiar characteristic of the English language is the presence of semantic tensions suggestive of oppositional significances resident within terms. This is nowhere more evident than in the fact that many terms carry among their meanings one that expresses the opposite of the accepted sense of that word. "Awful" is at once "disagreeable" and "awe inspiring;" "enormity" is both "immensely significant" and "monstrous;" "terrible" is both "terrifying" and "terrific."

This latter characteristic requires further comment. In natural languages, relatively free from the influence of formal theoretical contexts (scientific, aesthetic, philosophic, and so on), words carry within them polarities of meaning. This is a consequence of the fact that the experiential origin of linguistic expression is invariably a world of unreflective process in which "all things flow." In this naive original condition, words are employed to characterize processes and situations with the tendency to change into their opposites. Significant words, therefore, are bound to allude to both of two contrasting points of the same process. *Day* is recognized as "becoming-night," *darkness* as "becoming-light."

Early in the development of Ancient Greek thought, attempts were made to halt the flow of experience; to claim precedence for *being* over *becoming*. The movement had its first major expression in Parmenides's thought and reached its initial culmination in Plato's attempts to ground the search for knowledge upon appropriate formal definitions. The search for *univocity* remained a part of our tradition throughout the Greek period and found a second culmination in the terminological debates associated with late scholasticism. Later on, when the desire for univocity shifted from the theological context to the modern concern with physical cosmology, the basis for literal meanings found its final flowering. Language, when used responsibly in increasingly *professional* contexts principally defined by the methods of logic and science, led to the promotion of precision and clarity at the cost of richly ambiguous associations.

3. The Question of Style: A Cultural Contrast

One way of bringing the disappearance of personal "style" as a philosophically significant consideration into clearer focus is to tell the story of how style has been denigrated within the Western philosophical tradition. Another way is to contrast this classical Western experience with a tradition in which the pursuit of a homogenizing and essentializing univocity did not occur. In reporting on contrasts between the classical Greek and Chinese experience, Nathan Sivin makes several salient observations. He begins by stating flatly: "That fundamental claim, which we usually refer to as appearance vs. reality, has no counterpart in China."[1] As we suggested above, it is this ontological assumption of "Being" behind "becoming" that generates the reality/appearance distinction in classical Western philosophy, and that drives the search for the essential aspect of things, and for a literal and logically disciplined language that can report on this essential reality with veracity and precision. If the classical Chinese tradition does not entertain this ontological assumption, then one would expect there to be a greater emphasis on *meaning* as it is disclosed within specific contexts, rather than on *truth* as it is demonstrated through the applications of the formal structure of thinking, that is, *logic*. In the absence of a literal, objective, language that would articulate the "truth" about a given event, concern shifts to the appropriateness and efficacy of language as it shapes and is shaped by the world. As Sivin suggests, this is indeed the overriding concern in the Chinese experience:

> Much effort has been wasted by comparativists straining to find logic in early Chinese philosophy, but no one has yet come to grips with the complementarity of Greek logic and Chinese semantics. Semantics, after all, is what the people that historians lump together as *ming-chia* [*mingjia*] 名家 mostly discussed. . . . Logic has to do with the forms of thought or its expression, and semantics with the signification and meaning of words.[2]

This attention to "semantics" in Chinese literary culture is the substance of what is perceived as simply a matter of "style" within our own tradition. Importantly, this Chinese preoccupation with semantics entails the recognition that language does not merely describe a world, but actively valorizes and prescribes it. *Zhengming* 正名—conventionally translated as "the rectification of names," but better understood as "using terms properly"—is a recurrent, even pervasive, theme in the classical corpus. It is the performative and perlocutionary function of language that is the primary concern in the determined effort to "use terms properly." This ontological power of language is reflected in the homophony and interchangeable use of the terms, *ming* 名 and *ming* 命: that is, the "naming" of a world, and the "commanding" of that world into being. This preoccupation in the early philosophical writings with *zhengming* as "using terms properly" anticipates the flourishing of commentaries that continue to be woven around each of the canonical texts as they are passed on from one generation to the next. The need to constantly attend to language in order to "use terms properly" and the need to write revisionist commentary are acknowledgments of the processional nature of experience, and the unrelenting uniqueness of each historical moment and situation.

4. The Rise of Professionalism

What we have said thus far is in preparation for a discussion of the problem of style in English and, indeed, all European languages subject to the press toward univocity. That problem may be approached from a number of directions. It can certainly be understood as the problem of "professionalism"—namely, how to deal with the alienation of the metaphorical from the literal uses of language attendant upon the privileging of the scientific interest. Professionalism has forced philosophers, for example, to take sides in the dispute between "literature" and "science," a dispute born of the Greeks but perhaps best expressed as a peculiar problem of modernity. The postmodern version of this dispute is that between the logical and the rhetorical uses of language and argument.

Professionalized discourse promotes the perpetuation of its own disciplinary concerns. Specifically philosophical discourse has in modern times doubly entrenched itself through its claim to be the adjudicator of value conflicts among the various cultural interests. This claim insures, as well, the professionalized status of the areas of cultural interest that it purports to classify and organize.

The Enlightenment claim that science provides the ground of knowledge effected a shift from scholastic theology to scientific rationality as the guiding and grounding discipline of culture. This movement in the direction of rationalized science challenged philosophers, principally Kant and Hegel, to defend the role of philosophy as the presiding cultural discipline. This they did by employing philosophical thought to establish the role and limits of the scientific interest, and to insure autonomy to moral, aesthetic, and (to a lesser degree) religious interests within intellectual culture.

It was Hegel to whom we might give credit for introducing literary culture shaped by a Romanticism that qualifies the scientific pursuit of truth by appeal to a broader cultural vocabulary. The effect of Hegelian Romanticism was to substitute an essentially literary and historicist discourse for logic and empirical science as the guiding cultural discipline. In this organization of cultural interests, science is placed in an ancillary role with respect to the interests of art, religion, and philosophy.

The marginalization of science by the Romantics occasioned a counterassault from the Positivists in the early twentieth century that effectively brought philosophers back into the scientific fold, replacing the broad brush of the Romantics with the precision tools of Occam's razor and Hume's fork. For the greater part of this century, with the notable exceptions of the American pragmatists and the Continental philosophers, philosophy has had its greatest prestige when expressed in the empirical and analytical style of science.

The several movements sheltered by the umbrella term "postmodernism" are the culmination of post-empiricist counter trends. From Darwinian evolutionary theory to the paradoxes of relativity theory and quantum mechanics, science has finally yielded the usual senses of rationality and has itself shifted away from the literal toward the metaphorical. The challenge of theoretical relativism in general philosophic theory is best illustrated by the copresence of a variety of irreducibly distinct modes of speculation. A hundred flowers have bloomed. One must add to these factors the emergence of ethnic and gender-related movements that challenge the objectivity of rational methods by claiming them to be ideologically grounded. The final blow to the myth of objectivity has been felt through the increased encounter with alternative cultures that operate on the basis of values and understandings sufficiently distinct from our own as to suggest the provincial character of our Enlightenment rationality.

This complex shifting back and forth between the literal and the metaphorical, the scientific and the literary, the rational and the rhetorical, has shaped "the problem of style" in modern Anglo-European cultures.

5. The Strange Alliance of Truth and Style

The Latin root of the English word "style"—*stylus* (*stilus*)—meant a pointed instrument used for writing. The word still has associations such as "a surgical probing instrument" and "the gnomon of a sundial." (The gnomon is the attachment to a sundial that projects the shadow permitting us to tell the time.) *Gnomon* itself derives from the Latin *gnomon* and Greek, *gignskein*, "to know." The contemporary meaning of "style"—"the way in which something is said, done, expressed, or performed"—readily contrasts with this original sense. For the indispensable means of the act of both writing and coming to know, we now usually wish to substitute that which may be only its accouterment: "the dress of thought" (Samuel Wesley); "a vile conceit in pompous words expressed" (Alexander Pope). The sense of the seriousness and performative force of style is all but lost in its popular usage.

What of significance is restored to the philosophical endeavor by rehabilitating "style" and acknowledging its contribution to worldmaking? One way to recover its importance is to mine the etymology of the English word, "style," as we have done above, and to lay bare the original expectations of the term—namely, that "style," far from being simply window dressing, has an integral role in "knowing" and thus "making real" a particular world. Again, another way to recover the importance of "style" is to reflect on the Chinese experience in which "style" was never deprecated nor marginalized as a potential source of meaning.

The functional equivalent of "style" in the Chinese language is "*wen* 文 ": literally, "the incision of pattern," and by extension, the articulation of a world both physically and normatively, from the character wrinkles on an aged face (*zhouwen* 皺紋) to the generic name for "civilization (*wenming* 文明)" to the awesome design of the natural firmament (*tianwen* 天文). *Wen* is both the orthography of the culture (*wenzi* 文字) and the culture itself "culture (*wenhua* 文化)." There is nothing incidental, accidental, or superficial about "style" so conceived.

A more respectful attitude toward style is encouraged by the recognition that the stylistic elements of any formal expression are its only truly unique elements, the remainder being covered by grammatical rules, the strictures of theoretical principles, and ideas reworked from traditional sources. Very little is really new except for *style*.

> Style is a terrible thing to happen to anybody. As Miss Stein has already remarked, "the way to say it is to say it." Any attempt to devise a way of "saying" it that will tinge the subject with the writer's personality results in obscurity, mannerism, originality; and Mr. Eliot tells us that whatever is original is under suspicion. . . . If a man were to look over the fence on one side of his garden and see that the neighbor on his left had laid his garden path round a central lawn; and were to look over the fence on the other side of the garden and observe that the neighbor on his right had laid his path down the middle of the lawn, and were then to lay his own garden path diagonally

from one corner to the other, that man's soul would be lost. Originality is only
to be praised when not prefaced by the look to right and left.[3]

Several remarkable things stand out in this quotation. First, style is, indeed, a fear-
ful thing, terrible in its implications, for it presents an extremely formidable challenge to the author to expose herself in a most intimate fashion to her readers.
Readers, too, are challenged to yield their defenses, to enter into the personal
world of the writer, to accept her on her own terms. Secondly, style ought, according to the advice of Gertrude Stein, to originate in the straightforward effort to say
what needs to be said. Thus, a person's style, though unique to the individual, is
also unique to the situation, since different messages require different sorts of
media. Further, originality of style is "under suspicion" because what we think of
as "originality" is so often a consequence of the effort, first and foremost, *to do
something different;* an effort stimulated by "the look to right and left."

All three of these points converge in the thought that the enemy of good style
is self-consciousness. This, presumably, presents more of a problem to the philosopher than the poet since it is assumed that the philosopher, above all, must
champion self-conscious effort in the elaboration of his or her insights.

Leaving this questionable assumption concerning the philosophic enterprise
aside for the moment, it is clear that self-consciousness can threaten the poet as
much as anyone. In an interview shortly before his death, Ernest Hemingway
noted: "What amateurs call style is usually only the awkwardness in first trying to
make something that has not been heretofore made."[4] Surely this is one contribu-
tor to good style. To express the (relatively) new, a (relatively) new language is
required. The struggle to construct such a language can be a decidedly conscious,
even self-conscious, enterprise. Consciousness is little more or less than *attention
to task,* and self-consciousness is attending to the manner of one's attention.

Geoffrey Hartman's felicitous characterization of literary language as "a dic-
tion whose frame of reference is such that the words stand out as words (or even
sounds) rather than being at once assimilable meanings"[5] focuses the issue rather
well. The task of the poet *qua* poet is to present language whose meaning is secondary or at least a complement to the sound and meter of the words employed. The
Western philosopher, we must presume, has worked at the opposite end of the
spectrum. The "problem of style" was born out of the tension between the extremes
of this spectrum of sound and measure, on the one hand, and meaning, on the other.

Hartman's insight is that the relative importance of sound and sense, of rhyme and its reason, will vary according to context, and the poetic context privileges sounds and the words themselves. This view appears quite contrary to the notion that one should "take care of the sense and the sounds will take care of themselves."[6] But we take it that these words of Lewis Carroll are quite consistent with the contrast promoted by Hartman. Carroll, even in his most fantastic poetry, combined sense and sound.

> 'Twas brillig, and the silthy toves did gyre and gimble in the wabe.
> All mimsy were the Borogroves,
> And the momwraths outgrabe.[7]

Every good fan of Alice's adventures knows that "The Jabberwockey" makes good sense in "translation" (which Carroll graciously provided in his *Annotated Alice*). The point, however, is not that there is sense. Rather, it is that the sense is not the point of the poem. It is the sound and meter we enjoy. We are often quite pleased to take a holiday from sense-making.

The problem of style is appropriateness to context; to say what needs to be said. If one speaks as a poet, it is the metered words themselves that need to be said; if one speaks as a philosopher, meanings are at issue. *How* to say the words (when that is the goal) without the meanings getting in the way; *how* to express meanings (when that is required) without forcing readers to stumble over the words—this then, is *the problem of style.*

Recall the cartoon picturing two biologists at lunch, one of whom has reproached the waiter with these words: "There is a *Drosphohila melanagoster* in my soup." Appropriate word choice is at issue here. Imagine it were a poet who ran afoul of the fly: "Waiter, here lies a runty wingéd creature in my soup." Arguably, the locution "runty wingéd creature" stands out as words, while with respect to the term *Drosopohila melanagoster*, meaning is at issue. Nonetheless, both expressions refer to the hapless fly.

The problem of style is, therefore, how to use language appropriate to context. It is the context that determines whether words as words, or words as meanings, are to be stressed, and the degree of dominance that is required. Pure poetry on such terms would be sound and meter without meaning; pure philosophic discourse would be expressions whose meanings lay behind transparent words. Even if their attainment were possible, we neither need nor desire such pure extremes. Arguably, the problem of style would vanish at either end of the spectrum.

6. The Truthfulness of Style

Defining style as appropriateness to context provides a segue into a discussion of the philosophical career of Eliot Deutsch, and his manner of healing this breach between meaning and style that has plagued Western literary and philosophical expressions well-nigh from its beginnings. We have observed above that style is the way in which each thing expresses its uniqueness. Deutsch, keenly aware of what is at risk philosophically when style is dismissed or ignored, begins to re-claim style for philosophy with his ontological theory of truth. That is, Deutsch's cure for the rift between sense and style is rooted in his contextualist understand-ing of "truth" as achieved rightness.

Ben Jonson characterized style as "that where you can take away nothing with-out loss, and that loss be manifest."[8] This recognition of the identity of style with an eminent degree of *rightness* recalls Deutsch's formal definition of "truth:"

> X is true when and only when it achieves rightness through the articulation of its own intentionality. X is perceived by Y to be true when Y recognizes that there is no correct alternative to X within the matrix of its presentation.
> Where
> *X is anything that has the capacity to realize its rightness and Y is a person qualified to perceive that X is true.*[9]

This understanding of truth repeats the idea of appropriateness to context and precludes the reduction of truth to either of the extremes of literal or metaphori-cal expressions. There are distinct occasions upon which speaking of the fly in one's soup in scientific terms, or in literary terms, or in the terms of ordinary experience, may be most appropriate.

The recurring signature of Deutsch's philosophical reflection has been a chal-lenge to the hegemony of the formal structures of human experience, however defined (logic, impersonal reason, metaphysics, scientific and moral law, human nature), by giving *aesthetic* sensibilities a central place in the redefinition of these same structures. This is not to deny the formal aspect as a source of truth, but to reconsider what this means.

> By the term "form" in art we do not mean some kind of independently analyzable shape or structure but rather that blending of content and structure that appears as inevitable. Form is the artwork as a realized end that establishes those relationships that are right for itself.[10]

Deutsch's starting point, then, is the shaping of the work of art as a paradigm for the crafting of life's experience, a processional paradigm that resists dualistic thinking that would separate artist from medium, form from content, artifact from the creative process, the uniqueness of this kind of experience from its continuities beyond the making of art itself.

> The creative act is a kind of "letting be," but at the same time it is a shaping, a formative act, that involves expressive power. Together with the immanent purposiveness and cooperative control, the creative act is an infusion of power, an imparting of a felt life or vitality; it is a making of that which is alive with the very spirit of natural-spiritual life.[11]

If one is forced to characterize Deutsch's understanding of truth, it would be feasible to call it a distinctly *aesthetic* understanding. This is not to side with literary over scientific mode of expressions, but rather to recognize that scientific language is *aesthetically* appropriate in the contexts requiring such language. Moreover, it is to acknowledge that any severe separation between style and truth, between unique particular and context, involves a false dichotomy that presumes only one context—usually that of the objective language of fact—provides a vision of the way things are.

A singular insight that Deutsch has contributed to comparative philosophy is that a careful understanding of the non-Western traditions is a way of both challenging our entrenched philosophical sensibilities, and reintroducing us to our own cultural assets that have been driven to the periphery by professional philosophy. What one sees in the non-Western traditions—and here Deutsch is particularly dependent upon the sinitic cultures of China and Japan—is not, as first might be assumed, a mirror opposite to the Western dominant. The absence of transcendent formal structures is not immanence, the absence of objectivism is not subjectivity, the absence of impersonal reason is not intuition, the absence of absolutism is not relativism, the absence of atomic individuality is neither relationality nor the group collective. Deutsch requires that we seek out a third position.

Explicitly, Deutsch looks to the "special transitivity or mutuality that seems to obtain between creativity and what is created"[12] as a model for taking us beyond the dilemmas of dualistic thinking. The formal structures of experience both inform and are formed in a process in which the quality of the always specific achievement is the ultimate indexical of truth. This is a particularly important insight, because as Deutsch tells us in his ontology of language, quite often, saying it does make it so.

Over the entrance to London's Victoria and Albert Museum is the inscription: "The Perfection of Art lies in the Realization of Its Purpose." The perfection of art is the same as that of the scientific or the religious enterprise. There are a potentially limitless number of perspectives on experience, each an abstraction from the totality of overlapping contexts comprising the way of things. Each may achieve perfection through the realization of its purpose. *That* perfection is a perfected style—the only means whereby truth may be expressed.

7. Truth as Trust

When Deutsch builds upon this his definition of truth as "achieved appropriateness to context" and extends it to the project of the "crafting of person and world," the full connotative range of truth is mined to restore its original sense as that of "trust." Truth is fiduciary: It is the capacity to foster those constitutive relations which allow at once for the expression of our integrity as unified individuals, and the full growth and integration of this individuality in specific social, natural, and cultural contexts. It is certainly important that propositions be true, but perhaps even more important that husbands and friends be true.

This way of construing truth gives a much broader meaning to the biblical enjoinder, "You shall know the truth, and the truth shall set you free." That is, truth so conceived, is the fullest expression of personal freedom. It is the assertion of one's uniqueness. It is the fulfillment of *style*.

In constructing his theory of person, Deutsch uses the familiar vocabulary of "individual," "unity," "autonomy," and "freedom." However, these terms take on specific and often unfamiliar meanings as he pursues the central focus of his thesis: Person is a creative achievement in the attainment of what is appropriate for oneself. In his own words,

A person, I want to argue, is not a given but an achievement. A person is a creative articulation, in varying degrees of rightness, of his or her individuality within the matrix of social community and within the enduring reality of the self.[13]

To press this creative aspect and to distinguish this conception of person from more metaphysical assumptions about the givenness of human nature, Deutsch recognizes the social and political context in which his notion of person is to be achieved. He appropriates the Daoist notion of "non-action" (*wuwei* 無爲, a term we have translated elsewhere as "non-assertive action") to describe the optimum conditions for person-in-community, and thus the ultimate "style" of those who would govern. Rejecting alternative totalitarian conceptions of political life, Deutsch appeals to what he terms "creative anarchism" as the way of effecting the creative achievement of personal integrity within community. In such a community, the direction and design of the whole is conterminous with the aspirations of its individual members, with its most distinctive feature being the absence of coercion. Notably, this form of government is posited specifically in the language of style:

There is then the style of those who are in positions of authority that, according to creative anarchism, is one of authoritative leadership, of orchestrating the necessary involvements of other men and women, of harmonizing contributions in order to advance the welfare and dignity of all concerned. There is also, in the same spirit, the style of those who are participant subjects in the governmental political arena that, according to creative anarchism, is that of spontaneously acting in accord with others in imaginative ways to satisfy common needs, striving always to enhance human autonomy and dignity.[14]

In such a manner, philosophically serious terms such as truth, freedom, causality, necessity, and action give way to the more marginalized yet perhaps liberating vocabulary of aesthetic rightness, cooperation, creative possibilities, aesthetically necessary destiny, and play. Freedom, like truth, is ultimately a matter of style:

To act freely means, I think, to act skillfully in fulfillment of the natural grace manifest in every action-related process and thereby to attain an effortless power. To act freely is to express the achievement of personhood; it is to be fully self-expressive as a social being in action.[15]

And to live freely might well be to give personal style to what would otherwise be "a nonpersonal, boundless consciousness, a state of being that is an ever-present reality to be realized."[16]

8. Religion and the Spirituality of Style

One of the most provocative contributions Deutsch has made to the reinstatement of style is his curious volume entitled *Religion and Spirituality*. This work, a personal epistolary act addressed to his colleagues, is a collection of aphorisms, dialogues, prose-poems, tales, letters, meditations, and even plays that demands parity for sound and meaning, for rhyme and reason. Reminiscent of Plato's dialogical form, it will not tolerate the passive reader.

Deutsch styles this text a "postmodern" discourse in which "this author's voice is allowed as well to have something essentially to do with the meaning that is inscribed."[17] It is an attempt to illustrate the importance of personal spirituality in our most ambitious religious pretenses by reclaiming the center for inspired personal participation. Like Confucius some 2500 years ago, Deutsch is saying: "The expression 'sacrifice as though present' is taken to mean 'sacrifice to the spirits as though the spirits are present.' But the Master said, 'If I myself do not participate in the sacrifice, it is as though I have not sacrificed at all.'"[18] Unabashedly Deutsch has abandoned any and all of the protections offered by professional discourse, opening a window on his most personal thoughts and feelings for all to see and evaluate. Such playfulness is a most serious business. He exposes himself and says to his reader: "Is my spirituality worthy of your notice?" "How do you like my life so far?"

This recalls our remarks above:

> style is, indeed, a fearful thing, terrible in its implications, for it presents an
> extremely formidable challenge to the author to expose himself in a most in-
> timate fashion to his readers. Readers, too, are challenged to yield their
> defenses, to enter into the personal world of the writer, to accept him on his
> own terms.

Religion and Spirituality, in abandoning any theoretical conceits, reduces to the judgment: If good people write good books, then what kind of a person is Eliot Deutsch? What, after all, is the quality of his spiritual progress?

9. Deutsch and the Idiosyncrasies of Style

The importance of style is not simply expressed in the writings of Eliot Deutsch, but is evidenced in his personal journey, where his philosophical career has itself become an object lesson in the sense of creating the very object of its own discourse. In his own research, witness his passage from critical scholarship on specifically Indian philosophy to comparative philosophy on a more global scale, his passage from historical interpretation to philosophizing itself, his passage from metaphysics and epistemology to art and religion, his passage from the medium of philosophical treatise in discussing "truth" to a collage of poetry, plays, letters, and personal reflections in evoking religious and spiritual feelings, and his passage from professional dialectical arguments to his own personal philosophical style.

True to his own sense of personal realization as "achieved appropriateness to context," Deutsch has fostered collaborations both personally and professionally. For the academy generally, it was Deutsch who transformed *Philosophy East and West* from a periodical for a few hundred subscribers into an international journal with some 1600 subscribers around the world that, on its forthcoming fiftieth birthday, can claim to be a defining force for the community of comparative philosophers. It is hard to identify any other source that has done as much to promote Western literacy on non-Western philosophical traditions.

Heir to the comparative vision of Charlie Moore and Wing-tsit Chan, Deutsch has continued their legacy as a senior colleague in the Philosophy Department at the University of Hawai'i, taking a leading role in promoting world philosophy. The continuity of the East-West Philosophers' Conferences that date back to 1939 has, since his arrival in Hawai'i in 1967, been largely driven by his energy.

No small number of comparative philosophers would bear testimony to the profound influence that Eliot Deutsch has had on their lives. On a personal note, it was Eliot who was responsible for bringing the two authors of this essay into collaboration. As Editor of *Philosophy East and West*, he generously agreed to publish the first comparative efforts of David Hall. Upon reading these essays, Roger Ames recognized a student of Chinese culture who was dealing with issues similar to those with which he was concerned, and in ways that he could happily endorse.

Contact was made; discussions ensued. And the result has been a productive, and personally enjoyable, collaboration.

Our book, *Thinking from the Han: Self, Truth, and Transcendence in Chinese and Western Culture*,[19] is dedicated to Eliot with the words of Confucius: "In wanting to establish himself he establishes others; in wanting to succeed himself he helps others to succeed."[20] It was Confucius's judgment that a person so described is more than simply authoritative in his conduct (*ren* 仁); he can quite fairly be called sagacious (*sheng* 聖). On this judgment, as with so much else, we find ourselves in agreement with Confucius.

Notes

1. Sivin (1995) I:3.

2. Ibid. Chad Hansen begins his entry on "Logic in China" in the *Routledge Encylopedia of Philosophy* with the statement: "Technically, classical China had semantic theory but no logic. Western historians, confusing logic and theory of language, used the term 'logicians' to describe those philosophers whom the Chinese called the 'name school.'"

3. Crisp (1995):ix.

4. Donaldson (1986):137.

5. Hartman (1981):12.

6. Carroll (1974), chapter 9.

7. Carroll (1974), chapter 4.

8. Redwine (1970):11.

9. Deutsch (1979):93.

10. Deutsch (1992):156.

11. Deutsch (1992):155.

12. Deutsch (1992):157.

13. Deutsch (1992):3.

14. Deutsch (1992):206.

15. Deutsch (1992):171.

16. Deutsch (1992):230.

17. Deutsch (1995):x.

18. Ames and Rosemont (1998), 3.12.

19. Hall and Ames (1998).

20. Ames and Rosemont (1998), 6.30.

References

Ames, Roger T., and Henry Rosemont, Jr. (1998). *The Analects of Confucius: A Philosophical Translation.* New York: Ballantine.

Carroll, Lewis (1974). *The Annotated Alice: Alice's Adventures in Wonderland and Through the Looking Glass.* New York: New American Library.

Crisp, Quentin (1995). "The Genius of Mervyn Peake." Introduction to *The Ghormenghast Novels.* Woodstock, N.Y.: The Overlook Press.

Deutsch, Eliot (1979). *On Truth: An Ontological Theory.* Honolulu: University of Hawaii Press.

——— (1992). *Creative Being: The Crafting of Person and World.* Honolulu: University of Hawaii Press.

——— (1995). *Religion and Spirituality.* Albany, State University of New York Press.

Donaldson, Scott (ed.) (1986). *The Cambridge Companion to Hemingway.* Cambridge: Cambridge University Press.

Hall, David L., and Roger T. Ames (1998). *Thinking From the Han: Self, Truth, and Transcendence in Chinese and Western Culture.* Albany: State University of New York Press.

Hartman, Geoffrey (1981). *Saving the Text: Literature, Derrida and Philosophy.* Baltimore: Johns Hopkins University Press.

Redwine, James D. (ed.) (1970). *Ben Jonson's Literary Criticism.* Lincoln: University of Nebraska Press.

Sivin, Nathan (1995). "Comparing Greek and Chinese Philosophy and Science." In *Medicine, Philosophy and Religion in Ancient China.* Aldershot, UK: Variorum.

PART
2

Eliot Deutsch
Responds

Eliot Deutsch

One afternoon, not too long ago, I received a call from my very good friend Roger Ames inviting me to drop by his home later that evening, as he had something important to share with me. He wouldn't say what it was, and on the way to his home that evening I speculated that perhaps some good fortune had come his way: his discovery of an hitherto unknown ancient Chinese text? his receiving an inheritance from a long-lost uncle or a prestigious award for his outstanding creative scholarship? It was with considerable surprise that I then learned from Roger that, with the help of other of our friends, he had just received a signed contract from Open Court to publish a volume in my honor and that all the persons invited to contribute had gladly agreed to do so. I was, as it is said, struck dumb.

After assuring me that this tribute was not meant as a hint for me to retire—one does after all reach a point where a great deal more time stretches behind one that awaits one—Roger went on to explain that this volume would be part of a series published by Open Court to recognize "senior" philosophers with a global perspective—Herbert Fingarette, A. C. Graham, and David Nivison being my predecessors—and that the format of the volumes called for brief, but substantive, responses to each of the contributions. I might also, it was suggested, outline the various stages and facets of my work and indicate its general unity, if such there be, or barring that, the dominant interests and themes that have informed it.

My first impulse was to try to sketch such a trajectory of my work, but I soon realized that it would have to be a rather long story—a philosophical memoir, as it were, of considerable detail—if I were to avoid imposing, in the manner of many autobiographies, a rather artificial order of a step-by-step progressive development from where I began to where I now was to be located. Upon reviewing the various contributions by my distinguished colleagues, however, I realized that my individual responses to them might do the job of exhibiting something of the unity of my way and in a more natural manner.

I have noted on more than one occasion that the finest tribute one can offer a philosopher is not so much to talk about him or analyze his ideas as such, but to think with him; to extend, as far as one can, what one finds valuable in his work within the framework of one's own self-appointed tasks. I hope that my responses to the contributors, who have so graciously written in this manner, will likewise reflect that intention. I am deeply honored by their recognition and express, of course, my special and enduring appreciation to Roger Ames for his friendship and continuing support. The Director and Editors of Open Court should also, I think, be warmly thanked for their on-going efforts to sustain dialogue among different philosophical traditions and to encourage philosophers to challenge complacency and parochialism in philosophy wherever it is to be found.

Arthur C. Danto

I am especially pleased to have the opportunity to respond to Arthur C. Danto's incisive, clear-headed engagement with my work in aesthetics for, as he rightly notes, we have been friends since the late 1950s when he was a young Turklike assistant professor and I a rather rebellious doctoral student at Columbia, but that we seldom agreed then, and still do not agree now, on what philosophy—let alone aesthetics—is, or ought to be. I recall a little experience which perhaps makes evident this difference between us very nicely.

When Arthur with his family was visiting with us once in upstate New York, where after receiving my doctorate I was teaching for a time, I suggested that we take a long walk across the snow-laden fields and discuss some philosophical issues that concerned us. Arthur heartily agreed to the walk and to discuss the issues, but—sensing that this would not be an analytic exercise—on condition that it was understood that we would not be "doing philosophy." In order to have the discussion, I assented: "Ok, we will not do philosophy," while saying to myself, nevertheless, as far as I'm concerned, we will be philosophizing.

Arthur states that at Columbia, my "preoccupations were, centrally, religious in nature" and that my attraction at that time to the modern Indian philosopher Sri Aurobindo was because "one might have a genuine mystical calling without foregoing the secular imperatives of life." I think, rather, that it was Aurobindo's insistence on the inseparable relationship between philosophical reflection and the spiritual imperatives of life that most attracted me, especially at a time when what I perceived to be rather narrow and dry versions of analytic philosophy were indeed becoming dominant across the Anglo-American philosophical landscape and something called "critical naturalism" was the party line metaphysics at Columbia. With regard to the relationship between philosophy and art, however, Arthur does rightly point out that I "never felt a gap between philosophy and art, and found, from the beginning a certain internal relationship between artistic and religious experience."

Arthur has argued for some time now that we cannot distinguish a work of art from any other object simply by referring to how it looks; that whatever qualities are essential to art are not located in its appearance. In short, an object need not have any intrinsic discernible features or in any manner bear the direct imprint of the artist to have it count as a work of art. Arthur says he was driven to philosophy of art in the '60s "through the problems of Contemporary Art, in which it proved possible for works of art and quite ordinary objects to look so alike that there need be no relevant perceived differences between them." He goes on then to say that "The difference between Eliot's view of art and mine is that, for him, such problems do not arise. He has a very clear idea of what a work of art is, as something that could hardly be confused with an ordinary object . . ."

In opposition to what many of us are inclined to believe today, that in every act of perception and use of descriptive language we integrate various conceptual and value structures in our seeing and talking in such a way as to make our perceptions and language-use inevitably interpretive, Danto seems to hold to an "innocent eye" view of experience: we do see and hear, he argues, the *same* thing as the thing it is whether as art or as mere ordinary object. Nothing we may know or learn about an object will affect our "perception" of it as being a uniquely discernible object. I don't think that my idea of a work of art precludes the possibility that a work of art "could hardly be confused with an ordinary object"—Arthur's innumerable examples of indiscernibility in his work would surely suggest otherwise—but I do think that it is possible and philosophically imperative to spell out what a work of art intends to be in such a way as to allow recognition of its distinctive qualities.

Referring to a "performance" of John Cage's notorious *4′33″*, which consisted of a silence framed, as it were, in Carnegie Hall by a "pianist" sitting unplaying with his hands on the piano keys, Arthur cites a witness to the performance who allows that the audience caught-on to what was non-happening when "everyone there . . . began to say 'Oh. We get it. Ain't no such thing as silence. If you listen, you'll hear a lot . . . . It made available to a number of us not just the sounds [of chairs creaking, people coughing] but all phenomena.'"

I am quite prepared to argue that "music" rightly calls attention to itself as a *created* organization or form, invites our concentrated participation in what *it* has to offer, and that it is not its primary office, and certainly not part of its very definition, to awaken our capacity to hear any sounds that happen to be present in our immediate environment more keenly—important as that exercise might be therapeutically to liberate us from our humdrum habituated ways of negotiating aurally our worlds. Music, I argued, in *Essays on the Nature of Art*, is silence-and-sound; the silence, however, understood not as an absence of sound but as something that becomes, especially in the hands of a master composer, part and parcel of what is articulated in the composition and, in any event, is centrally ingredient to what we mean by "music."

Danto allows that his sense of the performance of *4′33″* "is that the message is not quite that there is no such thing as silence. It is rather that some silences are music and some are not, just as with sounds which are noises when not music *without sounding different in any way* from when they occur in music [italics mine]." So when people enter and sit in a concert hall (presumably paying for the privilege to do so), expecting to listen to a performance of a certain kind, anything whatsoever there that draws their auditory attention can rightly be regarded as music. As a kind of conceptual shaking-up, a pulling of the ear, if you will, well and good, but that this "artistic gesture," if I may call it that, has anything interesting to do with music, other than perhaps inspiring one to think more clearly about its very nature, seems to me to be ludicrous.

Danto states that it is bold of me to proffer an essentialist account of art and to develop it against the background of an ontology, and allows that he too is an essentialist. "I too," he states, "am convinced that an adequate philosophy of art must be compatible with art of every sort, irrespective of cultural differences." We differ, he says, in our respective ontologies. His "holds that there is no object which cannot be a work of art: a siren sound, a fortuitous shadow, a Brillo box, a block of fat, a urinal. . . . Whatever we understand the concept of art to be, it must be compatible with any object being a work of art."

On the contrary, it seems obvious to me that while any object whatsoever can become represented in art as a subject-matter, it is not the case that the alleged fact of look-alikes means that any object whatsoever can be a work of art. For Arthur the ontology of a work of art is that it is an object *plus.* The ontology of a work of art, in my view, is that art has its own intentionality to present meaning, power, form—and uniquely in each particular work—in its own special way as *integral* to its being a work of art. I don't think a work of art is an object which can be perceptibly indiscernible from an ordinary object *plus,* but that it bears the truth of its being in the manner in which it attains a certain qualitative authenticity or achievement. An artifact whose very nature, according to its maker, disallows any conceivable criteria for judging its intrinsic worth as a work of art cannot thereby, I think, be a work of art. Analytic to our understanding of "art" is that artworks are candidates for appreciation and evaluation and not just occasions for external conceptual analyses. One cannot argue that "anything goes" in art without undermining the very idea of art and thereby what it might mean to be an artist—and for that matter, an art critic or philosopher of art.

Arthur's ontology would place me, and anyone else of a similar persuasion, in the impossible position of chasing him forever around a circle of his making. "I find it difficult to see," he says, how Eliot's "definition [of art], when it is put in place, can be extended to cover the art from which I take my philosophical inspiration." I simply fail to see how the kind of "essentialism" I develop (which, incidentally, does take strongly into account cultural differences) obligates me "to cover" the examples (for example, the Brillo boxes) that "tirelessly" inspire him, without my having to abandon the very understanding of what art is which informs my definition.

In this context, Arthur takes up the question of beauty "as a component in the essence of art," but misses here, I believe, crucially what I had to say on the matter. He assumes that I hold, or at least that I am obliged to hold, that beauty is a property of an artwork. Beauty in art, I argued to the contrary, has to do with what is right for the individual, particular work of art as an expressive form. Forsaking the traditional quest to identify some objective feature or other that is necessary and sufficient for beauty to be present, I argued that "the history of the opposition between those who thought beauty could be determined as some objective feature of the object perceived and those who, despairing of ever finding such a feature or set of them, claimed that beauty resided in some essential way in the subjective response of the beholder lends credence to the possibility that the whole problem was framed wrongly in its assumption that beauty is a property of an object and not the object itself as *shown* rightly" as, what I called, a "radiant form." Danto then rather curiously (for the basic idea would seem to be highly congenial to his own ontology) states that "this conception of beauty may . . . be as true of [Duchamp's] *Fountain* [which is highly doubtful] as of Giorgione's *La Tempesta* or Piero's *Resurrection*. But that would not be the beauty aestheticians have in mind of thinking of art as beautiful"—precisely!

In closing, Arthur suggests that the artworks which he supposes I especially prize furnish us with experiences that "are close to mystical experiences." Yes and no: yes, I believe that art has an intimate kinship with religion, but no—as I argue quite extensively—the differences between the making of artworks and what I called religious-works, and as well the experience of them, are profound—as are the differences between all of this and "mysticism."

The kinship between art and religion, however, I also believe, and as Arthur so generously suggests, is much the same as between us; it is deep and complex—and being someone who is inclined to celebrate philosophical differences, I was pleased to realize that all those between Arthur and me—from the time of our earliest friendship in the late 1950s to the present—are still happily in place.

Graham Parkes

I am very grateful to my colleague Graham Parkes for his carefully crafted and insightful essay "Further Reflections on the Rock Garden of Ryōanji." Together with presenting a rich historical background to the tradition of the art of Japanese gardens, Graham offers a number of subtle reflections on his own experience of the Garden which do indeed "further" the account and analysis I gave in *Essays in Comparative Aesthetics* of my encounter with it some thirty-five years ago.

Graham rightly points out that the Rock Garden of Ryōanji is not, as I had put it, of just stone and gravel, for there is "also *moss*, as well as thin layers of lichen in the larger rocks" and that these "touches of life provide a striking contrast to the unremittingly inorganic nature of the rest of the garden." I would only add that for much of Japanese sensibility rocks are not *just* inorganic objects: as a Zennist might say, "you need first to see that rocks are not just rocks before you can see that they are." The point, however, that Graham wants to make "that without these touches of green life the garden would look very different" is well-taken.

He also rightly points out that although our experience of most gardens call, as I noted, for a kind of multi-perspectival engagement, "the rock garden of Ryōanji can be viewed only from the platform that runs along (the larger part of) its northern side—or at least intended to be viewed only from points on this platform—the number of available perspectives in it is actually quite restricted."

Graham finds that his experience of the Rock Garden is "less one of being drawn into oneself than of being drawn out of oneself," and although at the beginning of my account I did say that the Garden demands our inwardness, I also indicated later on, in a different context, that "the realization of *yūgen* in art calls precisely for a highly disciplined openness—an *ekstasis*, a playful 'stepping-out' on the part of both artist and experiencer."

It is primarily in this sense that I referred to the experience at Ryōanji as an invitation to contemplation.

Graham believes that the best single-word translation of *yūgen* may be "grace" and that "only the feature of 'half-revealed or suggested beauty'," as developed by Zeami, "seems apposite to the rock garden at Ryōanji." He goes on to conclude that "It is hard to see how the idea of *yūgen* as developed by Zeami helps us understand the aesthetic effect of the rock garden aside from the way, mentioned above, in which its beauty seems to derive from something's remaining unrevealed." As I understand the concept of *yūgen*, however, it is not so much a matter of "something's remaining unrevealed" but that, as Makoto Ueda puts it in his *Literary and Art Theories of Japan*, "*yūgen* . . . is the beauty not merely of appearance but of the spirit; it is inner beauty *manifesting* itself outwards" (italics mine). In good Zen fashion, the unrevealed becomes that which is most revealed.

One of the most helpful ideas, I think, that Graham applies to the Rock Garden of Ryōanji is that of *kire-tsuzuki* or "cut-continuance." He shows nicely how in haiku poetry a syllable, *ya* at the end of the first line, represented in translation by a dash, "is a syllable that cuts to the next line in much the same way as a director 'cuts' from one scene to the next in a film, breaking and yet maintaining continuity at the same time." He then calls our attention to the fact that at Ryōanji the major cut is effected by the wall which runs along the rear of the garden and describes with great sensitivity the various aesthetic functions it performs.

What, I asked myself, might one learn from the Rock Garden of Ryōanji and the concept of *yūgen* regarding the nature of beauty. "Beauty," I argued, "the concept of *yūgen* teaches us, is the *presence* of the object as it is in truth of being. Beauty in art is thoroughly paradoxical in this, that it gives rise to the qualities by which it is apprehended; it becomes the essential being of that which it is thought to qualify." Beauty in art, I maintained—and still strongly believe—is not a quality among qualities; it is not something that is superadded to the materiality of an object; it is not properly (ontologically) a qualifying adjective which may give rise to a class of "beautiful things." It is rather thoroughly constitutive of a work of art: it is the artwork itself as a fulfillment that is right for itself. Beauty is thus experienced in art not as an isolatable quality or formal arrangement but as the very expressive form that the work of art is. In short, "I don't perceive the artwork as beautiful; I perceive beauty as the artwork."

In the end, the task of "comparative aesthetics" as I understand it—and I believe Graham Parkes shares this understanding—is to engage other traditions for the opportunity it affords to learn from their distinctive achievements in such a way as to bring about a re-examining of one's own cultural presuppositions and the developing of new approaches and insights for understanding the nature of art and its role in our lives.

J. N. Mohanty

In *On Truth: An Ontological Theory* (1979), I suggested that "we start our thinking about the nature of truth—about what truth is—by looking first to our aesthetic and religious experience." I proposed that

> we ask first 'What sense of "truth" is appropriate to artworks and to religious language?'; from these analyses to develop a new conception about propositional truth (aiming to avoid at least some of the apparently insuperable difficulties in traditional and contemporary correspondence, coherence, pragmatic, redundancy, performative, and semantic theories); and finally to formulate a general, unified notion of truth which may apply to all its varied forms and kinds.

The general ontological theory that emerged from the particular analyses then was summed-up in the notion that truth was *rightness*, the fulfillment of the articulation of the intentionality of a thing.

Professor Mohanty allows correctly at the outset of his essay that most philosophers take it as a commonplace that there is no (or better, there cannot be a) unified concept of truth. In working out his critique of my "unified concept," it is not clear to me just how far Mohanty is in agreement or disagreement with the overall project, as he indicates that he will "develop a Vedāntic theory of truth with regard to cognitions" and then will suggest generally how the theory he arrives at "fares in the case of works of art and religious discourse."

The order of his presentation—"I will begin at the opposite end to Deutsch's"—from the truth of cognitions to what amounts to some very brief passing references at the end to truth in art and religion, strongly suggests, however, Mohanty's unwillingness to accept the general program or direction I set forth that moves from what are assuredly among the most complex and richly value-laden forms of human experience to problems of propositional truth, culminating in a "unified" notion of truth as rightness. I feel compelled, then, to examine Mohanty's own reflections on truth here with the aim, not so much of spelling-out or defending further my own position, but of pointing out where importantly the two of us seem to meet and then separate.

In "cleaning up" some terminological matters, Mohanty urges that we follow the more traditional understanding that a "proposition p is the thought expressed by [the sentence] 'p.'" The sentence *expresses* the proposition. In the communicative mode, by asserting the proposition one also *reports* (to the auditor) the fact, namely *that* p." In my less elegant usage I stated that a proposition presents a fact, which itself reports a state of affairs or what is the case, and that a proposition is true *iff* it articulates its intentionality to present a fact.

Mohanty says that there are two ways the locution—"the intentionality of a proposition"—can be understood and that both are admissible. "If a proposition is the *Sinn* of a sentence, and through the *Sinn*, the sentence, or its utterance, or the utterer, refers to a fact, then by 'intentionality' of the proposition may be understood either the intentionality of the speaker's consciousness (what the speaker intends to refer to) or the reference of the *Sinn* itself." He goes on then to say that "Deutsch is right in bringing the idea of intentionality into his theory of truth. . . ."

My understanding of the intentionality of a proposition, however, differs rather markedly from Mohanty's, for my general use of "intentionality" has to do, as I stated explicitly, with "whatever a thing qua the individual thing that it is aims to be by its own nature." I stated further that "the intentionality of a thing gives rise to the conditions under which its own authenticity is discerned. We grasp intentionality, not by any mysterious peering into the inside of a thing, but rather by our noticing its 'direction,' by our recognizing its possible fulfillment as the thing it presents itself as being. The intentionality of an artwork is discerned in terms of our noticing, with whatever content is available to us, that the artwork is an artwork and is the artwork that it has sought to become. The intentionality of an utterance is determined in terms of our perceiving what the language as language is doing or trying to do in its particular way within its own mode of functioning." I concluded with the idea that "The truth of a thing calls for realizing its own rightness through the articulation of its intentionality."

Mohanty wonders whether or not by "articulating its intentionality" is meant "saying what it means and meaning what it says"; and also states that "When Husserl held that truth is evidence, what he meant is that truth is experienced in the experience of the fulfillment of a meaning-intention. I think this comes very close to Deutsch's view." But this is not at all what I meant by "articulating an intentionality," for it is surely clear throughout, as indicated above, that I give a primary *ontological* not *semantic* content to it. Mohanty's à la Husserl's concern with "*meaning*-intention" takes the whole issue of truth in a very different direction from my own.

Or so it would seem, until Mohanty sketches his own "Vedāntic theory." Relying on Davidson's "two types of theory of truth"—the *epistemic* (coherentist, pragmatist, idealist) which understands "truth" in terms of our knowledge and the evidence available to us, and the *non-epistemic* (mainly realist) which explains truth as "evidence-transcendent" in such a way that it is possible "that reality always and irremediably diverges from our beliefs"—Mohanty looks for a way to reconcile them and, as far as I understand his argument, appeals to the Vedāntic theory known as *svataḥprāmāṇyavāda*, the theory of the self-validity of knowledge. This theory holds that knowledge is intrinsically valid insofar as validity arises, not from external, inferential justifications, which could go on *ad infinitum*, but from the very conditions that make for belief in the first place. We don't so much demonstrate positively the truth of our beliefs as we fail to falsify them in our on-going experience. As Mohanty puts it: "A cognition is true in case it is not false, that is, not contradicted," and he rightly notes that on this view epistemic truth "would always be provisional, open to revision," while what he calls "metaphysical truth" (for Vedānta, the "cognition" of Reality) will remain uncontradicted forever."

I held that indeed all judgments of rightness in the articulation of intention-ality, the realization of a thing's own aim to be, are "open to revision." I stated that "the realization is within the matrix of the existential conditions of the thing, and it is, necessarily, a dynamic realization. The articulated is not just a finished thing; rather, it is the thing as still open to development, to our discerning new meanings and values in it, to its being 'corrected' in the light of new experience." I also con-cluded the work with the assertion that "Truth of being [Mohanty's "metaphysical truth"] is inaccessible to philosophy," but, presumably contra to Mohanty, not to "metaphysical" experience itself.

In the concluding portion of his essay, Mohanty makes reference to art and religion, and it is here that the different directions we take toward the whole prob-lem of truth, as noted in the beginning, become especially apparent. Following once again the traditional insistence on the proposition being the natural and original home, as it were, of truth, Mohanty seems to allow, if truth has any initial bearing at all in art, only a metaphoric significance. The very predicates, he says, "great," "genuine," and "authentic" "can do the same job as 'true' in the case of works of art." Although Mohanty and I are in considerable agreement about the nature of art as having its truth reside within itself, I rather profoundly disagree with his refusal to allow for the possibility of a "unified" concept of truth that would not only accommodate works of art but arise out of giving central impor-tance to the nature of art, and I went to considerable pains to so present that case.

It is, however, with his very brief discussion of religion that our differences, I think, become altogether transparent, and here I must confess my inability to ap-preciate at all what now seem to be Mohanty's "realism" and "pragmatism" and where they take him. He states oddly enough that he finds the distinctions I drew between three kinds of religious language—"language of," "language for," and "language about"—"most interesting, as also his remarks on each"—I say, "oddly enough" for he then goes on to make claims about the objective truth of religious utterances that would be unintelligible within the framework of my analysis of religious language.

His question, he writes, is "is experience of sacredness, *no matter in what context, where, and on what occasion* (italics mine), a merely subjective feeling or is it objectively true?" He wants to contend, then, that the distinction between what "is really sacred" and "only seems to be sacred" cannot rightly be made for it "is not available as it is in the case of 'red'. It would follow then that if one experiences a thing, a space, a time, an idol, a life, as sacred, then it *is* sacred." I find nothing in the articulations of the intentionalities of religious language that could allow this to be the case.

In closing, let me remark that I have the highest respect for my dear friend Jiten Mohanty, both for his outstanding contributions to world philosophy (most notably Husserlian phenomenology and Indian analytic thought) and for the re-markable integrity of his person. I am deeply honored by the consideration he has given to my work on truth.

Thomas P. Kasulis

I appreciate very much Tom Kasulis's close reading of my work on truth and, of course, being the astute philosopher that he is, his agreement with its general ap-proach and conclusions. With some few exceptions, to be noted, Tom understands me correctly and, in a very constructive manner, offers some "augmentations" to my theory. I was also extremely pleased to have his report on our initial contact when he was a graduate student at the University of Hawaii and participated in a seminar I gave in 1973 on the problem of truth. I recall vividly his being by far the liveliest and most challenging among a number of very thoughtful and well-pre-pared students from many different countries and cultural backgrounds.

In summing-up and questioning a few points with regard to my treatment of truth in art, Tom states that I understand the work of art "as expressing only one possibility." Although he goes on to clarify this nicely, his statement can, I think, be somewhat misleading, for it suggests that there is a certain pre-determination in artwork-making which I don't believe is the case. I would prefer to say that a work of art presents its own unique expression, which is then subject to many different valid interpretations. Tom also raises some questions regarding the status of folk art—which he wrongly, I think, characterizes in terms of artifacts of use. "We now have," he says, "museums full of beautiful objects that were originally created not for display, but for everyday use. Can," he asks, "a blanket or a pitcher that was created to be used as a blanket or pitcher be a work of art according to Deutsch's theory?" Now "folk art" is indeed sometimes identified with "beautiful objects created for everyday use," but is more often understood today in terms of its nature as "craft work." When "folk art" is so understood, not infrequently such work does strive to fulfill the intentionality of art as I have tried to understand it and rightly finds its place in mainline museum exhibits. In any event, the distinction between so-called fine-art and craft-art has been considerably—and happily—blurred in our time.

Tom's treatment, however, of the way in which a finely made tea bowl functions aesthetically in a traditional Japanese tea ceremony was, I thought, extremely insightful and helpful. He shows here how an object not intended to be a work of art as such in terms of modern Western notions of expressive values nevertheless becomes art-like as it functions in a performative, ceremonial context which is throughout aesthetic as well as highly ritual in character. A tea bowl is art-like in virtue of the actions (and non-actions) of the participants in the ceremony in which it functions. The ceremony does not exist as such apart from its being performed. The closest analogy we might have today would be various forms of so-called "performance art," where the art-object likewise has its being only in being acted out, although here, of course, the work is being performed *for* an audience and ceases thereby to be primarily ceremonial. In any event, Tom's way of understanding the Japanese tea-ceremony should, I think, become a model for understanding better the aesthetic significance of a wide range of cultural artifacts (for example, pre-historic cave paintings) which were not intended to be works of art in our modern sense of the term.

Turning to Tom's treatment of my analysis of truth in religious language, here, too, some initial misunderstanding of what I meant by various modes of "religious language" needs some clearing-up. I distinguished several kinds of religious language, what I called "language *of*," "language *for*," and "language *about*," and characterized them in terms of their respective intentionalities, the fulfillment of which was the criteria for their "truth." Tom, I think, largely misses the point about "language *of*" (which may very well have to do with my failure to attain clarity here) when he identifies it with what a particular religious community takes as scripture or revelation. He (mis-) states that religious "language *of*" "is the expression of an authoritative sacred source" and that "the speaker must believe in the sacred source of the utterance." In explaining why I refrain from giving an example of religious "language *of*," he argues that "although all of us may not be able to decide unanimously whether a particular utterance of this sort is true, we should (at least theoretically) be able to agree that 'X' serves as such an instance of truth for community 'C'."

My understanding of religious "language *of*," however, as I tried to make clear, was that it was not to be identified with what a particular religious community or tradition took to be authoritative in virtue of its sacred source, that it was not essentially a bearer of a message, teaching, or proclamation, but that in religious language *of* "there is content but no subject-matter—nothing that can be adequately translated or transposed into a set of independent statements or propositions. . . . The content of religious 'language *of*' is the spiritual rhythm and power of creative being. Religious 'language *of*' is surcharged and suffused with an integrative vitality. It is thereby revelatory of spiritual being" (p. 48). In short, by religious 'language *of*,' I meant that very rare form of non-personal utterance which, through its inherent power, appeared to embody spiritual being. It bears, I suggested, a kinship with poetry, but is "symbolic in a special way; for it is at once wholly transparent, pointing to a divine presence, and entirely opaque, partaking of that presence in its own vital being" (p. 49).

I am calling special attention to this understanding of religious "language *of*" for it enables one, I think, to examine questions of the truth of this form of utterance quite apart from the old debates over the truth of scripture and the conflicts between reason and revelation, and because it enables us further to get clearer regarding the distinction between this kind of performative utterance and other forms of religious language such as "language *for*" and "language *about*," to whose nature Kasulis is especially sensitive.

Religious "language *for*," as I defined it, is essentially a teaching language. It is intended primarily "to point the way for another. Advisory, exhortative, celebrative utterances are intended, in this domain of religious discourse, to incite the hearer to follow some inner-outer path," and its truth then becomes largely a matter of its pragmatic efficacy. Tom accepts this characterization, but also wants in certain important cases to integrate religious "language *for*" with what I call religious "language *about*"—with that "which appears to be reducible semantically to propositions and statements" and whose "truth or falsity can be agreed upon in principle by logical and empirical verifying procedures. . . . It ["language *about*"] is the language which we use to interpret experience conceptually . . . and, when used in a theological and not just a philosophical context, to transmit a religious tradition, both in creedal and systemic terms" (p. 54).

I then tried to show how it also performs a function of shaping and directing consciousness, even in such activities as theist proof-making of the existence of God. Tom nicely elaborates on this notion when he points out that while my treatment of this tends to be individual rather than communal, I do recognize that this kind of religious language can be part of the transmission of religious tradition. "Yet," Kasulis rightly notes, "that transmission would seem to be at least in part a function of 'language *for*' . . . That is, religious reflection about the nature of reality may be inevitably related to how 'language *for*' points to a particular religious path." In short, he says that he "would argue that religious 'language *about*' may also, in a critical sense, be *for* the religious person expressing the language" as this takes place in a communal context. He then goes on to show how "religious praxis, especially communal religious praxis, . . . connects the three types of religious language" by taking as his example a "spirit-filled sermon." Tom's description of this is, I think, something of a gem from which all philosophers of religion could learn a great deal.

Lastly, Tom turns to my analysis of truth in propositional language and indicates how my "ontological theory," building on the discussions of truth in art and in religious language, might lead to a better understanding of what truth means in this traditionally central area of philosophical concern and attention. As with the other areas discussed, he has himself a number of important insights that augment my main argument, but allows nevertheless that I "have found a way of avoiding all the traditional problems associated with correspondence theories." Would that that were so! Any ontological theory of truth will, I think, have to incorporate some sense of correspondence in its formulation of what truth of statement means (although, to be sure, in virtue of its need to be highly contextually-situated, not simply among the standard variety), and I doubt very much that I have avoided "all the traditional problems" involved therein—as Jiten Mohanty and Tom Kasulis himself, in their very different ways, have so thoughtfully made evident.

Gerald James Larson

I pointed out at the beginning of "Knowledge and the Tradition Text in Indian Philosophy," the article which Gerald James Larson addresses, that quite frequently Western philosophers with some interest in Asian thought tend to engage that thought straightaway, in fine analytic style, as a series of arguments that can be lifted out of the forms in which they are embedded (and not merely presented) and dealt with in strict truth-value terms. I argued that the forms of philosophical expression that are to be found in various traditions have direct bearing on their conceptions of truth and knowledge, conceptions which must be understood before the comparative, critical engagement can rightly take place.

I called the general form that dominated Indian philosophy the "tradition text," by which I meant the authoritative sources, namely the *sūtra*-s and the *kārikā*-s of the different "schools" together with the ongoing exegetical work that was based on, but not rigidly bound to, them. The commentarial work, in short, formed part of a continuing creative effort that sought to refine and modify arguments, construct new ones in the face of various challenges, and to attain an ever-greater systematic coherence to the basic ideas of the school—and indeed the sub-schools—that constituted a particular tradition.

What was both presupposed in and followed from this form of philosophical expression was the idea that knowledge was as much a recovery as a discovery of truth; that it was an *appropriation* of meaning, a special kind of self-knowledge or removal of ignorance which, for most of the "orthodox" schools, was thought to be liberating.

Philosophers who engage classical Indian thought need indeed to be primarily concerned with truth-values, for that is what philosophy is all about, but we need to do so, I concluded, with a careful listening to what the tradition is saying and the distinctive manner in which it is said.

I was delighted to find that my good friend and colleague Gerry Larson found this notion of the "tradition text" in Indian thought helpful to his "own work in trying to piece together certain developments in the history of Indian philosophy, specifically, with respect to the traditions of classical Sāṃkhya, classical Yoga, Abhidharma Buddhist thought, and early Vedānta." Larson not only accepts this notion but very convincingly extends it in the direction of understanding how the terminology of tradition texts "have tended to overlap in the unfolding of these traditions" and have often, in that overlapping, given rise to what amounts to new tradition texts.

He very nicely illustrates this in the way in which the classical Yoga philosophy as represented in Patañjali's *Yoga Sūtra* appears as "a hybrid formulation derived from the 'tradition text' of the old Sāṃkhya philosophy . . . and the early 'tradition text' of Buddhist philosophizing as found primarily in the *Abhidharmakoṣa* and *Bhāṣya* of Vasubandhu." Larson goes on to allow that "this philosophical conflation [between the old Sāṃkhya philosophy and the early Buddhist philosophy]" suggests that it "becomes the ground upon which much of the later Vedānta philosophizing of Gauḍapāda and Śaṃkara develops." This bold claim, however, is not further developed or defended in this essay, and one hopes that he will do so in the future.

Larson nevertheless shows us quite properly that the traditional schools of Indian philosophy with their respective tradition texts were not only in contention with one another as such but were actively interacting and assimilating and appropriating each other's terminology and ideas and, I would emphasize, their arguments as well. One of the unusual features of Indian philosophizing, which I pointed out in the article, is the manner in which a particular argument became a kind of public property which any school or philosopher could use for their own purposes and with little concern for temporal boundaries. This disregard for ownership and historical context often breeds considerable frustration among students of Indian philosophical texts where, especially in Vedānta, old arguments taken from rival schools are simply incorporated as valid within their own Vedāntic tradition text. Śaṃkara, for example, in his treatment of causality borrows directly certain stock arguments developed primarily in Sāṃkhya regarding the manner in which an effect pre-exists in its cause (*satkāryavāda*) in his opposition to various Nyāya and Buddhist formulations, but then goes on to argue for a very different kind of theory in the context of explaining the ultimate relation or non-relation between Brahman and the world. Who, then, the student is lead to wonder, is in fact the real opponent (the *pūrvapakṣin*) in the discussion?

In any event, Larson concludes his excellent essay by acknowledging first of all the way in which the notion of a tradition text was helpful to him in understanding how there can be growing, evolving tradition texts that emerge in the interaction of the different schools, but more importantly how the notion puts philosophers on notice that Indian philosophy is not only an object for philological, scholarly studies but is itself a tradition of rich creative thought that is indeed worthy of close study for the intrinsic value of its distinctive achievements. To have a distinguished scholar and thinker such as Gerry Larson join me in this conviction is a source of great satisfaction.

Herbert Fingarette

"Suffering" is not a central theme or concept in my *Religion and Spirituality*, to which Professor Fingarette refers, or in any of my other writings. Fingarette's brilliant and sensitive analysis of the notion, however, strongly suggests that it ought to have been, and a close reading of his understanding of "suffering" indicates, I believe, that without my realizing it, it has in fact played a significant role in my thinking—but not necessarily in the way or context indicated.

Fingarette asks: in "what appears to be the intrinsically undesirable nature of the experience, how could suffering, in and of itself, have positive value, whether spiritual or not?" He answers boldly: "It is the only way to achieve anything of spiritual value." In order for this to be the case, however, we have to appreciate that what appears to be an "irradicable association between the notion of suffering and that of pain or, at least, distress or malaise" can be set aside if we retrieve an older, more authentic, meaning of the term which has to do with being patient, "allowing or permitting something or someone to be or to act without interference." This meaning, Fingarette argues, is a "fundamental human concept," it is "universal," having a "generic meaning," it involves our being "open, not to impose the ego-will or interfere, to suffer reality to be and to show forth."

He illustrates this meaning most effectively, I think, with respect to our experience of art, namely music, where we attain a kind of attunment with the aesthetic structure and power of the composition, turning ourselves over, as it were, whether as listener or performer, to its dynamic order, "suffering" its presence: "I must patiently suffer the music to perform itself, to live through me."

Fingarette then goes on to relate this "authentic suffering" to a concept of "spiritual passivity" which I develop in *Religion and Spirituality*. Now although there are several common features that can be noted between Fingarette's "suffering" and "spiritual passivity," I don't think they function in the same or similar way. I treat spiritual passivity (incidentally, a very active condition) as an intervening stage between solitude and the attainment of wisdom, which I define in terms of an on-going process of awakening. "Passivity" contains but, unlike "wisdom," does not have Fingarette's authentic suffering as among its essential features.

Fingarette's "suffering" finds a central place, however, I think, in a very different context in my work, namely in the notion of "acting freely" that I develop in *Personhood, Creativity and Freedom* (chapter 5) and in *Creative Being: The Crafting of Person and World* (chapter 10). "To act freely," I argue, "means to act skillfully in fulfillment of the natural grace manifest in every action-related process and thereby to attain an effortless power." The achievement of this manner or style of acting requires a special attitude on the part of the actor, an attitude which is precisely that of non-attached participation. It is one's willingness to turn oneself over to the action that contributes to the special power that is then realized in the act. When acting freely, then, the purpose of the act and the reason for it coincide insofar as any justification for the way in which the act is being carried out would do no more than specify that it is being carried out for its own sake. Actions that are performed freely, in other words, require no justification apart from what is realized intrinsically in their performance.

Fingarette developed his notion of authentic suffering by reference to what he believes is the key role it has played in various Asian traditions, namely in Daoism and in Hindu thought. Following his lead, let me proffer a few observations on these concepts with respect to what it means to act freely in relation to authentic suffering.

The teachings of the *Bhagavad Gītā* on action are subtle and somewhat elusive. Its central doctrine about human action is that if one acts with a certain attitude or spirit, one which, to be effective, must be a natural expression of one's spiritual being, then one can attain a complete freedom or liberation while engaged in the doings of the world. This attitude or spirit involves a special kind of non-attachment to the results (fruits) of one's action (*niṣkāma karma*: lit. "action without desire").

Preparing the way for a radical notion of free action, the *Gītā* affirms a kind of strict conditioning in ordinary action. "No one can remain, even for a moment, without performing some action. Everyone is made to act helplessly by the *guṇas* [qualities, strands, energies] of *prakṛti* [material nature]" (III, 5). Nature, for the *Gītā*, which here follows the ancient Sāṃkhya system, is constituted by various *guṇas*, energy states or dispositions which, in varying degrees of emphasis, are distributed throughout nature's many forms and products. Every human being is said to represent a special combination of these qualities which form the basis for his or her personality. Within a single life-span of an individual the *guṇas* are simply the limiting conditions of one's physical and psychical being. At this level of action the individual as such is not a genuine actor. "All actions are performed by the *guṇas* of *prakṛti* alone. But he who is deluded by egoism thinks, 'I am the doer'" (III, 27). What the *Gītā* seems to be arguing is that with the presence of "ego" we misunderstand the nature of action and of ourselves as actors.

> He who sees inaction in action and action in inaction, he is wise among men; he does all actions harmoniously. (IV, 18)
>
> Having abandoned attachment to the fruits of action, always content and independent, he does nothing even though he is engaged in action. (IV, 20)

This is surely authentic suffering *par excellence.*

Daoism, with its doctrine of *wei wuwei* or "actionless action," also introduced a teaching on the nature of action which points in the direction of "patiently" acting freely. *Wuwei* has been translated (and interpreted) in a variety of ways by commentators on, and scholars of, the Daoist tradition. They go from "action that is actionless" (Waley), "accomplishment apart from work" (Blakney), "taking no action" (Chan), to "non-interference" (Chang). Some of the key passages in the *Daodejing* in which the concept is set forth are: (Chan translation)

> Tao [Dao] invariably takes no action, and yet there is nothing left undone. (37)
> [The sage] accomplishes without any action. (47)
> Few in the world can understand teaching without words and the advantage of taking no action. (43)
> By acting without action, all things will be in order. (3)
> The man of superior virtue takes no action, but has no ulterior motive to do so.

The man of inferior virtue takes action, and has an ulterior motive to do so. (38)

He who takes an action fails.

He who grasps things loses them.

For this reason the sage takes no action and therefore does not fail. (64)

What does it mean to act without acting and thereby to accomplish one's end? The key term, I believe, in answering the problem is *de*, which may be translated here not as "virtue" but simply as "power." One who has real power never has to exercise it. Power here means "compelling presence." It grows out of a kind of *niṣkāma karma*, action without desire for its fruits; it means acting *without need*. Being centered in the Dao, in reality, the sage "has" all that is worth having, and is able thereby to be a presence and to exhibit *de*. *Wuwei*, actionless action, means then "not to have to do anything further in order fully to be," which state of being, in virtue of its inherent power, becomes—in a proper Confucian sense—compelling, as it were, for others.

The actor who acts freely for both Hinduism and Daoism achieves—and experiences directly—a power in action, which power, is effortless and thus becomes an expression of freedom—it shows freedom as intrinsic to the action performed as it is a quality both, indeed inseparably, of the actor and act.

This power is compelling for others. It attracts, because it is evident; it calls because one recognizes its possibilities for oneself; it demands because it sets a standard by which one measures, as it were, one's own attainment as a person.

I am greatly pleased to discover that I share deeply with Herbert Fingarette—one of the finest persons I know—a common philosophical understanding and aspiration to realize what it means "to suffer."

Daya Krishna

Daya Krishna's contribution to this volume, "Reconciling the Irreconcilable: Some Critical Reflections on Deutsch's *Humanity and Divinity* and *Creative Being*," provides the occasion for me to review the central metaphysical and philosophical anthropological positions I set forth from my earliest work *Humanity and Divinity*—to which Daya curiously devotes over ninety percent of his paper—to my more recent effort *Creative Being*. A first draft of *Humanity and Divinity*, with only minor subsequent refinements, was—as I noted in the Preface—written while I was a graduate student at Columbia University (1956–1959) and exhibits both a good deal of youthful enthusiasm (Daya graciously regards it as "boldness") and uninhibited philosophical reflection that was very much against the current fashions of the day. Daya sets the vision animating this work in rather sharp contrast to that informing *Creative Being*, a somewhat more sober, yet wider-ranging discussion of various ontological, anthropological, metaphysical, linguistic, ethical, social, and political issues. Rather than putting these in "irreconcilable" opposition to one another, I am more strongly inclined to see them as part of a process of development—and hopefully one not yet completed.

In Daya's extended treatment of *Humanity and Divinity* he draws attention to my interests there in the classical school of Indian non-dualistic philosophy *Advaita Vedānta*. It is certainly the case that during the early sixties I did extensive post-doctoral research (at the University of Chicago and in India) in this extraordinarily rich tradition and published several works as a result of that research, most notably *Advaita Vedānta: A Philosophic Reconstruction* and, in collaboration with the distinguished Sanskritist J. A. B. van Buitenen, *A Source Book of Advaita Vedānta*. At the time of writing *Humanity and Divinity*, however, I was not particularly engrossed in, or knowledgeable about, classical Advaita and made only a number of passing references to it, albeit large portions of that work were devoted to drawing out what I conceived to be the implications of a kind of non-dual metaphysical form of experience. With that youthful "boldness," I wrote *Humanity and Divinity* for the most part entirely in my own philosophical voice rather than in the more typical "academic" manner. I call attention to this, for Daya's essay as I read it is devoted mainly to a philosophical-social critique of Advaita Vedānta and, to be sure, my affinity with it, and to a forceful expression of his own somewhat over-heated antipathy to it (Advaita "makes all human enterprise meaningless"; the Absolute of non-dualism is "something that is apprehended as an ideal to be actualized and realized by a spiritual praxis which can only hypothetically postulate it as something to be apprehended"). In developing his critique, Daya does raise a number of specific issues which are discussed in *Human and Divinity* and developed more fully in *Creative Being* which I would like to address briefly. The problem of the nature of consciousness, which Daya addresses in particular, has been given considerable attention in traditional Indian philosophy and, of course, for some time now in modern Western thought. The differences between them, however, in describing, characterizing, and understanding the phenomena are so deep and wide that one might ask whether or not they are in fact referring to the same thing (for example, Vedānta, unlike in the modern West, lays considerable stress on the possibility and importance of realizing, within the framework of a multi-leveled ontology, a "pure self-illuminating state of awareness"). Daya nevertheless makes a number of assertions that cut across these traditions and emphasizes throughout that consciousness is *always* dependent upon "external conditions."

In *Humanity and Divinity*, I discussed the idea of a "transcendental consciousness" in non-dualistic terms and contrasted it with the intentionality of consciousness as understood in phenomenology and with those "everyday fluctuations of consciousness" which Daya says "seems to find no place in the [non-dualist] literature." Our ordinary waking consciousness, I wrote then, "is never wholly fixed or stable . . . it ceaselessly shifts to different objects and to different aspects of a single object, it constantly lapses into disinterest and is freshly stimulated by other interests." In *Creative Being*, I attempted a more thorough-going account of consciousness as a multi-leveled power of awareness which, in its fullness, achieves a certain boundlessness, but which functions for the most part as bound to the limitations and constraints of its waking and subwaking modalities. The main point which I tried to establish, and one which is central to my analysis of how personhood may be realized, is that human consciousness is not simply a given that one possesses in virtue of being human; rather it is most fundamentally an achievement—something that each person realizes uniquely from within and through the rich intricacies of his or her experience. Persons, I argued, *appropriate* their various mental capacities, their power of discernment as reflected in and exhibited by their perceivings, their reasonings, their evaluatings, and so on, in ways that make these capacities, in varying degrees, their own.

I then offered a brief analysis of "madness" as a kind of fallen consciousness, for I saw madness as the great impediment to the very possibility of achieving personhood, followed by an elaboration, at the other end, of the idea of a free, creative consciousness. Drawing from the entire range of appropriated experience, the creative imagination of a person is, I stated, a disciplined openness to reality that gives rise to new forms of insight and value. I concluded that one is free in consciousness when one is able to exercise fully one's cultivated capacities of intellect and feeling, when nonegoistically, unselfconsciously, one is one's activity in virtue of one's being properly attentive to reality, and that freedom is integral to the achievement of personhood.

What does it mean to be a person? Daya Krishna argues that "Once one has accepted the identity of the Self and the Absolute as already accomplished, one cannot meaningfully talk of crafting a person except in the sense that one tries to actualize on the phenomenological plane what is already realized at the ontological level." I have always thought that something important was missing in both traditional mainline Indian and Western thinking about the self and what it means to be a person. With the kind of all or nothing attitude, the liberated *ātman* or karmic-bound *jīva* (empirical self), in Indian conceptions, there seemed to be little space for the very idea of autonomous personhood, and with the emphasis either on non-ontologically grounded, socially-constituted, or atomically individualized ego-centered selves characteristic of Western thought, culminating perhaps in existentialism and today in various "post-modernisms," the very possibility of a genuinely free acting person, as I wanted to understand it, seemed to be ruled out. What was needed, I thought, was a viewpoint and way of life which— once again—acknowledged a non-dualist ground of being that not only allowed for but called for the crafting of creative, playful persons and which indeed made possible a "reconciliation," which Daya seems to disallow, "between the vision that is unfolded in *Humanity and Divinity* and the task that is envisioned in *Creative Being.*" Let me explain.

In *Creative Being* and elsewhere, I have argued that a human being realizes herself as she ought to be to the degree to which she becomes a person. A person, as I used the term, is a dynamic integration of the particular conditions and universal features of his or her individuality, an integration that is then articulated in a manner that, while allowing for multiple appearances, is appropriate for oneself. He or she becomes a person, in varying degrees, who realizes the abysmal depth of being and makes the conditions of his or her individual being opportunities for nonegocentric, socially informed growth. I thus have an identity as a person only insofar as I realize the spontaneity of my spiritual being and, in and through the conditions of my individual being, attain what I ought to be, as that "ought" is itself dynamically determined within the creative process of my historical becoming.

I distinguish clearly then between *the self*, as the atemporal ground of my being, as it is a pure spontaneity; *an individual*, which is whatever is objectifiable empirically—the total conditions, in short, of my peculiar, historical individuality; and *a person*, which I understand to be the dynamic, creative integration of selfhood and individuality. A person is an articulation of unique possibilities whose rightness is secured through the affirmation and creative transformation of the constraints, limitations, and conditions of his individual being—all of which is carried out in a spirit of play.

Throughout my work, and most recently, in varied ways, in *Religion and Spirituality* (1995) and *Essays on the Nature of Art* (1996), I have been concerned with the idea of play as a kind of liberated creativity that is carried out "disinterestedly" for its own sake, and as this idea has considerable bearing on the achievement of personhood. "Play," here means a highly disciplined and skillful, yet essentially non-egocentered, acting out of the freedom attained in the realization of the self. It is the joyful bringing forth of that which then becomes inherently meaningful and valuable as the articulation of a particular human being. By its very nature, the playful making of personhood is non-obsessive (it is not an anxious discovery of who *I*, as a personality, really am; it is not an angst-filled concern with one's own immortality), rather this playful making exhibits throughout precisely that lovingness and openness to reality which is integral to creative consciousness and imagination. It becomes, then, a loving state of being.

In *Creative Being*, I argued that it is important to give full recognition to the ontological grounding of personhood, for views of personhood *qua* development and realization are often accused of harboring a peculiar amorality; they allow, it is argued, for there to be no incompatibility between being a fully developed person and being able to commit heinous acts. Your Hitler, your Ghengis Khan, your everyday pedestrian murderer could be true to himself. But by insisting that the content of personhood is grounded in spiritual being we have as sharp an incompatibility as is possible between personal realization and acts of destruction and exploitation. To be a fully developed person means to be a loving being, not in a sentimental, self-centered, romantic way but in a manner that exhibits a sensitivity, informed by knowledge and understanding, which expresses an affirmation (celebration) of one's own being and that of the other.

With respect to this entire notion of crafting ourselves as nonegocentric, so-cially-informed, loving persons, Daya asks: "But where in all this is the fact of mutual-dependence and collective creativity without which no thinking about the human situation can be complete . . . ?" *Humanity and Divinity* paid little atten-tion to the ethical, social, and political (it was after all an essay in "metaphysics"), but in *Creative Being*, I tried to develop the implications of the crafting of personhood for these central areas of human life. When developing the idea in the first place of *an individual* as an insubstantial locus of empirical attributes, I ar-gued that such a notion discloses clearly that various social dimensions of experi-ence are constitutive of that very individuality. We cannot, I insisted, conceive of an individual apart from others, for the interactions between a human being and his or her world are always socially mediated.

Part III of *Creative Being* includes chapters on "A Creative Morality" and "Cre-ative Anarchism." I asked at the outset: If human beings are more or less persons, having realized their spontaneity and having achieved freedom in varying degrees, should not some human beings count for more than others and enjoy special privileges and be accorded exceptional rights? Ought not societies to be structured, as indeed they often have been, hierarchically in ways that take these differences between human beings into account? The answer, I allowed, is that when one achieves personhood and freedom, one has precisely the nonegoistic, loving sensitivity and concern that carries along with it the recognition of a non-discriminatory spiritual worth obtaining throughout life. A person affirms quite spontaneously and naturally the intrinsic worth, the dignity, of every human be-ing—and it is this recognition, this affirmation, which makes possible a political/moral understanding commensurate with the spiritual potentialities of human-kind.

This is not the place to elaborate upon all that was said with respect to the moral, the social, the political, but I would like to note that the freedom attendant upon becoming a realized person, I strongly believe, needs express itself quite naturally in that intersubjective, interdependent world that is itself necessary for the very realization of personhood. That expression in all its many dimensions remains indeed, I would affirm with Daya Krishna, the supreme task for our time.

Leroy S. Rouner

Taking his lead from Paul Tillich's distinction between two types of philosophy of religion—the "ontological" (nondualistic) and "cosmological" (dualist/theist)—and setting aside for his purposes the many sub-types or "varieties" within each category, Leroy S. Rouner in his very thoughtful and wise paper acknowledges implicitly that the central issue for both philosophy/theology and the rich fabric of actual religious experience is the relationship between these "two types." Putting this issue in the form of a long question, one might ask: Can the claim of the ultimate, spiritual identity between self and reality, and the consequent radical qualitative difference between our true self and our everyday self, which functions in a less than fully-real practical world (*māyā*) that follows from it, ever be reconciled with the assertion of an essential separateness obtaining between the human/the natural world and the Divine, with the latter taken to be inescapably "other" to, and standing in a hierarchical fashion over against, our finite and vulnerable human being which resides in a world that is irreducibly real and constituted by a multiplicity of particular, differentiated things? While the non-dualist, as Leroy sees it, does secure a radical peace and blessedness, he nevertheless eliminates in the end all forms of I-Thou relationality and thus becomes something other than genuinely human. The unrepentant dualist, on the other hand, as Tillich argued, while remaining very much human indeed, runs the risk of forever being a stranger in the world, threatened by doubt, fearfully confronting his inevitable death and, while living, suffering an ever-possible estrangement from his spiritual nature.

This central issue, as Leroy astutely recognizes, has indeed from the beginning been an overriding problematic in my work. Leroy traces this concern back to my interests in Indian philosophy, namely in the nondualistic (Advaita) school of Vedāntic thought. On a personal note, as I have already stated, my interest in nondualism preceded both my formal study of Advaita Vedānta and my engagement with the *Bhagavad Gītā*, which was sustained precisely by its varied attempts to effect an integration of nondualist and dualist ways; its ultimate inability to do so satisfactorily being highly instructive.

In this context, Leroy refers to my "philosophy of religion." If a designation is required, I would prefer "religious philosophy" for, as he rightly observes, I am concerned essentially with the "religious spirit" as it centers and defines a person and as it might inform philosophy at its core, enlivening its disciplined reflections and influencing its treatment of many issues. I have not been concerned academically in any central way with "religion" as an orthopraxy or as an object of anthropological or doctrinal inquiry as such, important as these studies might be in their own terms.

One other little point before getting to the heart of the matter: Leroy refers often to nondual awareness as a kind of possible personal experience and raises the question whether in its absence one must, if so oriented, embrace a kind of Jamesian "will to believe." This emphasis on personal experience can, I think, give rise to various misunderstandings. From a nondual standpoint at any rate, it doesn't make much sense in the first place to talk of that awareness as an *experience* of "mine" or of anyone else, for its very nature is such that there is no subject confronting, knowing, or otherwise engaging an object. Undifferentiated awareness is thus not best described as an episodic, occurrent happening, but rather as a self-transforming process of realization, in a very real sense, without beginning or end. One cannot, then, in any meaningful sense that I know of, "will to believe" this process: it simply is or is not part and parcel of the fabric of one's life.

How, then, as a philosopher can one integrate the dual and the nondual, "reconcile the irreconcilable"—to use Daya Krishna's expression? Must one after all, in the end, have simply to choose between them as different metaphysical or theological "perspectives" (as John Hick would seem to have it) or struggle to derive one from the other (as not a few philosophers and theologians going back to Plato have attempted), or just let stand the apparent contradiction between them and, as with so many other dimensions of our human living, muddle through and move among them as the occasion seems to call for?

My own approach, as I have tried to outline it more fully in my response to Daya Krishna, has been to look to "creativity" as a kind of play that is naturally consequent to nondual spiritual consciousness and manifests itself in the crafting of persons and worlds. This "liberated creativity," as I call it, rests on the affirmation of a very special kind of absurdity of being as disclosed in nondual consciousness; "absurdity," not as the meaninglessness of it all as an existentialist would have it, but as a joyous letting-go of the very need for cognitive certitude in the light of an apprehension of that "no-meaning" (to use a happy Zennist phrase) which may ground all subsequent meaning and value. A liberated creativity becomes then—as I try to describe, elaborate, and understand it—the transformation of the natural constraints of our being in the world into opportunities for person-making and world-making that yield a non-ego-obsessive creative way of belonging rightly with others in various natural-social environments as a knowing and *loving* being.

In *Religion and Spirituality*, to which Leroy refers, I wrote that genuine belonging is not something "possessed by a self that is simply pleased with itself in its relations to others and the world; . . . it is rather what possesses a self as it celebrates its finding where it properly belongs, in spirit." It becomes then "a kind of homecoming, a return and yet a re-making of the enduring that is always new: it is a renewal, a finding of the self as it is taken hold of in love." This love, I believe, is at once personal and impersonal: it has a deep, nonpersonal ontological grounding that becomes "actual" in and through intersubjective togetherness. The dichotomous characterizations of "dualistic or nondualistic," of "human and non-human" seem here to be altogether inadequate and inappropriate. Love is an essential reverence for all being; love is a celebration of others in the full integrity of their own particular being; love is a universal calling which demands a creative response. With love, as Leroy S. Rouner knows so well in his exemplary way of being, the mystery of being, untouched by our ruminations, shines forth in its full splendor.

Henry Rosemont, Jr.

In my *Creative Being: The Crafting of Person and World*, to which Henry Rosemont frequently refers, and as I indicated earlier in my response to Daya Krishna, I stated that:

> A person affirms quite spontaneously and naturally the intrinsic worth, the dignity of every human being—and it is this recognition, this affirmation, which makes possible a sociopolitical understanding that is commensurate with the spiritual potentialities of man.

And further that:

It would be inherently contradictory for a person who has realized to the full his or her own dignity to act immorally—that is, to willfully deprive another of his or her personhood and freedom or, given the opportunity, to fail to enhance the personhood of the other.

Rosemont, in his fine, sympathetic essay, wants to extend, while critically engaging, my conception of personhood and freedom to the social-political arena more fully than I have done and see how far that extension accords with his own thinking in this area—and, I should also note, with his deep, passionate commitment to the ideals of justice and equality. I am pleased to say, with a few reservations, that I find myself in very close agreement with Rosemont's project.

He begins by contrasting the U. S. Bill of Rights with the U. N. Universal Declaration of Human Rights and shows, as many others have done, how the latter, unlike the former, includes "fundamental economic, social, and cultural rights ('second generation' rights)." He sees these rights as placing a special obligation on persons, and especially in a philosophical context which understands freedom as something to be achieved and not merely given. If, Henry argues, freedom "is something to be achieved, then it may well be that I have moral obligations to assist you on the path thereto, just as you have obligations to assist me on the path as well."

If we are "co-members of a human community," rather than simply autonomous individuals in a society, then we are "obliged," I think, to act as Rosemont would have us do. I would strongly prefer, though, to set aside—as Henry seems to want to do as well in a somewhat different context in his essay—obligation-talk altogether in favor of recognizing the kind of moral sensitivity that flows quite naturally from human beings who do realize in some considerable measure what it means to become, as I understand it, a genuine person. It is not, then, so much that, on the basis of a rational assessment of my duty, I am obligated "to assist," as that morally as a person I wouldn't, nor indeed couldn't, feel or act otherwise.

Henry says that "while individuals and persons are very different for him [me], he uses the same adjective for both: 'autonomous.'" I think he misreads me here. I defined "an individual" as a "concentration of the limiting conditions of his or her being—the accidents of birth, language, environment. An individual is a concatenation of empirical constituents that interact with the world in continuous patterns of experience. . . . An individual, as I use the term, is the locus of whatever is objectifiable in and of the human being as the given [physical, mental, social, cultural] conditions and materials of his or her being." The autonomous person, on the other hand, "is one who transforms social dependencies into care-filled relationships where one's own autonomy is seen to be realized only as one promotes as well the autonomy of others."

Rosemont is no doubt right, though, in pointing out that I do not dwell sufficiently on "history, tradition, and ritual when describing the actions—aesthetic, moral, spiritual—of persons," and I am grateful to him for both pointing this out and showing the way for one to do so.

One part of Henry's argument, however, which seems to be central to his concerns, is I believe rather confusing. He first contextualizes the discussion of freedom in the framework of human rights which, he allows, "presupposes the view of human beings as rational autonomous individuals." He then goes on to say that "For myself, I would do away with rights language, especially as technically employed in moral, political, and legal discourse" and concludes by asking: "Is it not, then, that human beings must first understand themselves to be free, rational, autonomous individuals before they can strive to be achieved persons?"

I argued that "through complex functions of learning, of adaptation and acculturation, we become socially informed organizations of various traits and habits that yield a personal identification (not just identity) that we call 'me'. . . . We become centered in and though certain dominant values and interests that, while often partly imposed upon us, are nevertheless selected by us—and are often created by us—within the framework of our culture. We become differentiated into identifiable personalities with our own characteristic ways of acting and reacting. A person, then, must appropriate one's individual being in order for one to rightly articulate that being; one must acknowledge and assimilate that which one is as an individual." Individuality is ingredient, then, in one's becoming a person, and further, I would agree with Rosemont that "not everyone in our society, and very few people in developing countries, can have a genuine opportunity to become a person," that is, be able to exercise their free will as rational agents. I acknowledged that situation explicitly, and deplored it. Rights-language is, I believe, necessary for individuals striving to become persons to be able to fulfill that striving, but takes on a very different shape and form for those who do attain co-membership in communities as autonomous persons.

Rosemont concludes his essay with the suggestion that "a more radical model of co-members of a human community is needed than Deutsch constructs, one in which personhood, and freedom, are only in part to be seen as achievements of the person; they must equally be seen as being conferred on us by other persons . . . ." I must confess that I don't understand what it means "to confer" personhood and freedom on another person. If it means—and this might be something of a reach here—that a genuine person is one who thinks and acts, in an unselfconscious manner, in such a way that she strives to empower and enrich others within her web of relationships as all of us are "co-members of a human community," then I think we are saying much the same thing. If, on the other hand, "to confer" means, as a dictionary would have it, "to bestow from, or as if from, a position of superiority," "to give to someone or something," then quite clearly we are saying very different sorts of things. But knowing Henry Rosemont as I do, I don't believe the latter is the case. Get rid of "conferrals" and we are, I think—or surely I want to presume that we are—on the same path.

I have always rejoiced in knowing that Henry Rosemont and I have been, and remain as, members—in deep friendship—of a community with others in sharing our work and aspirations. It is just this sort of relationship, among one's most intimate, that makes one's life worthwhile.

Tu Wei-ming

Tu Wei-ming believes that much of my later work in "philosophical anthropology" is "characteristically Confucian in nature." Knowing how dedicated and committed Wei-ming is to understanding and seeking the contemporary relevance of Confucianism, I am, of course, deeply flattered by his placing me in that context. His very clear and concise exposition of the salient features of the Mencian tradition of Confucianism makes evident to me several important topics to which I have not yet paid sufficient attention in my published work, namely the idea of "the human as a learner," and how the concept of *li* as a ritual process may further human togetherness.

I have thought a good deal about how, in a Confucian spirit, one might be educated toward the achievement of personhood and freedom, but I have not yet worked out how this can be done within a liberal, pluralistic society with its requisite democratic educational institutions. My intuitions are that a rather thorough revamping of the entire structure from kindergarten to Ph.D. is needed; but perhaps what is more important here is the need to recognize that the playing field for "the human as learner" is less that of one's formal education and more that of one's actual web of social engagements and relations. I do not doubt but that Confucian wisdom would be a rich resource for thinking through this complex issue. Also, with respect to *li*, I have argued for the need in social relations for a style of communitarian participation which involves a special, cultivated openness and sensitivity on the part of the participants that engenders a power that is then "experienced as an inherent quality of the community." The question remains as to how this can be accomplished in a cultural situation where *li*, as traditionally understood in Confucianism, is for the most part notably absent in favor of our having many and ever-changing codes or standards of behavior. The very exciting work of Herbert Fingarette on this topic, as well as of Tu Wei-ming himself, might, however, indeed provide a way for answering this question.

Tu Wei-ming points out a number of areas where he finds a "sympathetic resonance" and a "natural fit" between the contours of my "philosophical probing and the Confucian project" as he understands it, and also where he sees "several areas of disagreement" between us. I think this calls for some clarification, for I sense that where he sees disagreement there really is agreement, and where he sees agreement there are important differences in emphasis if not in substance. Let me explain.

Near the end of his essay Wei-ming makes much of a rather small comment I made in the context of a discussion regarding the concept of destiny to the effect that the attainment of what I called an "artful destiny" oftentimes "requires abrupt discontinuities and dislocations (alienation)—for it is these that present the challenge to imagination to realize a design." In context, this certainly was not a call for some kind of existentialist angst which necessitates "that personal freedom entails an experienced alienation from convention, tradition, culture, and society." I too have faith in the possibilities of "harmony between self and community" of the sort advocated by Confucianism.

Wei-ming also states that what I regard as the "aesthetically necessary" is not a sufficient ground for the notion of human destiny (as it lacks a necessary dimension of transcendence), and that I seem to advocate the idea that a human being, strictly speaking, can be a work of art. Perhaps I should have been clearer here, but I thought it quite evident that I see the crafting of self as a person in a number of respects as *analogous* to what happens in art-making but hardly *identical* to that making. Where we probably do differ here quite significantly has to do with Wei-ming's insistence that the "Confucian anthropocosmic vision" and its associated idea of the "Mandate of Heaven" are centrally necessary or important for the fulfillment of personhood and freedom. Other ontological grounds, many of which can be found in various traditions of Western as well as of non-Western philosophy can, I think, be drawn upon to do the job. "Heaven" for some may be *a* "source of the Way," but philosophically I don't see that it is *the* source for all of us.

Tu Wei-ming, I take it, sees a "natural fit" between our ways of thinking regarding the place of "the Human Species in Nature." He states that: "The Confucians always considered 'forming one body with Heaven, Earth and the myriad things' not only as an exalted human aspiration but also as attainable common experience." Nature, Tu states, is "the proper home for our existence."

I would agree that phenomenally, a person is an embodied consciousness and, as a member of a species, has at once a "place" in nature, which is the same for all other persons, but that she enjoys as well a mode of being in her environment that is, while shared, her own. The later particularity has, I think, qualitative variability and provides the basis for what is genuinely distinctive in our human being in the natural world.

Nature, we have come to believe, is that total organic/inorganic, apparently lawful or lawlike system of energy and events (however best described and understood in changing ways and models by physical science) of which we are inextricably a part in virtue of the givens of our evolved biological being. Organically we are thus said to be in perfect continuity with the rest of physical nature—our atoms, electrical discharges, and the rest are as such not restricted to us but are, on the contrary, to be found throughout the myriad forms of life and structures of the universe. Our place in nature, in these the most general physical terms, although having a distinctive configuration, is thus not different from any other identified being's place in nature. As embodied we are natural: ashes to ashes, dust to dust.

One can, however, with some confidence say (and without commitment to some kind of mind-body dualism) that it is our powers of consciousness (as mind, feeling, awareness) which, as it is so often pointed out, and seems also to be assumed in Confucianism, gives human beings a special place in relation to everything else that is natural, as it affords us a measure or degree of freedom apparently unknown to other forms of organic being. It is we, and we alone (at least on this planet), who ask the very question of our "place" and thus in the very asking exhibit a dimension not bound to (albeit perhaps still an inextricable part of) the brute necessities of nature. And the very moment the question is asked, some degree of specificity, if not particularity, even here within the structures of universality, obtains, for it is evident that our place in nature changes relative to the different stages of one's life. In the beginning and near the end the freedom associated with the very fact of consciousness is highly restricted, one's actions and being are fundamentally the result—much like those of other living things—of various natural forces and dependencies; it is only in-between, as it were, that they may be largely self-initiated and determined. Our place in nature thus has temporal variability. Psychologically, as one grows older the energies needed for successful sublimation diminish and one is left with the wild play of the subconscious and the vivid memories of one's historical waking consciousness. Old age, without sentimentality, is where one usually becomes abandoned to oneself—a subject so full of itself that, not infrequently, it becomes entirely object.

One's place in nature might also vary in virtue of sex-differentiation—a topic that not unsurprisingly is hardly addressed in classical Confucianism. The question certainly remains open as to whether sex differences (and not just gender constructions) are sufficiently radical to divide humankind into two sub-species, as it were, and thus to see them having different universalized places in nature.

In any event, the very question regarding our place in nature, if it is addressed simply as it stands, tends to presuppose just that one-sided emphasis on the universal at the expense of the particular that is characteristic of so much modern philosophy. *Which* person's place and at what point in its life is not often asked about philosophically, as though we all had only the same nontemporal place and that is the end of the matter. But the strictly universal dimensions, important and perhaps even phenomenally central as they are, do not exhaust our "place" but rather point the way to our actual "placing" of ourselves in an environment.

In other words, it is only as we are instances of humankind, exemplifications of the universal terms of being human, that we have as such a place in nature. As the particular persons that we are in our actual living we make our place in an environment (which is usually a highly complex one, socially and historically).

In short, I don't have a place in an environment as such, rather I place myself there in terms of everything that goes with the extent and manner of my relationships to the regional nature(s) and culture(s) to which I belong. We append the plural here, for my environment is wherever I make identifications and establish relationships; my neighborhood, and the extended geographical area in which it resides, my workplace, and all the places, in varied degree, where I might have lived or visited or indeed imagined myself to be.

And the placement varies qualitatively in many complex and subtle ways. Some relationships are harmonious, others not—some indeed to the point of being utterly destructive. We may happily belong with our environments and we may become estranged from them. In any event, the placing of ourselves in an environment is a dynamic process, one subject to political vicissitudes, rapidly changing technologies and social values, and all the vagaries of our personal lives. This somewhat more vitalistic and particularistic view is, I think, more central to understanding our species in relation to Nature than that of "forming one body with Heaven, Earth and the myriad things." Is it, though, perhaps only another way of formulating a kind of Confucian perspective?

David L. Hall and Roger T. Ames

David L. Hall and Roger T. Ames begin their insightful essay "The Style of Truth and the Truthfulness of Style" with a brief polemic against the prevalent postmodernist denial of the importance of the author of a text, and consequently of authorial style, in favor of reducing authorship to a play of political and social voices which shape, if not entirely determine, literary events. Authors disappear: critics replace them as givers of meaning. Hall and Ames do note that there is good reason to be aware of and combat political dominance whenever it is to be found in both literary and philosophical expression, but they rightly resist drawing the conclusion that this awareness frees us from addressing seriously the question of authorial style. After all, they argue, "This question is central to the understanding of the shape of our Western intellectual culture from its beginnings."

When exploring the historical origins of the meaning of style in ancient Greece and, as expected, contrasting this with the Chinese experience, David and Roger note that among the salient features of the Western approach has been the taming, as it were, of "the naive original" tendency to regard words as a means to express a "world of unreflective process in which 'all things flow'," and subsequently to give precedence to "Being" over "becoming," culminating in the Platonic endeavor "to ground the search for knowledge upon appropriate formal definitions." Ironically, it was thus Plato—the supreme philosophical stylist—who fathered the search for univocity of meaning in philosophy and which led to the privileging of literalness and the precision and clarity in expression characteristic of the methods of logic and science.

In contrast to this Western ontological assumption of "Being" behind "becoming" that generates the reality/appearance distinction and "drives the search for the essential aspects of things, and for a literal and logically disciplined language that can report this essential reality with veracity and precision," the Chinese tradition concerned itself primarily with "the appropriation and efficacy of language as it shapes and is shaped by the world" and thus emphasizes semantics (the signification of words) over logic (the forms of thought)—all of which gives rise to attending importantly to questions of style.

According to Hall and Ames, for the Chinese tradition, language "does not merely describe a world, but actively valorizes and prescribes it"—an understanding of language interestingly enough, in both its theoretical and practical employments, that is rather au courant today in much post-empiricist Western philosophy of science and epistemology. Many philosophers now accept the idea that "objectivity," in the traditional sense, is a myth; that *we* "make" our worlds; that there cannot be a 'one, true account' of anything. Combining the classical Chinese and the contemporary West suggests strongly the need for a new global understanding of the role of "style" in philosophy as well as in literature.

In tracing further the roots of the English word "style," and its functional equivalents in Chinese, Hall and Ames, I think, do some mischief in initially accepting and then overstating the distinction between opacity and transparency in linguistic expression by way of attending to the special offices of the poet and the philosopher. Recognizing that the "original expectations" of "style" as being far from simply window dressing, as is so often the case in ordinary language use, having as it does "an integral role in 'knowing' and thus 'making real' a particular world," they insist nevertheless that the "task of the poet *qua* poet is to present language whose meaning is secondary or at least [only] a complement to the sound and meter of the words employed" with the typical Western philosopher working "at the opposite end of the spectrum," that is to say, aiming that his or her utterance could, without conceptual remainder, always be translated into propositional form and determined to be either true or false.

Now certain symbolist poets, to be sure, held the dream of creating a poetic language that would be free from all conventional meaning and whose significance would be had in "pure" poetic/musical form, but even they (for example, Paul Valéry) recognized the futility of this dream and, in any event, were hardly typical of Western poetic sensibility and aspiration. Likewise with philosophy: the ideal of our having a purified formal language for science and philosophy, so strongly favored by the logical positivists, has been put largely to rest. We still, of course, have a keen sense of the difference in degree between semantic arrest and semantic transparency in both poetry and philosophy, but are adverse to seeing this as a difference in kind. It is enough, I think, that Hall and Ames note that "the problem of style is appropriateness to context," which appropriateness may play itself out differently in poetry and philosophy, without insisting that "If one speaks as a poet, it is the metered words themselves that need to be said" and "if one speaks as a philosopher, meanings are at issue." If "style" rightly means appropriateness to context then linguistic form and content can never be radically disassociated. David and Roger do seem finally to acknowledge this when they say that "arguably the problem of style would vanish at either end of the spectrum." The remainder of "The Style of Truth and the Truthfulness of Style" deals with my work over the years and I appreciate deeply the recognition they accord my "manner of healing this breach between meaning and style that has plagued Western literary and philosophical expressions well-nigh from its beginnings." I especially appreciate the way in which they relate my concern with "appropriateness to context" to questions of "truth" and how an understanding of the meaning of style may enter into the very definition of truth—a connection in my work of which I was not explicitly aware.

David and Roger say so many nice things about my concern to learn from the nature of art and from non-Western traditions, as well as from my own Western background and training, in treating of a range of philosophical issues and in celebrating diversity in the articulations of meaning, that I can only return the favor by pointing out that the characterization of style that in the end they appropriate from Ben Johnson's "style is where you can take away nothing without loss, and that loss be manifest," is so wonderfully exhibited throughout their own work. David and Roger have *almost* convinced me that I too am, or at least aspire to be, a good Confucian.

Published Works of
Eliot Deutsch

Books

The Bhagavad Gītā: An English Translation from the Sanskrit with Introductory Essays and Philosophical Analyses. New York: Holt, Rinehart, and Winston Co., 1968. Selected for inclusion in *Encyclopedia Britannica: The Great Ideas Today,* 1985.

Advaita Vedānta: A Philosophical Reconstruction. Honolulu: East West Center Press, 1969. French translation by Sylvie Girard. *Qu'est-ce que L'Advaita Vedānta,* Paris: 1982. Spanish translation forthcoming.

Humanity and Divinity: An Essay in Comparative Metaphysics. Honolulu: University of Hawaii Press, 1970.

A Source Book of Advaita Vedānta (With J. A. B. van Buitenen). Honolulu: University of Hawaii Press, 1971.

Studies in Comparative Aesthetics. Honolulu: University Press of Hawaii, 1975. Monograph Number 2 of the Society for Asian and Comparative Philosophy. Korean translation forthcoming.

On Truth: An Ontological Theory. Honolulu: University Press of Hawaii, 1979.

Personhood, Creativity and Freedom. Honolulu: University Press of Hawaii, 1982.

Interpreting Across Boundaries: New Essays in Comparative Philosophy. Edited with Gerald Larson. Princeton: Princeton University Press, 1988. Indian Edition published by Motilal Banarsidass, 1989.

Culture and Modernity, ed. Honolulu: University of Hawaii Press, 1991. Indian Edition published by Motilal Banarsidass, 1994.

Creative Being: The Crafting of Person and World. Honolulu: University of Hawaii Press, 1992.

Religion and Spirituality. Albany, New York: State University of New York Press, 1995.

Essays on the Nature of Art. Albany, New York: State University of New York Press, 1996.

Introduction to World Philosophies. New York: Prentice-Hall, 1996.

Companion to World Philosophies. Edited with Ron Bontekoe. Oxford: Blackwell Publishers, 1997.

Articles and Reviews

"Sri Aurobindo's Interpretation of Spiritual Experience: A Critique." *International Philosophical Quarterly* 4, no. 4 (Dec. 1964). Excerpted in *Twentieth-Century Literary Criticism,* edited by Jennifer Gariery (New York: Gale Research, Inc., 1997).

"The Nature of Scripture." *Vedānta Kesari* 50, no. 9 (Jan. 1965).

"Karma as a 'Convenient Fiction' in Advaita Vedānta." *Philosophy East and West* 15, no. 1 (Jan. 1965).

"The Justification of Hindu Polytheism in Advaita Vedānta." *East West Review* 1, no. 3 (Feb. 1965).

"Śakti in Medieval Hindu Sculpture." *Journal of Aesthetics and Art Criticism* 24, no. 1 (Fall 1965).

"Levels of Being." *Darshana International* 5, no. 4 (Oct. 1965).

Review: *Ways of Thinking of Eastern Peoples,* by Hajime Nakamura. *Journal of Philosophy* 62, no. 22 (Nov. 1965).

"The Self in Advaita Vedānta." *International Philosophical Quarterly* 6, no. 1 (Mar. 1966).

Review: *Dr. S. Radhakrishnan. International Philosophical Quarterly* 6, no. 1 (Mar. 1966).

Review: *Radhakrishnan and Integral Experience,* by J. C. Arupura. *Journal of Asian Studies* 26, no. 4 (Aug. 1967).

"Types of Philosophical Problems in Classical Vedānta." Abstract in *Proceedings of TwentySeventh International Congress of Orientalists.* Ann Arbor, Michigan, August, 1967. (Wiesbaden: Otto Harrassowitz, 1971).

"Western Approaches to Comparative Philosophy." *Proceedings of the Indian Philosophical Congress,* Banares, India, December, 1967.

Review: *Emptiness: A Study in Religious Meaning,* by Frederick J. Streng. *Journal of Asian Studies* 27, no. 2, 1968.

"Aesthetics East and West: Tentative Conclusions and Unresolved Problems." *Philosophy East and West* 19, no. 3 (Jul. 1969).

"Introduction to Violence and Non-Violence East and West." *Philosophy East and West* 19, no. 2 (Apr. 1969).

"Speaking About God." *Journal of Religious Studies* (Punjabi University) 1, no. 1 (Sept. 1969).

"Commentary on J. L. Mehta's 'Heidegger and the Comparison of Indian and Western Philosophy.'" *Philosophy East and West* 20, no. 3 (Jul. 1970).

Review: "Śāntarasa and Abhinavagupta's Philosophy of Aesthetics" by J. L. Mason and M. V. Patwarden. *Journal of Asian Studies* 30, no. 1 (Nov. 1970).

"Philosophy and Freedom of Consciousness." In *Philosophy: Theory and Practice*, Proceedings of the International Seminar on World Philosophy, edited by T.M. P. Mahadevan. Madras: The University of Madras, 1974.

"Commentary on Dr. Fernand Brunner's 'Theory and Practice in the Evolution of Western Thought,'" in same.

"Vedānta and Ecology." *Indian Philosophical Annual*. Vol. 6, 1970. Centre of Advanced Study in Philosophy, University of Madras.

"The Nature of Freedom," in same.

Review: *The Philosophy of India and Its Impact on American Thought*, by Dale Riepe. *Journal of the American Oriental Society* 92, no. 1 (1972).

Review: *Freedom and Consciousness*, by Pratima Bowes. *The Journal of Philosophy* 69, no. 8 (April 20, 1972).

Review: *The Structure of Indian Thought*, by Ramakant Sinari. *Journal of the American Oriental Society* 92, no. 4 (1972).

"The Multi-Leveled Ontology of Advaita Vedānta." In *Studies in the Languages and Culture of South Asia*, edited by Edwin Gerow and Margery D. Land. Seattle and London: University of Washington Press, 1973.

"Some Reflections on Rasa." In *Festschrift for Professor T.M.P. Mahadevan*, edited by H. D. Lewis. Madras, 1974.

Review: *Contemporary Indian Philosophy*, by Margaret Chatterjee. *The Journal of Asian Studies* 35, no. 1 (Dec. 1975).

Foreword to David Kalupahana, *Causality: The Central Philosophy of Buddhism*. Honolulu: University Press of Hawaii, 1975.

"On the Concept of Art." *Journal of Chinese Philosophy* 3 (1976).

"Vidyā and Avidyā." *Proceedings: World Philosophy Congress.* New Delhi, 1976.

"On Meaning." In *Self, Knowledge and Freedom,* edited by J. N. Mohanty and S. P. Banerjee. Calcutta: World Press, 1978.

"A Reply to 'How to Help Advaita Vedānta Refute Itself.'" *Insight: A Journal of World Religions* 2, no. 2 (Winter 1977–78).

"Causality and Creativity." *International Philosophical Quarterly* 18, no. 1 (Mar. 1978). And in *Man and Nature,* edited by George F. McLean. Oxford University Press, 1978.

Review: *Encyclopedia of Indian Philosophies, Indian Metaphysics and Epistemology,* by Karl H. Potter, editor. *Journal of Asian History* 12, no. 2 (1979).

Review: *Faith and Belief* and *Belief and History,* by Wilfred Cantwell Smith. *Philosophy East and West* 30, no. 4 (Oct. 1980).

Review: *Śaṁkara on the Absolute,* by A. J. Alston. *Numen* 27, no. 2 (1980).

"Reflections on Some Aspects of the Theory of Rasa." In *Sanskrit Drama in Performance,* edited by Rachel van M. Baumer and James R. Brandon. University Press of Hawaii, 1981.

Review: *Asian Philosophy Today,* by Dale Riepe. *Teaching Philosophy* 5, no. 4 (Oct. 1982).

"A Radical Discontinuity in Being: A Dialogue." In *Rationality and Philosophy,* edited by V. K. Bharadwaja. New Delhi: Northern Book Centre, 1984.

"On Art and Religion." In *Religious Pluralism,* Boston University Institute for Philosophy and Religion Series, edited by Leroy S. Rouner. Notre Dame: University of Notre Dame Press, 1984.

"The Bhagavad Gītā." Article for *Encyclopedia of Religion,* edited by Mircea Eliade. New York: Macmillan, 1985.

"The Ontological Power of Speech." *Journal of Chinese Philosophy* 12 (Fall 1985).

"Knowing Religiously." In *Knowing Religiously,* edited by Leroy S. Rouner. Notre Dame: University of Notre Dame Press, 1985. And in *Philosophy, Religion, and Contemporary Life,* edited by Leroy S. Rouner and Janes R. Langford. Notre Dame: University of Notre Dame Press, 1996.

"Participation: The Metaphysical Grounding of Social Relations." In *Philosophy, Society and Action.* Delhi, 1985. Translated into Chinese, in *Philosophical Research,* Beijing, no. 5 (1986).

"A Metaphysical Grounding for Natural Reverence: East-West." *Environmental Ethics* 8, no. 4 (Winter 1986).

Review: *The Face of Truth,* by Julius Lipner. *Idealistic Studies* 19, no. 1 (Jan. 1989).

Review: *Religion and Human Purpose: A Cross Disciplinary Approach,* edited by William Horosz and Tad Clements. *The Journal of Religion* (University of Chicago) (Jan. 1988).

"Breugel and Ma Yüan: Principles of Comparative Criticism." In *A Selection of Famous Works on Western Aesthetics of the Twentieth Century* (*Ershi shiji xifang meixue mingzhu xuan*). Shanghai: Fudan University Press, 1988.

Foreword to N. K. Devaraja's *Humanism in Indian Thought.* New Delhi: India Publishing Company, 1988.

"Time and History: East and West." In *Radhakrishnan Centenary Volume.* Indian Council of Philosophical Research, 1990.

Review: *An Interpretation of Religion,* by John Hick. *Philosophy East and West,* (Oct. 1990).

"Community as Ritual Participation." In *On Community,* edited by Leroy S. Rouner. Notre Dame: University of Notre Dame Press, 1991.

"The Concept of the Body." In *Self as Body in Asian Thought and Practice,* edited by Thomas P. Kasulis et al. Albany: State University of New York Press, 1992. And in *Phenomenology East and West: Essays in Honor of J. N. Mohanty* (Kluwer Academic Publishers and Motilal Banarsidass), 1993.

Review: *Nonduality: A Study in Comparative Philosophy,* by David Loy. *International Journal for Philosophy of Religion* 32 (1992).

Feature Review: *Indian Philosophy: A Counter Perspective,* by Daya Krishna. *Philosophy East and West* 42, no. 4 (Oct. 1992).

Review: *The Word and the World* and *Moral Dilemmas in the Mahābhārata,* by B. K. Matilal. *Journal of the American Oriental Society* 112, no. 3 (1992).

"On the Comparative Study of the Self." In *Selves, People and Persons,* edited by Leroy S. Rouner. Notre Dame: Notre Dame University Press, 1992.

"The Person as Knower and Known." *Journal of Indian Council of Philosophical Research* 10, no. 1 (1993).

"Truth and Mythology." In *Myths and Fictions,* edited by Shlomo Biderman and Ben-Ami Scharfstein. Leiden: E. J. Brill, 1993.

Review: *Reason and Tradition in Indian Thought: An Essay on the Nature of Indian Philosophical Thinking,* by Jitendra Nath Mohanty. *International Philosophical Quarterly* 34, no. 2 (Jun. 1994).

Review: *Phenomenology and Indian Philosophy*, by D. P. Chattopadhyaya, et. al. *Philosophy East and West* 44, no. 2 (Jul. 1994).

Review: *Mysticism and Language*, by Steven T. Katz. *Journal of the American Oriental Society* 114, no. 3 (1994).

"Creative Friendship." In *The Changing Face of Friendship*, edited by Leroy S. Rouner. Notre Dame: University of Notre Dame Press, 1994.

Review: *Life and Thought of Śankara*, by J. C. Pande and *Shankara and Indian Philosophy*, by Natalia Isayeva. *Journal of Asian Studies* 54, no. 4 (Nov. 1995).

Review: *Majesty and Meekness*, by John B. Carman. *Philosophy East and West* 46, no. 2 (Apr. 1996).

"Self-Deception: A Comparative Study." In *Self and Deception*, edited by Roger T. Ames and Wimal Dissanayake. Albany, NY: State University of New York Press, 1996.

Foreword to Alexander Eliot, *The Timeless Myths*. New York: Continuum Publishing Company, 1996.

Review: *Art and Philosophy*, by S. K. Saxsena. *Journal of Aesthetics and Art Criticism* 54, no. 2 (Spring 1996).

"Outline of an Advaita Vedānta Aesthetics." In *Relativism, Suffering and Beyond*. New Delhi: Oxford University Press, 1996.

"Loneliness and Solitude." In *Loneliness*, edited by Leroy S. Rouner. Notre Dame: University of Notre Dame Press, 1998.

Review: *Aesthetics East and West*, edited by Grazia Marchianò. *Journal of Aesthetics and Art Criticism* 57, no. 1 (Winter 1998).

"Comparative Aesthetics." In *Encyclopedia of Aesthetics*, edited by Michael Kelly. Oxford and New York: Oxford University Press, 1998. Italian translation in *Il paesaggio dell'estetica* (Università di Siena, 1998).

"Seyyed Hossein Nasr's Philosophy of Art." In *The Philosophy of Seyyed Hossein Nasr*, Library of Living Philosophers, edited by Lewis E. Hahn. Chicago: Open Court, forthcoming.

Review: *Aesthetic Value*, by Alan H. Goldman. *International Studies in Philosophy*, forthcoming.

Review: *The Fruits of Our Desiring: An Inquiry Into the Ethics of the Bhagavadgītā for Our Times*, Julius Lipner, editor. *The Journal of the American Oriental Society*, forthcoming.

Contributors

Roger T. Ames is Professor of Philosophy and Director of the Center for Chinese Studies at the University of Hawai'i. He is editor of *Philosophy East & West* and *China Review International*. His recent publications include translations of Chinese classics: *Sun-tzu: The Art of Warfare* (1993); *Sun Pin: The Art of Warfare* (1996) and *Tracing Dao to its Source* (1997) (both with D. C. Lau); and the *Analects of Confucius: A Philosophical Translation* (with H. Rosemont) (1998). He has also authored interpretative studies of Chinese philosophy: *Thinking Through Confucius* (1987), *Anticipating China: Thinking Through the Narratives of Chinese and Western Culture* (1995), and *Thinking From the Han: Self, Truth, and Transcendence in Chinese and Western Culture* (1998) (all with D. L. Hall).

Arthur C. Danto is the Johnsonian Professor Emeritus of Philosophy, Columbia; and Art Critic, *The Nation*. His most recent publications are *After the End of Art: Contemporary Art and the Pale of History* (Princeton), and two volumes of essays—*The Body/Body Problem* and *Philosophizing Art* (California).

Herbert Fingarette is Emeritus Professor of Philosophy in the University of California, Santa Barbara. In addition to his studies of the Book of Job and the concept of suffering, he has published studies of the *Bhagavad Gītā*, and of the Confucian *Analects*. His book, *Confucius: The Secular as Sacred*, has appeared in Japanese and in Korean editions, and will soon appear in a Chinese edition in Beijing. Professor Fingarette has also written extensively in the fields of ethics and philosophical psychology, psychoanalysis and psychiatry, alcohol and drug abuse, and criminal law.

David L. Hall is Professor of Philosophy at the University of Texas at El Paso. He is the author of *The Civilization of Experience: A Whiteheadian Theory of Culture; The Uncertain Phoenix: Adventures Toward a Post-Cultural Sensibility;* and *Eros and Irony: A Prelude to Philosophical Anarchism*. With SUNY Press, Professor Hall is coauthor of *Thinking Through Confucius, Anticipating China,* and *Thinking From the Han* (all with Roger T. Ames); and author of *The Arimaspian Eye* and *Richard Rorty: Prophet and Poet of the New Pragmatism*. His most recent publication with Open Court is *The Democracy of the Dead: Dewey, Confucius, and the Hope for Democracy in China* (with R. T. Ames).

Thomas P. Kasulis teaches in the Department of Comparative Studies at Ohio State University. In addition to co-editing *Body as Person in Asian Theory and Practice* (1993), *Self as Person in Asian Theory and Practice* (1994), and *Self as Image in Asian Theory and Practice* (1998), he annotated and translated *The Body: Toward an Eastern Mind-Body Theory* by Yasuo Yuasa, and co-edited *The Recovery of Philosophy in America: Essays in Honor of John Edwin Smith* (with Robert C. Neville).

Daya Krishna taught philosophy at the University of Saugar and Rajasthan (India). He has been Visiting Professor at Carleton College, Northfield, and the University of Hawai'i; Senior Fellow, East-West Center, Hawai'i; Fellow of the Rockfeller Foundation; and National Fellow of the Indian Council of Social Research and the Indian Council of Philosophical Research. Presently he is Editor of the *Journal of the Indian Council of Philosophical Research*. Professor Krishna has written extensively on theoretical issues in the realm of philosophy, sociology, economics, and literature. His major works include *The Nature of Philosophy; Social Philosophy: Past and Future; Political Development: A Critical Perspective; The Development Debate* (with Fred Riggs); *Indian Philosophy: A New Approach;* and *Prolegomena to any Future Historiography of Culture and Civilization.*

Gerald James Larson is Rabindranath Tagore Professor of Indian Cultures and Civilizations, and Director of the India Studies Program, Indiana University, Bloomington; and Professor Emeritus, University of California, Santa Barbara. He is the author of numerous books and articles on Indian philosophy and religion. His most recent books include *India's Agony over Religion* (SUNY, 1995, and Oxford University Press, Delhi, 1997), and *Changing Myths and Images: Twentieth-Century Popular Art in India,* co-edited with P. Pal and H. Daniel Smith (Indiana University Art Museum, 1997).

J. N. Mohanty is Professor of Philosophy at Temple University and Woodruff Professor of Philosophy and Asian Studies at Emory University. His latest book is *Logic, Truth, and the Modalities* (Dordrecht: Kluwer, 1999). A forthcoming book is *Classical Indian Philosophy* (Rowman & Littlefield).

Graham Parkes is Professor of Philosophy at the University of Hawai'i. He is the editor of *Heidegger and Asian Thought,* and *Nietzsche and Asian Thought;* translator of *The Self-Overcoming of Nihilism* by Nishitani Keiji, *Heidegger's Hidden Sources* by Reinhard May, and *Reading Zen in the Rocks* by François Berthier; and author of *Composing the Soul: Reaches of Nietzsche's Psychology.*

Henry Rosemont, Jr. has written *A Chinese Mirror,* and edited and/or translated six other works, the most recent of which (with D. J. Cook) are *Leibniz, Writings on China,* and *The Analects of Confucius: A Philosophical Translation* (with R. T. Ames). He is George B. and Willma Reeves Distinguished Professor of Liberal Arts at St. Mary's College of Maryland, and Distinguished Consulting Professor at Fudan University in Shanghai.

Leroy S. Rouner is Profesor of Philosophy, Religion, and Philosophical Theology, Director of the Institute of Philosophy and Religion, and General Editor of Boston University Studies in Philosophy and Religion, at Boston University. He taught for five years at the United Theological College in Bangalore, India, in the 1960s, and drove his family overland in a Land Rover to England during1966–67. He is the author of *Within Human Experience: The Philosophy of William Ernest Hocking; To Be At Home: Christianity, Civil Religion, and World Community;* and *The Long Way Home* (a memoir). He is also editor of some 18 volumes in the Boston series, and is co-author of seven of those. During 1998–99 he was a Phi Beta Kappa Visiting Scholar.

Tu Wei-ming has been Director of the Harvard-Yenching Institute since 1996. His research interests are Confucian humanism, Chinese intellectual history, the philosophies of East Asia, and comparative religion. He has served as Chair of the Committee on the Study of Religion and Chair of the Department of East Asian Languages and Civilizations at Harvard University. He is currently chair of the Advisory Board of the Institute of Chinese Literature and Philosophy, Academia Sinica; vice chair of the Board of Directors of the International Confucian Association in Beijing; co-moderator of the Aspen Seminar of the "The Chinese in the Global Community," and fellow of the American Academy of Arts and Sciences. Recent publications of his include *China in Transformation* (Harvard, 1994); *The Living Tree: The Changing Meaning of Being Chinese Today* (Stanford, 1995); and *Confucian Traditions in East Asian Modernity: Exploring Moral Education and Economic Culture in Japan and the Four Mini-Dragons* (Harvard, 1996).

INDEX